WARRIOR of TWO KINGS

Also by Birgit Constant

The Northumbria Trilogy

Prequel: *Squire and Sword*

Book 1: *Warrior of two Kings*

Find out how the story continues:

For Lord and Liege. Book 2 of the Northumbria Trilogy

Coming in 2025

About the Author

Birgit Constant has a PhD in medieval studies, has learned eleven languages and worked her way through translation, IT and Public Relations before ending up in the world of books.

She writes historical novels for language nerds and has also published a handbook for budding authors.

Her monthly newsletter *Medieval Motes* brings exclusive reading material and news from the Middle Ages, her projects and books.

Subscribe at www.birgitconstant.com/newsletter.

BIRGIT CONSTANT

Warrior of two Kings

THE NORTHUMBRIA TRILOGY

BOOK ONE

© 2024 Birgit Constant All rights reserved.

Birgit Constant, c/o Sissis Autorenlounge, Steig bei der Warte 15, 67595 Bechtheim, Germany

www.birgitconstant.com

ISBN: 9783911199032 (e-book) / 9783911199001 (paperback)

Book Cover by Patrick Knowles (www.patrickknowlesdesign.com)
Editor: Miranda Summers-Pritchard

Maps by John Wyatt Greenlee of Surprised Eel Maps

ESCOCE

Bebbanburh

Noef Chastel

Dunholm

NORTHUMBERLAND

Riche Munt

Use

Everwic

De

NORTHGALES

Snotingeham

Lincolia

MERCE

Trente

Burg

Sauerna

Waruuic

Use

Elig

EST ANGLE

Grentebrige

Tamise

Londres

Melduna

WEST SESSOINE

Wincestre

Cantwarebyri

Sandwice

Wiht

Peuenesel

Hæstinga

ENGLAND

AD 1070

NORMANDIE

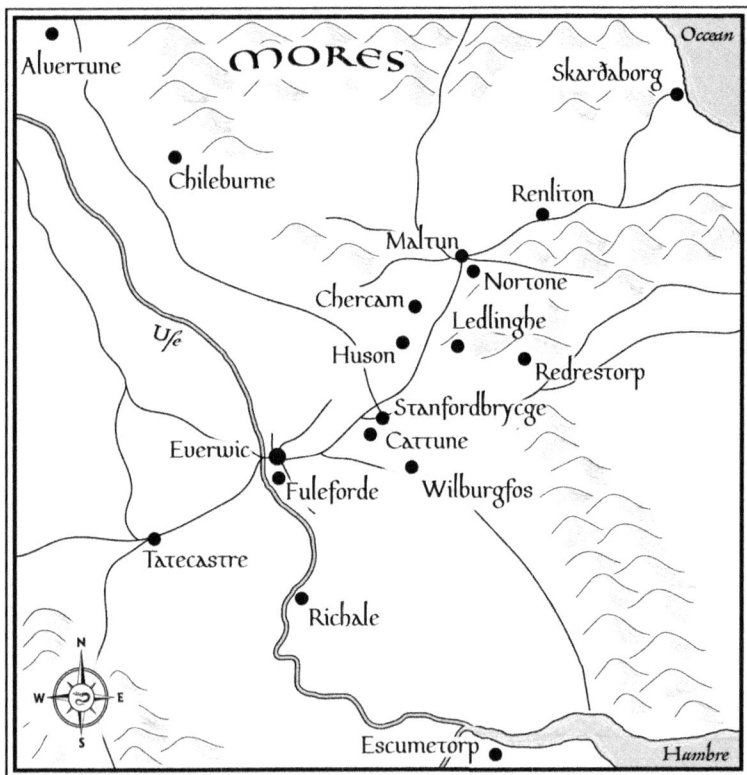

Alvertune

MORES

Ocean

Skardaborg

Chileburne

Renliton

Maltun

Nortone

Chercam

Ledlinghe

Huson

Redrestorp

Stanfordbrycge

Everwic

Cattune

Fuleforde

Wilburgfos

Tatecastre

Richale

Escumetorp

Hambre

N
W   E
S

YORK AND YORKSHIRE AD 1070

Cast of Characters

Historical persons are marked with an *

Ledlinghe
Oswulf: son of an English ðegn
Osfrið and Æþelgifu: English nobles, Oswulf's parents
Æðelflæd, Wassa, Wigstan, Oswine and Eda: Oswulf's siblings
Ulfgar: son of Godric the smith, his friend and brother-in-arms
Godgifu: Oswulf's fiancée/wife
Stígandr Olafsson: son of Olaf, the Norwegian shoemaker
Dunstan: an old Englishman
Erik and Wulfnoð: messengers

Wilburgfos
Edeva: English noblewoman, lady of the manor and healer
Kjetil: Edeva's first husband
Geoffrey de Bernaium: Norman baron, Edeva's second husband
William and Adelais (both from Geoffrey's first marriage) and Roger/Hroðgar: Edeva's step-children and child, respectively

English servants
Hild: healer woman

Cenhelm: seneschal during Kjetil's time, cupbearer at the Norman manor

Cenric: Cenhelm's son

Father Leofric: priest from Cattune

Norman inhabitants

Walchelin le Engleis: wealhstod (language master)

Thibault Braz de fer: master of arms

Frederic de Lisieues: seneschal

Hugues de Borre: bailiff

Jehan Colbert, Roul le Blanc, Eustace Landry, Eudo FitzRou and Jeannot Marteleau: squires assigned to Oswulf for training

Quentin de Lisieues: Roul's uncle

Travellers

Morwenna: a Breton noblewoman

Solen: Morwenna's daughter

Others

Morkere (eorl)*: Morcar, Earl of Northumbria after the deposal of Tostig Godwinson*

Gospatric (eorl)*: Earl of Bernicia (northern part of Northumbria) and Earl of Northumbria after Morcar's capture by William I

Harold Godwinson (Harold cyning)*: son of the mightiest Earl in England; from January until October 1066, King of England

Willelm (eorl) of Normandig*: William I, "The Conqueror", Duke of Normandy and vassal of the French King Philippe I; from December 1066 King of England.

Eadgar Æðeling*: Edgar Atheling, grandson of the English King Edmund Ironside and last descendant of the House of Wessex after the death of Edward the Confessor* (the brother of his grandfather) in 1066; chosen by the witan as king in October 1066, but never crowned

William "Als Gernuns" de Perci*: vassal of the Comte de Cestre, tenant in chief, Hugues d'Avranches* and Liege Lord of Geoffrey de Bernaium

Ælfred cyning*: Alfred the Great; from 871, King of Wessex, from 886, King of England

Hereward*: Hereward the Wake, English rebel

For old/foreign-language expressions and locations, please refer to Places and Glossary.

Chapter 1

There are too many of them. We will neither escape their bloodstained lances nor the ravenous fires with which they burn down our houses and villages. Perhaps I die today, but my scramasax will make sure that I am not the only one.

I gaze over the dismembered bodies that cover the ground. It will be a feast for the wolves when the scent of death beckons them hither. Whoever survived the slaughter amongst us will not linger to save the fallen from the scavengers and give them a decent burial. For the hordes will return and spare no one, not even women and children. Norþhymbre is dying of raging flames, murder and destruction, and the enemy will not stop until they have broken our will and made us submit to their rule. Or until the last one of us is dead.

My tongue sticks to the roof of my mouth. We have been battling them for what feels like an eternity, trying to keep their fierce riders from our life and limb, our goods and chattels. They are relentless. Anyone who stands in their way is skewered with a lance or struck down with a well-directed blow from a sword.

We cannot but stand in awe as Byrhtnoð and his men did in the Year of Our Lord 991 when they watched the Norþmenn wading over to them near Melduna. Wodon þa wælwulfas, for wætere ne murnon... But our enemy fears neither water nor fire – possibly not even God or the Fiend. Our weapons are no match for their merciless thirst for blood, which they greedily quench on thousands of my fellow countrymen.

I have fought until the end, but now, hope is leaving me. I am exhausted. Our weapons drip with the blood of many of their riders and horses, but we cannot win. I have lost everything. Their horsemen have butchered my father, raped and stabbed my mother and two of my sisters, set fire to my homeland. They round up the helpless like cattle and slaughter them with a single blow of their swords. May God keep my three younger siblings safe in the woods, to which they have fled. They may yet survive. But for how long?

I take a deep breath and put down my makeshift fire sling – the flames in the stuffed bucket are all but extinct. Another rider joins the rows of warriors surrounding us and urges his horse forward. There is a large dark spot on the instep of his foot. The Frenchman I fought with in our kitchen. His helmet shields his face, and I search in vain for a sign of hate. Instead, he looks down on me almost benignly. Is he waiting for his brothers-in-arms to drive their lances through my body and make me pay for the wound I inflicted on him?

Another rider shouts something, whereupon the others make way for what seems to be their leader. Like a king, he sits on his mighty warhorse and rides forward with his chin held high until he is right in front of us. The one who shouted pulls up beside him, and they eye us from head to toe.

With a sneer, the leader sits up and speaks, but I do not understand a single word. The rider next to him asks, in an accent I do not recognise, "Hwæt is þin nama?"

They have a wealhstod who speaks my language? I tighten the grip on my shield and the rope of the bucket with its weakly flickering flames. Then I lift my chin, "Ic hatte Oswulf."

"Hu eald eart ðu?" the language master continues.

"Ic eom nigontinewintre."

From the corner of my eye, I see that, like me, Ulfgar has not lowered his spear and shield, as if he were expecting an attack at any moment.

My foe from the kitchen makes his way past the other riders to the leader. They talk briefly. The leader nods. With a stern look at me, my foe points to his foot. Then he turns to the language master. While he is talking to him, his gaze keeps going back to me, with only intermittent glances at Ulfgar.

The language master introduces my foe as the French master of arms, who has been watching me since the fighting began. It has surprised him to see the two of us hold our ground against some very experienced warriors.

"You are a worthy fighter, young Englishman," says the wealhstod. "Thibault would like to see you fight on our side."

Thibault? Who is Thibault? I look at the master of arms, who nods almost imperceptibly. My hands tremble with anger. I tighten the grip on the handle of my shield and pull tight the rope on the bucket. "Næfre ic sceal wigan for wuldre Angla banan."

The wealhstod raises his eyebrows. How much of my words he passes on, I cannot say, but the leader continues to stare at me without even batting an eyelid. "Hwær sind þine ældran, Oswulf?"

"You want to know where my parents are? Why do you not ask your spears and swords with which you slaughtered them?" If they were not sitting on their horses, I would spit into their faces. Instead, I lift the bucket and swing it over my head in ever-increasing circles. "Min fædre wæs Osfrið, Morkere eorles and Haroldes cyninges ðegn, þe ge acwealdon. They are both dead. But I am still alive."

With a shrill neighing, two horses jump back from the thing that comes flying at their nostrils, but the riders quickly bring them back under their control. The circle of spears around us is closing in.

"I would rather die than betray my country," I cry out.

The leader's face darkens. He hisses something incomprehensible. The wealhstod and the master of arms give him a look that swings between worry and annoyance. It seems their liege lord is slowly running out of patience with this stubborn Englishman.

My friend Ulfgar stands in silence, watching, shield up, spear at the ready.

The two Frenchmen talk at their leader. I stop whirling the bucket and pointlessly try to read their lips. Finally, the leader raises his hand, and the two fall silent. He speaks at length. I put the bucket down slowly and listen. Again, I do not understand, but some words sound like the names of the English eorles. I eagerly wait for the wealhstod to explain.

He confirms the names, but his words are like lumps of earth thrown onto someone being buried alive. The eorles are at King Willelm's manor house in Normandig. The language master does not call them prisoners, but how could it be otherwise? In Eoforwic, the French have rebuilt the two castles, this time in stone, so that they will not again fall victim, like dry twigs, to the flames. A French abbot who is an old friend of King Willelm's is soon to take over the office of archbishop. The few English nobles and rebels still alive in Norþhymbre will perish because the French destroyed their land and all the food supplies, from Snotingeham through Eoforwic to Dunholm. Famine, misery, disease, infirmity and agony await all those who oppose the king, and death will be a welcome relief to their suffering.

Every sentence from the wealhstod hits me like a spear being thrust right into my heart. The southern and eastern parts of Englaland are firmly in French hands, and the north will not hold out much longer.

What are we still fighting for? The French are taking our land, and we cannot stop them.

With his eyes sparkling like a deceptive layer of ice reflecting the rays of the winter sun, the leader beckons, and two of his men emerge from nowhere, pulling at some ropes with three little human figures attached and stumbling behind them.

As I look at the prisoners, my whole body goes limp. I close my eyes and take a deep breath. As I exhale, the last hope escapes from my body.

"We found these children up a tree," the wealhstod explains to me in a calm, almost soothing voice. "They kept shouting your name as my men here were trying to get them down."

The leader grunts a few words in French, and it takes a sharp command from him to prompt the wealhstod to translate his words. "Do you know these three… urchins?"

I chew on my lip and exchange a look with the trembling children, who stare at me with pleading eyes.

"Are these your brothers and sister?" the language master is asking, but he already knows the answer. Surely, he has spoken to them, and they have told him everything because he speaks their language.

I take a step forward, followed by the spearheads, and look the leader in the eyes, "If you kill them, you are next."

The wealhstod translates. A scornful smile spreads across the leader's face. With a voice like hoarfrost, he speaks to me. The language master lowers his eyes briefly before translating the words into English. "Are you threatening me, Englishman? Look around you! Who do you think will die first if you make even one false move? You are lucky that my master of arms appreciates the way you fight and wants you in his service, for if he did not, your filthy English mouth would have been kissing the dirt of this forsaken village long ago." He points to the three children, "We will take them as a pledge. If you do not do as you are told, Sire Geoffrey will have all of them killed."

Sire Geoffrey. Lord Geoffrey. So that is the name of my family's butcher. The man I am to work for from now on. My new lord. If I refuse, they will kill my brothers and sister. Ulfgar and I will take some more of them to their graves before we also die. If I agree, I will betray my country, my family, my king, but I will save the lives of my siblings. Can I trust the words of a Frenchman? Will he not kill them anyway? The French claim to be powerful, yet the leader needs a pledge for me to surrender. Is he afraid of me as long as I am not lying dead in the mud in front of him? Should he not in that case make sure that his watchmen keep a close eye on me instead of using children against me?

"Well, young Englishman," the wealhstod interrupts my thoughts, "how do you decide?"

My brothers and sister are waiting for my answer with open mouths.

"Where are you taking them, and how can I be sure that you will treat them well?"

Lord Geoffrey squints his eyes, but before he can say anything, the master of arms talks to him and then nods to the wealhstod. "Thibault himself will vouch for the welfare of your siblings."

It is hard to see Thibault's face behind the nose guard, but he lacks the pride of the leader. He does not gloat over the misfortune of others and almost looks at me like a father trying to save his son from certain death. If there is one Frenchman whom I should and can trust, it is probably him.

With a sigh, I let the rope slip through my fingers. The fire in the bucket is only a flickering little flame that the next breath of wind will blow out. My will is broken, my strength exhausted. I can hold out no more. "I believe you, and I agree. But before you take us away, I must give my wife, my parents and sisters a burial that is worthy of good Christians."

The Frenchmen exchange baffled looks as the wealhstod translates. To my relief, the leader nods. They do not dare to refuse me this. At least they are in awe of God's power.

Ic ðancige ðe, Dryhten min.

But relief soon gives way to an eerie feeling in my belly, as Lord Geoffrey turns to the language master, pointing to Ulfgar. "Are you Oswulf's brother?"

Even before Ulfgar answers, a burning pain passes through me, a foreboding of death that drives beads of sweat onto my forehead. My mouth opens, but no sound comes out. My body is numb, and I hear Ulfgar's words, only muffled, as if he were speaking through a heavy wooden door.

"I am his friend and brother-in-arms. My name is Ulfgar, son of Godric the smith."

I slowly shake my head. I feel a "No!" forming on my tongue, but a gag of air seems to block its way out. *He will die.*

A word from the leader. A thrust with the spear. A gurgling sound. Ulfgar's heavy body collapses.

"No!" My scream comes too late. I rush to Ulfgar, who was alive just a moment ago and who now lies dying on the thin blanket of snow.

At Lord Geoffrey's muttered command, the wealhstod and five other Frenchmen dismount. Two of them pull me up and take away my armour and weapons.

"We will also bury your friend as befits a Christian," I hear the language master murmur. "Where can we find your family, Oswulf?"

I am only half listening, but I nod and point to our manor. The language master grabs me by the shoulder and pulls me along, "Come, before Sire Geoffrey regrets his decision."

We stomp across the ground, littered with dead bodies, towards my father's manor, which, rather than being a home, is now an early grave for most of my family.

I press one last kiss on my wife's icy lips before we wrap her and the others in linen sheets. We lower the blood-smeared corpses of Godgifu, my sisters and my mother down into the trenches that we dug in the garden behind the great hall. Then it is Ulfgar's turn, and it takes three of us to lift him.

"We shall meet again in a better life, Ulfgar," I whisper and throw the first clod of earth onto my loud friend, who, from now on and forevermore, will be silent.

Next to my father's body, I fall to my knees and bury my face in his tunic. My body trembles – in grief at my father's death, in anger towards those who killed him, in guilt for my shameless pride and disregard for my father's words. It is my fault that misfortune and doom came upon my family and my home village.

I clutch my father's upper arms. How often did these strong arms shield me when I was little, and what did I do when they needed me? I sob and cry like a little child. One last time, I lean towards my father's ear. "The French will pay for what they have done to us," I whisper, fearing that the wealhstod might hear. "I will avenge you, Father."

I nod to a Frenchman and reach under my father's shoulders. Together, we put the body into its final resting place and shovel the earth back onto this last grave.

My head is humming and buzzing as if someone has hit me with a stone. The life I have known is over. I have lost my wife, my family and my friend. I am leaving my home village for good and will spend my life as a servant to a Frenchman. Instead of upholding the honour of my homeland as a ðegn of Eorl Morkere and King Harold, I trample it with the feet of a traitor.

Silent on the outside, full of questions on the inside, I mount the horse that one of the Frenchmen is holding for me. One last time, I look back at what I leave behind. Ledlinghe is burning – but they have not destroyed everything. In fact, some huts and sheds stand unaffected by fire and weapons. Here and there, a chicken clucks and dares to come out of its hiding place. Those who survived, here or in the woods, may not have lost everything, at least for the moment. I failed to save my family, but Ulfgar and I may have spared a few others a terrible fate. We lost the battle, and yet we may have won after all.

As a last memory of Ledlinghe, I seal this glimpse of hope in my heart before I urge my horse on and follow my new lord to his manor house.

We head southward. Dusk slips its icy fingers under my clothes, and I can feel the sweat freeze on my skin. My body aches, I am tired, hungry and thirsty, and I pray to God that I can get off this horse soon and have a piece of bread and a cup of ale. Should I not have died on the battlefield like my fellow countrymen? What will become of me amongst the French? They will make fun of me and order me to do all the dirty work they do not want to do themselves. Should the son of a ðegn really spend the rest of his days living in thrall to a French nobleman? What if the master of arms finds that my fighting skills are not as good as he thought? What happens to me when he no longer needs me?

The riders around me could not care less about my fate and what happened in Ledlinghe. They chat away cheerfully in this language that sounds like a thick brew of snuffling and singing. I hear them, but I can neither understand nor turn a deaf ear to their words. Like ravenous maggots, the sounds eat their way through my ears into my head. If the French let me live, I will one day, surely, lose my mind from hearing them speak.

The sun melts into the horizon and bathes everything in a red-golden light. In the distance, the roof of a manor house rises up, surpassed only by the tower of a nearby church. The buildings and the area seem familiar and yet strange, as if I have been here before, although I cannot remember when and why. Good and bad memories flow through my mind, but my tiredness obscures them from recognition.

Behind me, two Frenchmen lead the horses that carry my siblings. The two younger ones seem to be asleep. Their slumped bodies sway along to the rhythm of the hoofbeats. The eldest sits tensely in the saddle, frowning as he looks at the passing landscape. Our eyes meet. I am unable to smile at him encouragingly, so we only gaze at each other, both of us lost in the turmoil of our own thoughts.

As we pass some peasant huts, it slowly dawns on me why I know this place. Pictures shoot through my head like lightning. Stanfordbrycge. Father. The night ride with Ulfgar. A torch. Curious people. A little woman smiling at me. The herb hut. Father lives. King Harold is dead. *Wilburgfos!* What are we doing here? Is Lord Geoffrey planning to raid another village? Is that why they've taken me along?

The Frenchmen show no sign of aggression or restlessness. As if they were going home, they follow their leader, past the wooden building of the Benedictine monastery and on to Wilburgfos Manor. Little patches of snow glow on the muddy ground like guiding lights. Apart from a few pigs and a flock of chickens, which flutter wildly from the horses' hooves to safety, nobody pays attention to us. Have we become so used to seeing French riddan passing through our villages since the bastard became King of Englaland?

It has only been a few years since I was here, and yet a lot has changed. Is it just the season? When I first came to Wilburgfos, it was autumn. Now, it is winter, but the snow is melting, and the first buds are already heralding spring. The last peasants drive their oxen back home from the fields where they have ploughed the soil for the forthcoming seed and spread the dung. But where are all those who do not work in the fields? Weaving clothes at home, mending tools, feeding the animals?

At more than a man's height, a fence surrounds the manor and shields it from the peasant huts of the settlement. The wood looks fresh – there are no rotten spots or other signs of weathering. Even in the dark, we would have noticed such a high barrier. They must have built it after we left, but what for? It would be of little use to Kjetil to fend off a group of French warriors. Perhaps a pack of wolves or a band of robbers is roaming the woods around Wilburgfos.

Two elderly women fall silent as we approach them. They watch us with a mixture of curiosity, caution and disgust and start whispering as we pass. A group of children playing just outside the gate of the fence pauses and stares at us, wide-eyed. A boy, no older than the French rulership in Englaland, points at me and calls out to his playmates, "Englishmen!" In spite of all the evil that has befallen me, I have to smile at the little boy's excitement.

We finally reach the yard in front of the great hall. Four men approach us. A smile plays around the lips of the first one as he greets Lord Geoffrey in French and lets his curious eyes glide over me and my brothers and sister. Next to him, I recognise the man who welcomed us at the manor back then and supplied us with clothes and weapons. *Cen... Cenhelm?* The father of the high-spirited Cenric! My English heart leaps. I would like to have a few words with Cenhelm, but he is already leading two of the horses to the stables.

As I dismount, I wonder what the purpose of our visit here in Wilburgfos is. Perhaps we are still too far away from Lord Geoffrey's lands, so we will spend the night here. Or maybe we do not have to go there at all because Lord Geoffrey does not want any Englishmen at his manor house and is leaving us here in Kjetil's care. I take a deep breath and look at my brothers and sister, who huddle closely together between the big Frenchmen like young birds in a nest who have just caught sight of a foe.

"Ic eom Frederic. Wilcume!" Two friendly blue eyes look at me. Before me stands the man who greeted Lord Geoffrey a moment ago.

"Ic ðancige eow, Frederic," I reply. "Min nama is Oswulf."

"Frederic insisted on welcoming you in your language," explains the wealhstod. "He is Sire Geoffrey's seneschal and looks after the manor when the liege lord is travelling. And since the two of us will be dealing more often with one another from now on, let me also introduce myself – my name is Walchelin."

"I thought Cenhelm was in charge of the manor."

"You know Cenhelm?" Walchelin asks.

"We met him when we brought my father here after the battle of Stanfordbrycge."

"Well," Walchelin begins, after translating for Frederic, "a lot has changed here since then."

"So I noticed." I point to the wall of wooden stakes around us, "I do not remember the fence being there then. Does Kjetil fear for the safety of the people in his manor?"

The look of the two does not bode well. *Another seneschal. A fence around the manor.* "This is not Kjetil's manor anymore, is it?" Secretly, I pray that they will contradict me.

A translation is not necessary. Frederic shakes his head.

"Kjetil is dead," Walchelin says. "Almost two years ago, Sire Geoffrey took over the manor as a reward for his services here in the north."

Kjetil is dead. Sire Geoffrey is the new owner and Lord of Wilburgfos. Lord Geoffrey of Wilburgfos. We are not travelling any further. We have reached the end of our journey. I will live at Lord Geoffrey's manor house and work as one of his English slaves. Surrounded by Frenchmen whose orders I must carry out and whom I must serve. Oh, Father! What shame I have brought to our family and our country!

I feel a hand on my shoulder and look up. Frederic smiles as he speaks to me.

"Frederic invites you to the great hall," says Walchelin. "You need to eat and drink. Come!"

As if it had been waiting for its cue, my belly grumbles. Although I am still dazed by what I have just experienced, I nod and follow Walchelin into the manor house.

In the great hall, the warmth of a blazing fire caresses my aching body. I stretch my limbs and inhale the smell of food and sweat. The large, golden-yellow flames in the hearth throw flickering shadows onto the faces of the people inside. Servants hurry back and forth with bowls, loaves of bread and jugs to supply their masters with food and drink.

Surrounded by a handful of Frenchmen, Lord Geoffrey sits at a raised table from which he can overlook the entire room. With a fleeting glimpse at us, he turns to the man beside him, a ruffian with wild, dark hair and hands that move about like flushed-out birds.

Frederic points to two empty seats at one of the long tables, says goodbye and takes his place at the feudal lord's table. While I make my way to our seats with Walchelin, many observers follow our movements. Some of them need no words to show their disgust at the uninvited guest. Others look in amazement. Only a few look curious.

Where is Cenhelm? What about Hild the healer? How is Lady Edeva? Is she dead too?

My eyes search in vain for a familiar English face. I am surrounded by clean-shaven Frenchmen with ridiculous haircuts.

Maybe I should take my meal somewhere else. It is only a matter of time before they close in on me.

"Sit down, Oswulf!" Walchelin's voice tears me from my thoughts. He points to the space next to him.

I step over the bench and slowly sit while staring at the tabletop in front of me to avoid their gaze. I feel hot. *This is what a bear must feel like when they lead him to the fairground, only to be torn apart by wild dogs as dozens look on.* "Walchelin, I really do not think I should—"

"Do not think, Oswulf, just do as I say!" Walchelin beckons a servant. "You are now part of Sire Geoffrey's retinue, so you will eat when and where we eat."

The girl fills our cups. She is still young, not fifteen winters old, with long blonde hair. She smiles at me before turning to other thirsty guests in the great hall. I watch her go. We share a single fate. We serve the same French ruler. Trapped amongst foes who stole our fatherland from us.

Opposite, a man lifts his cup in my direction and shouts something that I cannot hear amidst all the noise. He nods resolutely at me and lifts the cup to his mouth.

I nod, hurriedly reach for my cup and put it to my lips. I am so thirsty that I take several gulps at once.

A tingling sensation trickles down my throat. It tightens my cheeks. My tongue rears up like a young horse that is feeling a saddle for the first time.

Ðis is laðlic! I spurt out a broad mist of spray.

The man next to me bursts with laughter, and others join in. I wipe my mouth and stuff a piece of bread into it to get rid of the disgusting taste.

Walchelin bends over to me with a worried face. "I suppose you have never tasted French wine before?"

"How can you drink this stuff?" I say, chewing. "Is there no decent ale at a French manor house?"

Walchelin sends out a servant, who soon returns with a jug and pours me a yellowish-cloudy liquid. "This is probably more to your liking."

I carefully take a sip. The herbs in the cool, tart barley juice tickle my throat, before I greedily empty half the cup. As I wipe my moustache in relief, two children are watching me from behind the tables and benches. The older of the two is a blonde boy, perhaps four winters old, leaning against the wall with one shoulder and wrinkling his nose at me. He looks like a fox cub sniffing at something, only to move on in disgust. He withstands my gaze.

I sense an aversion – dare I say, hostility? – in his inexperienced eyes. *How the French must hate us, when even small children look at me with such contempt.* I take another sip and peer over at the girl next to him.

While chewing away on one finger, the little thing smiles at me with a mischievous glint. She takes the hand of a woman, probably her nurse, and points in my direction. Then she drags her companion towards me, stops at a safe distance and looks at me with sparkling eyes.

"You already seem to have an admirer," mumbles Walchelin. "Who is this?"

"This is Adelais, Sire Geoffrey's daughter. A clever girl, though very headstrong."

I smile at the little one, and she smiles back broadly. *Like little Eda, when she was her age.*

"That boy over there is her older brother, William. Sire Geoffrey loves him dearly, especially since his..." Walchelin pauses and peeks at Lord Geoffrey, who is still engaged in heated discussions with his hairy neighbour and Frederic, "since his first wife died while giving birth to Adelais."

The little girl utters some scraps of words and sounds that are obviously aimed at me.

"I assume Sire Geoffrey married again?" I ask.

Walchelin rises, "Indeed, he did. And here comes his wife. Let me introduce you to her. She will be pleased to meet a fellow countryman."

A fellow countryman? So, Lord Geoffrey is married to an Englishwoman?

Walchelin leads to me a tall, slender woman with a baby in her arms. I meet them halfway and bow to her.

"Dame Edeva," Walchelin says, "this is Oswulf, son of a ðegn and English warrior from Ledlinghe. He will assist the master of arms Thibault in teaching the squires. Oswulf, this is Dame Edeva, Sire Geoffrey's wife and your new mistress."

Dame Edeva. I know this woman. That is Lady Edeva, Mistress of Wilburgfos.

Lady Edeva regards me, "Ic ðe wilcume, Oswulf. Your face looks familiar. Have we met before?"

She may only be five winters older than me, too young to show signs of old age. And yet the three and a half winters since we last met have left deep marks on her youthful face.

"After the battle at Stanfordbrycge, you were kind enough to save my father's life. My friend and I brought him to your manor that night, badly wounded."

"That was more than three years ago." She stares into the void as if the memory were taking shape in the air in front of her. "You came with a friend. How young you were back then!"

She is almost as tall as me but slimmer. Her light skin looks pale. In her eyes lies a sorrow that I do not remember from the time when her first husband, Kjetil, was still alive. But that was a long time ago. Maybe she is just exhausted from the upheavals on her manor, her new husband and his new customs, maybe from a stressful birth.

"I guess there is no need to ask about your father's health." The bitterness in Lady Edeva's voice is unmistakable.

"He is now in a world without sorrow. My friend Ulfgar has gone with him. They will wait for me there."

Lady Edeva lowers her head. On her arm, her son gargles to himself. A bonny little fellow with attentive blue-green eyes and light-blonde, fluffy hair. He stretches out his left hand and tries to grab me.

"Hwæt dest ðu, Hroðgar?" Lady Edeva looks at the little boy, who eagerly continues to stretch out his arm.

When he catches hold of my moustache, he giggles and fumbles with the hairy structure that he knows only from the English servants and peasants and not from his father or his fellow countrymen.

What am I doing? While I am drinking ale and amusing the lord's children, my siblings might be sitting in a dark hole, with only just enough water and bread to keep them alive as long as the French need me.

"What about my brothers and sister?" I ask the wealhstod.

"Fear not," Walchelin replies. "They are being taken care of. You can see them again tonight before you go to sleep. Tomorrow, Sire Geoffrey will send them to the manor houses of other French barons. Wilburgfos Manor is too small to accommodate four more Englishmen. They will be fine there, Oswulf. Not all Frenchmen are monsters, though it may seem so to you."

I am not convinced by Walchelin's words, but I cannot change the decision. At least Lord Geoffrey's men captured my siblings alive instead of killing them like most of the others.

Lady Edeva gently pulls back the little boy's hand. A painful smile flits across her face. "If you want to ease your heart and pray for the dead, speak to Father Leofric. He will gladly stand by you in this difficult hour, as he did with me."

"Leofric is still alive?" I dimly remember the slender figure of the priest.

"The French are devout people. In their homeland, there are many cathedrals in honour of the Almighty, and they have also built many places of worship in Englaland. They need the English priests to convey the Good Tidings in our language and to keep the services going."

It hurts to know that the cleric was luckier than my family. I thank Lady Edeva and promise to see Father Leofric first thing in the morning. It will do me good to speak to another Englishman.

"Come, Oswulf!" the language master beckons. "Thibault wants you to meet the barons. None of them knows yet that you will be taking over some of their sons' weapons practice."

An unpleasant heat rises in my body as I follow Walchelin to the elevated table in the great hall. "I am to teach Frenchmen how to fight?"

Walchelin nods with raised eyebrows. It is hard to tell which one of us believes more ardently that the master of arms has lost his mind. "Be prepared for some unpleasant remarks, but stay calm, and nothing will happen to you."

I shrug my shoulders, "How can it be otherwise? I do not understand your language and will not know what people are saying."

"I shall translate what is necessary for you," says Walchelin.

So, only part of what they say. Not all the slander and abuse they will let loose in the face of an Englishman amongst them. What gift have I that Thibault or another Frenchman wants? They will hate me. How could I ever agree to this? I would never have entered their service of my own free will, but I had no choice.

Thibault asks for silence. His voice is restrained, but it does not allow any contradiction. The hairs on my forearms stand up. It becomes quiet in the great hall. The ordeal begins.

It does not take long before the first men heckle the master of arms. The tone of voice and the grim face of the callers leave no doubt that I am not welcome here. I feel like a horse at the market that the buyers consider too expensive for what they see. *Who would buy such an animal? No one. Especially not if it is of English descent.*

I listen to the protestations and try to memorise the faces and the voices, even though I do not understand the words. It will not be the only time that these men will make my life difficult. I must be prepared for it.

Thibault takes the hecklings calmly. He answers briefly but firmly, silencing the grumbling barons.

"What did they say?" I murmur to Walchelin without taking my eyes off the crowd, which continues to eye me suspiciously.

"Oh, nothing we did not expect. What is this English bastard doing here? Do we not have enough able French warriors? You are just waiting for an opportunity to take revenge on us. It is understandable that these thoughts will concern them."

My heart and soul are rebelling against the prospect of spending the rest of my life at a French manor house, pretending to be one of them. I am not, and will never be, one of them, even if I am to teach their sons, who are hardly younger than me. The French hate me because I am English. The English will hate me because I sup with the Fiend. I work for the French, and yet I am neither a servant like the English nor of equal rank to the Frenchmen. I am an outsider to both sides, outcast from my father's lands and a stranger in my new home.

Despite the warm food, the fire and the many people heating the great hall, I am freezing. The glances cast at me pierce through my skin like the cold steel of a metal blade. *With Ulfgar at my side, I would show them why I am here if they dared to compete against me and my friend. My friend.* I press my lips together. The French must not find any weakness in me, for they are like wolves who mercilessly follow the bleeding game and once they have ensnared it, tear it to pieces. But they shall not succeed. Not now, and not as long as I can prevent it. The son of an English ðegn does not give in so easily.

I clear my throat, "Thibault?"

Thibault pauses in his explanations and looks at me.

I clear my throat again and step forward. Two men put their heads together and whisper a few words. I nod to Walchelin and speak.

"My name is Oswulf, son of Osfrið. My father was a ðegn of Eorl Morkere and the last English king, King Harold, who liberated this country from the Norþmenn. As a young warrior, I fought in the battles near Eoforwic and at Stanfordbrycge, at an age when your squires know the battlefield only from stories and tales. In battle, I defeated many Frenchmen who were older and more experienced than me, and together with my brother-in-arms, I saved my home village from being pillaged and destroyed. Your master of arms has seen me fight. In fact, we faced each other in single combat." I turn to Thibault, who points to his foot with a quick nod. "As you can see, I survived this fight. If your master of arms, of all people, wants to save the life of an Englishman, he will not do so without reason. If you are still not convinced, then I challenge each one of you to fight against me. On your own, if you dare."

Walchelin reluctantly translates my last sentences for the breathless audience. For a long time, there is silence. Some rub their chins, others exchange glances showing amazement or indignation or both. Initially, they just whisper, then the first men rise and speak up.

A cry in French from behind me tears through the noise, "Silence!"

All fall silent. Lord Geoffrey speaks angrily to his men. The standing ones sit down one after the other and do not dare raise their voices again. When Lord Geoffrey has finished, he turns to Thibault, who gestures at us to get back to our seats.

"Come!" says Walchelin and heads for our bench. "We have waited long enough for food."

I chase after him, "What did Sire Geoffrey say?"

"That he expects his men not to question his decisions and that they should pass on any complaints about you to Thibault, as he is personally responsible for you and your behaviour."

Further down the table, Thibault is picking up some bread and dunking it into his bowl. He lifts the slice, dripping with thick vegetable soup, in my direction and then takes a hearty bite.

As I dip the spoon into the steaming pottage in front of me, I watch the master of arms chatting with the men who surround him. My life depends on him. Losing his favour means certain death for me. And the same fate for my siblings.

Most of the Frenchmen could not care less and simply shovel the food into themselves or cast fleeting glances at me while chewing away on the vegetable pieces of the soup. Some, however, do not touch the food but follow my every move, frowning, as if they are waiting for me to pull a dagger out of my sleeve and fly into a frenzy.

I try not to lower my eyes when they look at me. They must not think they have already won.

Again and again they exchange short sentences with others while keeping an eye on me. They are talking about me. If I let their words and behaviour intimidate me now, I will have a hard time in their midst. I would be a disgrace to my father and my family.

The pride of being English suddenly burns and gnaws at the feelings of hopelessness and cowardice that cloud my thinking. Like two wild animals, the two sides fight in my chest. *"He who does not fight is worth nothing."* It takes a while, but my pride finally gets the upper hand and forces my despair to its knees. A wave of power floods my body, straightens it up, makes the stares bounce off me like blunt arrows on heavy battle dress. They will see that the son of a ðegn cannot be frightened by a few harsh words. I will show them that it takes more than that. One day, they will regret having turned against me.

My gaze wanders to Thibault and finally to the language master. *How far can I trust them? They seem to mean no harm, but they are French and bound only to their liege lord. How can I be sure that they will not betray me as soon as it is to their advantage?* "Tell me, Walchelin, how come you speak my language so well?"

The wealhstod wipes his mouth with a linen cloth, "That is very simple, Oswulf. My father was a baron from Normandig and came to Englaland when King Eadward was ruling. He took a liking to this country and the pretty women here, and he married one of them. So I grew up with a nurse who taught me French, but my mother spoke to me in the language of the local people. I am not a master of it, but it is enough to mediate between the two peoples."

"What do you think about bringing an Englishman to a French manor house to teach French boys how to fight?"

Walchelin laughs, "Thibault is a brave man. He fears no danger."

"You think he is mad?"

Walchelin shrugs his shoulders and scrapes out his bowl.

Maybe he is. But his word has enough weight to change his liege lord's mind and save me from certain death, at least, for the moment.

After dinner, I visit my brothers and sister in the shed. Eda is already asleep and lies, curled up in a heap of straw. Oswine is struggling to keep his eyes open and soon is also sleeping peacefully in the straw. Only the eldest, Wigstan, is still sitting upright next to them, staring at me.

"What will they do to us, Oswulf?" he asks quietly.

I stroke his blonde hair. He is the eldest of them, but still so young. Only a one-day-old chicken has downier cheeks than him. "They will take you to other manors tomorrow."

"But it is wrong."

"I know, Wigstan. But there is nothing we can do about it. You should give thanks to God that we are still alive."

"But what kind of life will we have? We are in the hands of the enemy. We—"

"I know it will not be easy, but you are alive, Wigstan. And so are Oswine, Eda and me. God has saved us from the fate that claimed Mother and Father, Æðelflæd and Wassa. Now, we must put our lives to good use."

Wigstan chews on his lower lip and looks at me for a long time. "One day, I will take revenge on him for this," he whispers with a coldness that is not like him at all.

He does not say the name, but I know he is talking about Lord Geoffrey. I nod and put my hand on his shoulder, "Yes, maybe you will. But you should try to sleep now."

When I come back to the great hall, two servants are clearing away the remains of the meal. Some people are already lying on the floor, tucked up in blankets and sleeping. A few French instructions echo through the room. Someone hands me an old woollen blanket.

I search for a free place and go to sleep with other Englishmen. *I wonder what they think about me. An Englishman brought here by the French. Maybe they know nothing about it. Maybe they do not understand their French masters any more than I do and simply carry out the orders they receive from a language master like Walchelin.* I look out for the wealhstod and Thibault, but I cannot see anything. The sun set long ago, and the fire in the middle of the great hall gives only a faint glow. I am too tired to look for familiar faces in this light, so I stretch out, pull the blanket up to my chin and close my eyes. *Dryhten min, you took my parents and my siblings from me today, but you spared me. Help me to be strong and to do my father honour as befits the son of a ðegn.*

In the morning, I bid farewell to my brothers and sister. Wigstan and Oswine go to the manor house of William de Perci, Lord Geoffrey's liege lord, in Cattune, north of Wilburgfos.

He will probably send them far enough away to stop them from conspiring with me. As for little Eda, Lord Geoffrey will offer her as a servant to one of his vassals, like cattle on the market. I pray to God that she will find someone to marry her in a few years' time and free her from a life of poverty and servitude. As the daughter of a ðegn, she deserves better than that.

The three of them are sitting on horses with an uncertain gaze as the animals carry them into their new lives. They have escaped death, but will their lives be better? I try to be grateful to God for protecting them during the battle of Ledlinghe and pray to him to continue to protect them on their new path. That is all I can do. The helplessness is killing me. I am doomed to watch the Frenchmen dispose of my brothers and sister as if they were goods for sale.

They disappear through the gateway of the fence. The Frenchmen who sent off the mounted troop turn to their daily work as if nothing has happened. I am left alone in the yard.

Thibault picks me up with two guards and leads me into the armoury. He talks to me, but only when he points to a stack of weapons do I realise that he wants me to clean them.

He leaves the armoury with a stern look at the guards. One of them stands at the entrance, the other takes a position directly in front of me at a due distance. He grunts some words and beckons with his chin for me to start. I look at the stack of weapons: a few swords and two lances. As I reach for a sword to inspect the blade, the Frenchman pulls his own and points it towards me. He says something – probably a threat, judging by his narrowed eyes and posture.

There are two of them, but they wet themselves with fear. It is hard for me to stifle a grin, but inside, I am laughing aloud.

What reputation must precede me at this manor house when two seasoned fighters startle as I pick up a sword!

I turn the sword in my hand and look at it from all sides. It has the right feel and shows not the slightest damage. Its blade is flawless and sharp. The French know their craft and look well after their weapons. It is all in exemplary condition, although a little dirty.

Sitting down on the bench, I reach for the rag that lies on a bucket full of ashes and wipe the blade with long strokes. From the corner of my eye, I can see my guard's sword hand twitch whenever I reach out for another weapon. It makes me chuckle.

When I have finished, my excitable watchman examines the result. He seems satisfied because he nods with a grim face and points to the door. As I rise from the bench, my gaze falls on a scramasax hanging in a leather sheath on the wall. I immediately recognise it as the scramasax that ended the lives of many Danes and Frenchmen on the battlefield. I know it well because it is my father's sword, crafted by Ulfgar's grandfather. He made the hilt from the horn of a deer that my father killed when he was sixteen winters old. The blade bears his name in runes to protect him. Now, the knife hangs there, unheeded and useless, so close and yet so far. I feel the urge to go and close my fingers around the rough horn hilt. To feel this infinite strength and power within me.

The guard gives me a push. I leave the armoury, followed by the two Frenchmen. They give me further orders and drive me forward to the small chapel of the manor. A man in a black robe is standing in front of the entrance, talking to a maid. When he sees us, the maid moves away, and he turns towards us.

"Father Leofric?" I ask.

With a merciful smile, the frock-wearer nods. "You must be Oswulf. Lady Edeva told me you want to make confession and pray for the dead."

"Yes, I do, Father. I am only a young warrior, but I have brought endless suffering to my family and my village. Many people had to die because of me. I was disobedient and disregarded my father's request. The Lord has punished me cruelly for this crime. I need to confess my sins to you so that you may free me from my heavy conscience and pray for my soul and those of the deceased."

Father Leofric points to the door of the chapel, "Let us go into the house of God then, so that you can repent your sins and ask the Lord to have mercy on you."

Chapter 2

IN THE SUMMER OF THE YEAR OF OUR LORD
1066

I am the eldest son of Osfrið, Đegn of Ledlinghe. Together with my parents and my five siblings, I lived peacefully at our manor, a longhouse made of mighty wooden beams, home to my father and grandfather, the ancestral home of my family.

Ledlinghe lies northeast of Wilburgfos, some three hours on foot, less than an hour for riders in a hurry with a good horse. It was once surrounded by fertile manor land, lush green meadows and large woods where we could freely hunt for game. This was a time when the English got on well with the sons and daughters of the Norþmenn who had settled down in Englaland over the last two hundred years. We shared fields and woods, tools and oxen, helped each other in times of drought, flood and disease, celebrated and mourned together.

I had everything I could wish for. I was the son of a ðegn, a rich nobleman who was loved by the people of Ledlinghe and respected among the ðegnes of the neighbouring villages. My mother's father had also been a venerable ðegn in Norþhymbre.

I had two elder sisters, but as the first-born son, I was the most important child to my father, for I would one day replace him as head of the family and Ledlinghe manor. To this end, he started early to prepare me for my role as a warrior and heir. He showed no mercy during weapons practice, but I liked fighting, and I was good at it.

When I was not practising, I shared happy moments with my brothers making arrows and bows and enjoyed the warm summer evenings carrying my little sister, Eda, on my shoulders and galloping through the colourful meadows and fields like a proud warhorse. I also took part in wrestling matches and did secret weapons drills with the peasant children, who would never be called up for military service but would be the first to fall in the event of an attack by enemy troops. All those things my father contemptuously called useless and a waste of time.

I remember a morning in the summer of the Year of Our Lord 1066, when I was practising swordplay in the yard with my father, as I did every day. The hot, humid air weighed heavy on my arms like chain mail, and even the breeze did not cool me down. Rather, it seemed to drive hither all the midges and flies from the river Deorwente, which meandered south about an hour's walk to the west of Ledlinghe. I constantly lashed out at the gnats, which greedily attacked my bare upper body and legs.

"If you let every fly bother you, you'll never become a huscarl," my father rumbled. "Every dead man on the battlefield lures more of this vermin, and your opponents won't wait for you to chase the flies away. Turn your thoughts to what really matters: your enemy and your sword. Forget everything else."

I hit another midge on my upper arm and growled. My body was drenched in sweat, but my mouth was so dry that I couldn't even swallow – and my father would not let me drink for quite some time.

In front of the stables, my older sisters Æðelflæd and Wassa were feeding the chickens, while little Eda carried her favourite chicken in her arms and stroked it. They didn't seem to mind the gnats, and for a moment I envied them.

A swing with the sword right in front of my face made me jump.

"Don't dream, Oswulf!" my father said. "On the battlefield, you would now be dead. He who does not fight is worth nothing. You want to be worth something, don't you? You want to become a huscarl and be one of the best and most respected warriors to protect the Eorl of Norþhymbre with your own life and limb, do you not?"

I took a deep breath and nodded with my head down. "Yes, Father, I do. Forgive me my recklessness."

"I am doing this for you, Oswulf. I want you to attain what I was denied. I have been gathering a large sum of money for you so that you can afford everything you need to become a huscarl."

Inwardly I winced. Yes, my father collected coins in a chest, but the money came from the pockets of the peasants and smaller landowners from whom he collected taxes for the king. I had seen him secretly put some coins in the chest while the rest went into the sack for the king.

"I make sure you have the necessary skills in using weapons. Every evening, I check that the chest with the money and your battle wear is well locked. Once we have the sword with inlaid gold inscription for you to present to the eorl, nothing and *no one* shall stand in your way."

He spat out the words "no one". The anger about failing to become a huscarl many winters ago still gnawed at him. He too had had such a sword, which he proudly showed to his friends after picking it up from the blacksmith. That very night, it was stolen from him. One of his friends then presented it to the eorl and became a huscarl. My father never tried again. Since that day, however, he hated his former friend's brother, our shoemaker, as well as the shoemaker's son with whom I used to spend time in the woods or at board games. "Never trust a Viking!" was a phrase he often repeated since then. But why should I do so, when we had been living peacefully with them as neighbours for many years?

"Are you even listening to me, or are you dreaming?"

"Yes, Father..." I had been listening to him, but another noise distracted me. A rattling and wild mooing that grew louder as it approached from somewhere beyond the manor.

Little Eda was running after her favourite chicken, which was trotting around in front of our manor house and seemed to be playing tag with her.

The rattling noise came rushing in like a roaring torrent of water that bursts a riverbed after the snow melts. My heart was pounding. Something big was coming. Unstoppable, with force – and fast.

I dropped my sword and took a few unsteady steps across the yard.

"Where are you going, Oswulf?" my father asked. "We are far from finished."

My steps quickened. *Faster, faster,* said an inner voice. A shiver ran down my skin. Suddenly, I no longer cared about midges and flies, nor the swordplay.

"You come back right now!" my father shouted.

The thundering of hooves on sandy ground was now loud and clear. I set off running. Eda was sitting on the floor, stroking the chicken in her arms. Out of the corner of my eye, I saw the yoke of oxen thundering round the corner.

My father yelled. I shouted. Eda shrieked.

I darted across the path, snatched my sister and leapt into the dirt on the side of the road. The ground shivered as the oxen rumbled past with the cart. Grit pelted my naked back. A cloud of sand rose above us. Then the rattling died away.

From the other side, I heard voices. Cautiously, I unrolled and looked up.

A few men came chasing after the oxen, trying to bring them to a halt. Two peasants hurried past us without even bothering to look.

I lashed out at the flies buzzing around us, stood up and helped Eda to her feet. "That was close," I said, brushing the sand-strewn hair out of her face.

"Hwær is Hen?" Eda sniffled and looked around with a worried face and empty arms.

From the yard, my older sisters rushed over. "Are you injured?" asked Wassa.

I wiped my face. A few grains of sand crunched between my teeth. "No, everything's fine."

Wassa fell to her knees and hugged her little sister. "Ic ðancige ðe, Dryhten min! Nothing has happened to you."

"I'm so glad you were there, Oswulf." Æðelflæd hugged me before stroking Eda's cheek. "Without you, the oxen would have run her down."

"Oswulf!" My father stood at the entrance to our yard and looked at me grimly. "I don't have all day."

"But, Father!" said Wassa. "He saved Eda's life."

"That was very brave of him. But also very foolish. He could have been hurt, and what chance would a cripple have of becoming a huscarl? His brothers are too young to be taught how to fight properly. I need a strong and able son to take over the manor one day. Let us go, Oswulf."

❧

So, I lived happily with my family and friends, but as the warm summer days passed, travelling minstrels and messengers brought news that both Norþmenn and the French wanted to take the crown from our king. Father stepped up the weapons practice, even my brothers became more involved in the daily fighting. At the time, I did not understand my father's concern. If our enemies were after the king, wouldn't they attack in the south, far from Ledlinghe, where the king usually held court?

I was pondering this question, the disturbing tales and what they possibly meant, as I looked after our equipment and weapons one day. Father had had chain mail made especially for me and two leather harnesses for Wigstan and Oswine and picked up three extra swords from the blacksmith. After removing the rust stains from father's chain mail with sand, cleaning the spear, sword and axe and checking the shield for cracks, I took my bow and arrows and set off in search of Ulfgar and Stígandr. A little trip into the woods would do me good and hopefully, take my mind off things. Besides, now was the best time to catch a careless roebuck.

I hadn't quite left our yard when I heard a harsh barking sound from the other end of the village, alternating with hoarse yelping. Sighing, I continued towards the noise. On the dry ground, an ochre-brown-black hairy ball was rolling around, kicking up dust. The sounds came from within, sometimes from a muzzle, sometimes a mouth.

I stood beside the bundle and put one end of my bow on the ground. "When the two of you have flattened the sand enough, perhaps you would like to come hunting with me?"

The hairy ball unrolled, and four eyes looked at me sheepishly. "Oswulf, my friend. Good to see you."

Before I could reply, the four-legged half of the bundle, tail wagging and barking, jumped at me and just about failed to knock me over. She was the size of a cow, with equal weight and power, and there was nothing I could do to stop her from greeting me joyfully as she licked my face with her oversized tongue.

Meanwhile, the two-legged half had also lifted himself off the ground. Looking at the two of them, you could see they were a perfect match. "Bargest missed you," said Ulfgar, my friend and trusted brother-in-arms.

"Sit! Sit, Bargest!" I said, gasping, as I pushed the dog away from me. At last, she let go, but continued to pant and wag her tail, four paws on the ground. Breathing a sigh of relief, I pulled my linen shirt back into place.

Like two giant pincers, Ulfgar's arms flew around my shoulders and squeezed the air out of me. "Let me clasp you to my bosom, dear friend!" Eyeing my bow, he loosened his embrace. "I see you are on your way to the woods. Do you need some company?"

"Do you have time?"

"There's nothing for me to do at the moment." The expression on his face, shaped like a small round shield, was rather bored, yet my friend was still an impressive sight. His ochre beard curled sparsely but evenly over his upper lip, chin and cheeks – a sight envied by many youths in the village who, like me, boasted a mere below their nose. With his beard and a thick mane of the same colour, darker at the hairline and sun-bleached towards the tips, Ulfgar looked like an oversized wildcat standing on its hind legs looking for something to eat – and eat he did, as anyone who saw him could tell. For my friend was not at all the slender, sinewy "wolf-spear" one might expect from his name. He was a stocky, strong and brave fellow who never backed out of a fight. Countless scars on his body and a missing piece of his right forefinger bore witness to this.

"Well, get your bow and come! I need to talk to you."

"Talk to me? Eala, I thought we were going hunting."

"Gleoman. My father rode to Chercam this morning to discuss something important with the ðegnes."

"Something important. I see. Now, I suppose you think I can tell you what it is." He stroked Bargest over the head.

"Just get on with it or the deer will all be gone before we even reach the woods."

But Ulfgar would not let himself be rushed. "Easy, Oswulf! Deer come to those who wait. Haste scares them away."

When he returned with the bow on his back and Bargest at his side, we went on to the shoemaker's house to pick up Stígandr. As usual, his father Olaf flinched when I appeared in his workshop. Perhaps he was still afraid that my father would one day punish him for what his brother did, since his brother was no longer around to avenge directly.

"We have a lot of work," Olaf said with a sweeping motion at all the leather rags, half-finished and damaged shoes that surrounded him in his workshop. "Can't you go another time?"

"We'll be back before you have finished even a single pair of shoes." Like a cat about to pounce on an unsuspecting

mouse, Stígandr skirted his father. His blonde hair, tied together at the nape of his neck, nestled tightly against his head
and made his bony face look even narrower than it already
was. "Just remember, a little more meat for the winter never
hurts." He smiled, showing a row of even teeth in his protruding lower jaw.

I was ashamed of my thoughts, but with that expression
on his face and the sparse strands of beard on his chin, he always reminded me of a goat chewing. Perhaps this appearance
was the reason he was still not married, for he was several winters older than me and Ulfgar. Or perhaps his father couldn't
bear the loneliness that had been spreading through the hut
since his last daughter married and his wife died.

His father sighed and waved his hand. "Then get out of
here. But you will make up the time tonight, son."

Stígandr indicated a bow. "Of course, Father."

So, off I went with my strange friends – a tall and chunky
one who my father appreciated because he came from the family of my betrothed, and a tall thin one whom he hated because he was the nephew of his cheating huscarl friend, a
Norþmann with the morals of the god Loki, as he said. More
than once, my father had warned me that names were not
given without reason, that Stígandr too would eventually live
up to his name "wanderer" and that he would change sides
like the autumn wind changes the direction from which it
blows. I did not feel so sure about this. Wasn't the name what
the parents saw in a newborn or what they wanted to ascribe
to him, rather than an evil prophecy that would someday fulfil itself like an inevitable curse?

We walked along the wide path to the woods while Bargest
ran, sniffing through the tall grass beside us.

"Do you think the Norþmenn and the French will invade Englaland?" I asked my friends.

Ulfgar sucked in his breath. "Both of them at the same time? That's going to be tough."

"One West Saxon less to oppress us?" asked Stígandr. "I think that's something to look forward to."

"How can you be so sure that our king will lose?" I asked.

Ulfgar leaned forward and looked past me at Stígandr. "And what if he does? Do you think the Norþmenn or the French will treat us better once one of them is king?"

"You mean, will they squeeze us even more than that wicked brother of the king?" asked Stígandr.

"My father and two hundred other ðegnes drove him out," I said. "We will also protect ourselves from any other men preying on us."

"Oh, yes, sure." Stígandr waved my words aside. "You are the son of a ðegn and have nothing to worry about. Everyone knows that the tax collectors slip some of the coins into their own money pouches before passing the rest on to the king. You have money, a manor, people who work for you."

"That is the God-given order," I said. "Do you want to doubt it?"

"Nowhere is it written that a man should not seize an opportunity when he gets one."

"What are you implying, Stígandr?"

"My father expects me to take over the workshop and be a shoemaker for the rest of my life. But look at my uncle, he has become a huscarl, lives a carefree life at the manor house of the Eorl of Norþhymbre and receives a nice sum of money for it."

"And is the enemy's first target when they try to get rid of the eorl," Ulfgar said.

"But you can't become huscarl," I said.

"Who said I wanted to be a huscarl?" asked Stígandr.

"Why else would you have mentioned your uncle? He would never have become a huscarl either if he hadn't..." I pressed my lips together.

Stígandr turned and looked me in the eye. "Not everyone can be born into a wealthy family like you, young Osfriðson. Your father never accepted that my uncle was better than him, so he made up that story about the stolen sword."

"Oh did he? And what if I become a huscarl too, and I'm better than your uncle? Will your uncle accept it then?"

"You want to be a huscarl?" Stígandr raised his eyebrows. "Why? Because your father failed?"

"My father did not fail!"

"So why does he then put you through weapons practice and battle preparations until late at night? You already excel among your peers. But your father wants to be absolutely sure that you meet the physical requirements to become a huscarl, while he is taking care of your armour, weapons and the money. He wants you to become a huscarl in his place because he didn't make it."

"That's not true. I'm just not good enough yet, so I need to practise more."

"So it is your very own wish to become a huscarl?"

"Yes, forsooth!" How could he even ask? Of course I wanted to become a huscarl. They were honoured and highly respected warriors at the manor house of the great eorles and even the king himself.

"That's enough now," said Ulfgar. "Otherwise, you'll scare away the few animals that haven't already fled with all your shouting."

We continued in silence among the tall spruce and beech trees until we reached a long row of thorny brambles in the middle of the woods, where a grassy clearing spread out over a gentle valley. From behind the brambles, we had a good view of the clearing. Now, we had to wait.

"Lay down, Bargest!" Ulfgar pointed his mangled right forefinger and looked at Bargest with raised eyebrows. The dog lay down at his feet and let him pat her head. "Good girl. Now, stay there." As if to confirm, Bargest nodded and rested her head on her front paws.

Stígandr crouched next to the dog and took out his snare traps. I peered over the thorny bushes. No deer, not even the tiniest beast in sight.

Ulfgar let his massive body fall onto the ground and laid the bow beside him. Then he interlaced his fingers and let his gaze wander over the ground as if he were looking for something. "We should have brought something to eat."

"You're a glutton, Ulfgar."

My friend held his palms up reproachfully. "Hey, not everyone can be a sinewy stripling like you."

"Eat the blackberries in front of you. That will keep you happy for a while."

Ulfgar rolled to the side, crouched against the bushes and began to eagerly gather berries. While he stuffed a handful into his mouth, he held out the other hand to me. "Want some?"

I looked at his hand, then turned my gaze back to the clearing. "M-m."

"Hm!" Ulfgar shrugged and after Stígandr had also declined, gobbled up the rest of the berries before gathering more. He was probably expecting a longer wait.

Stígandr disappeared between the trees to set some traps. As nothing budged on the clearing, I sat down next to Ulfgar to eat some berries, but suddenly, Bargest raised her head and started sniffing. Ulfgar and I gulped down the fruit and peered from behind the bushes as carefully as we could. On the far side of the clearing, some deer emerged from the undergrowth, nibbling the young buds of the small trees.

"We're lucky," I whispered. "The wind is blowing in our direction. They won't smell us."

Little by little, the deer's grazing brought them closer, but they were still about half a mile away. Bargest became restless, repeatedly looking from the deer back to her master.

Ulfgar fingered his bow nervously. "Can't they go a little faster? I'm about to wet my breeches."

"Can't you hold on? If one of them gets just a little closer, I can take a shot."

"You're mad. They're a good four hundred feet away. Even a king's archer would have trouble hitting them." Ulfgar stepped from one foot to the other. "You'll only scare the whole herd away."

"You too, if you don't shut up." Slowly, I placed the arrow on my bowstring. "Now, if you want to pee, let me finish this."

"Pff. As if!"

The deer pattered a few steps closer, stopped, raised its head and twitched its ears as if it had heard something.

"You see? It knows that we—"

The rebound of my bowstring silenced Ulfgar. In a high arc, the arrow whizzed through the air over the clearing and then took a dive like a hungry hawk.

"You're in league with the Fiend," Ulfgar breathed as the arrow pierced the deer's side.

It flinched and pelted off. The rest of the herd disappeared, leaping into the woods.

"Let's go!" I dashed down past the brambles into the clearing.

"Fetch, Bargest! Go, get that deer!" shouted Ulfgar.

Barking, the dog raced past me to chase the injured animal, and we soon found her sitting like a good dog next to the dead deer.

Ulfgar slowed his steps and finally stopped. "I don't believe it." He turned to me, stretched out his arms and bowed so low that the tips of his hair touched the ground. "Oh, Oswulf, great god of hunting and king of the longbow, forgive me for not believing in you and for daring to doubt your abilities. I am unworthy of your friendship."

I could not help laughing. "You madman. Shut up!" With Bargest watching me, I pulled the arrow out of the deer. "Now, do what must be done," I said with a glance at Ulfgar.

"Like... what?"

"Wasn't there something you wanted to do before we head back?"

"Oh, right."

Ulfgar hid behind the bushes, flooded the ground and came back with a satisfied smile.

"Let's get our guest ready to travel then." He pulled two leather straps from the pouch on his belt.

We felled a thin tree to which we tied the front and back legs of the deer, hoisted the ends of the trunk onto our shoulders and set off.

"I see your hunt was successful." Stígandr joined us on the way, lifting up a pheasant. "But the shoemaker's son also made a catch."

"Come on, Stígandr!" I said, patting him on the back. "We've lived together peacefully until now, and that's how it's going to stay, isn't it?"

Stígandr nodded. "God willing."

☙

Back in Ledlinghe, Stígandr refused his share of the deer – he had, after all, caught a pheasant and held it up once more as if to prove it – and left us outside his father's workshop. We took our hunting prey to Ulfgar's home so his mother could start gutting the animal. Later, my mother and sisters would help her carve, roast and smoke it.

With a loud bark, Bargest announced us and ran into the hut. Shortly afterwards, the blacksmith's daughter stepped out, Godgifu, God's gift – and that's what she really was: the prettiest girl in Ledlinghe, sister of my best friend Ulfgar and, for a few months now, my betrothed. I still see her face before me, her large, bright eyes in which I could see my reflection as in a clear lake, her rounded lips to which I owe many sweet moments, her delicate hands gliding over my face and body like a feather. She stepped out of the hut into the light, and the sun tried in vain to outshine Godgifu's beauty. The slender gold ring that bore our engraved names on the inside sparkled on her right hand as she held out her arms to me.

With my free arm – I needed the other to hold the trunk with the deer on my shoulder – I pressed her against me and gave her a long kiss.

"Take your time, you two," Ulfgar said. "Deer dries much more gently in the sun than in the kitchen."

Godgifu ran her hand over my shoulder and arm. "Eala, you're getting stronger all the time. You'll crush me one day."

"And you're getting more beautiful every time I see you, Godgifu," I said and kissed her again.

"Never stop saying that." Another kiss.

"Not in a hundred winters."

The shuddering on my shoulder brought me out of heaven and back to earth.

"The deer is already starting to smell," Ulfgar said, continuing to pull on the tree trunk. "Save your sweet words for another time."

Godgifu slipped into the house, and we followed her into the kitchen, where Ulfgar's mother had already prepared everything for butchering the animal. I said goodbye to go and fetch my mother, gave Godgifu a kiss on the cheek and hurried home.

As I was walking towards the great hall, my brother Oswine came calling. "A messenger is here, Oswulf. Come quickly! It's urgent."

My father and a stranger were sitting at a table, with Wigstan standing beside them. After taking a large sip of his ale, my father slammed the cup back on the table. "There's bad news, Oswulf."

The messenger turned to me and said, "The king's brother has left his exile and conspired with the Norse king against his own brother."

I frowned. "You mean they want to invade Englaland together?"

"He's already doing it. All along the south coast of Englaland, from Sandwice in the southeast to Wiht in the west, he raids and ravages the land. King Harold has sent scouts to find out what his brother and the Norþmenn are up to. He has also called for the fyrd to gather in the south in case Willelm

the Bastard and his Frenchmen decide to set sail for Englaland."

My father stared at the table.

"Will you take me south with you?" I asked him.

"No."

"But I could be useful to you—"

"I'm not riding south, Oswulf."

"But why not? The king is assembling his army there."

"If the Norþmenn attack – and they will do so sooner or
later – they won't sail down south first."

Of course not. From Norweg, they are much closer to the
English northeastern coast. Where we live.

"I can tell by your look, that you understood, my son."

I nodded, not sure whether to rejoice or weep. Should I
have struggled through all those hours of my father's ruthless
weapons practice honing my fighting skills just for the sake
of defending a manor house, stopping a few stray Norþmenn
from raiding Ledlinghe? Were not the pitchforks and pikes of
the peasants enough for that? Surely, no young man who
wanted to become a huscarl was needed for that. On the
other hand, what about my mother and my brothers and sisters? How were they to defend themselves against the Norþmenn? Those grim wælwulfas from the north would take
what they wanted with their greedy fingers – using an axe, if
necessary. My mother and sisters were helpless against them,
and my two brothers were too young to protect them. They
could hardly fight for themselves, so how were they meant to
stand their ground against a much older and battle-hardened
Norþmann?

The messenger continued. "The king will defend the south
against the French, if necessary. At the moment, the wind is

keeping Willelm from crossing the water between Englaland and the Frankish kingdom. As for a Norse threat to the northern part of Englaland, all the huscarles and ðegnes who live here will gather in three days. It will not be easy for us. In Norþhymbre, some people have been upholding their oath to the king's exiled brother and are waiting for his return. He also has strong ties with the powerful Scottish king who will come to his aid. They will all bring together their men in the north."

"You mean they will attack from Scotland?" I asked the messenger.

"No," he said. "Our scouts tell us that they are meant to sail along the coast and then up the Humbre as far as they can with their longships, that is, as far as Richale. From there, it is not far to Eoforwic, the only large town up here and the most important place for traffic, trade and politics. Once Eoforwic falls, other places will follow. If the huscarles and ðegnes who have sworn oaths to Eorl Morkere are not all ready to defend Englaland with their men, it will be easy for the Norþmenn to take the north by force."

My father nodded and looked at me. "Eorl Morkere needs every man."

I chewed on my lip. *Eorl Morkere needs every man. Every man?*

"Well, what do you say, Oswulf? Will you support me in the fight against the Norþmenn?"

"You want me to ride with you? But who will take care of the manor and Ledlinghe?"

"Are you surprised that you are to go to war?" My father raised his eyebrows. "Isn't that what I've been teaching you? True, as my first-born son, you would usually be overseeing the manor when I am not around, but these are not ordinary circumstances, Oswulf. The future of Englaland is at stake. Your future, not that of a single manor. We will find a way to gather enough men to defend Ledlinghe while we are away, should the Norþmenn come this far. In the meantime, we must prepare to catch the enemy as early as possible."

"Our scouts are following their every move on English soil," said the messenger. "We know exactly where they are and what they are doing at all times."

I will fight in the name of Englaland and for the good of a whole people against unlawful invaders? "But Father, I am still too young to fight in a battle. What could I possibly do against a skilled warrior?"

"Don't worry about that. I know I can rely on you. You are a brave and tough boy and wield weapons like no other. You will look after my horse, weapons and shield and, God willing, you will come to help me." He raised his cup to me and drank.

Afterwards, when I accompanied my mother and sisters to Ulfgar's home, thoughts were whirling wildly in my head. This would be my first real battle. Was I ready? Had my father really prepared me enough?

"I am scared, Oswulf," Godgifu said, squeezing my hand as if to keep hold of me forever. "What if something happens to you? If you get wounded or..." She turned her head away. "I don't even want to think about it."

I gently clasped her hands. "Fear not, Godgifu. My father has taught me well over the years. Besides, I am still too young to join the battle myself. I will only be watching my father's horse and weapons, way off from the fighting."

My voice was firm to take away Godgifu's fear, but inside I was trembling. I was no huscarl, no ðegn, not even a warrior.

I was just a sixteen-winter-old youth facing his first battle and not wanting to fail in meeting his father's expectations.

❧

In the afternoon, my father called a meeting to choose the men who would go with him into battle. It was with great relief that I heard that Ulfgar was to remain by my side, yet it broke my heart that as a result of that decision, Godgifu would now be fearing for both her brother and her beloved.

The Norse threat became a certainty in September when our scouts reported the first raids along the northeastern coast of Englaland. Only when the Norþmenn embarked on the Humbre did the raids stop, and the invaders eventually pitched their tents at Richale.

On the last day before we left for Eoforwic, we spent much of our time preparing horses, armour, weapons, tents, provisions and all that we would need for a prolonged stay at the town gates. After the work was done, I sat with Ulfgar, leaning against the wooden wall of our stable and watching the setting sun.

"Sitting here doing nothing until we leave is unbearable," I said.

"You can't wait, can you?" asked Ulfgar, taking a sip from his cup.

"It will be my first real battle. That is truly exciting."

"Get used to it if you want to be a warrior."

"Are you scared?" I looked at Ulfgar.

He shrugged his shoulders. "I don't know. Right now, I have a strange feeling in my stomach. Tomorrow, I'll know if it was fear or a bad meal."

I looked again at the sun, whose yellow hue was slowly turning a reddish orange. "I want to get it all over with as quickly as possible and return to Ledlinghe." *Back to the everyday life that I must give up for this battle.*

"How many Norþmenn do you think we'll have to fight?"

"The scouts mentioned several hundred ships. Not all were warships, but there must be thousands of warriors." I shuddered at the thought of facing such a vast army of axe-wielding enemies.

"Then let's hope they don't bother with us but go for the warriors of the eorles."

The warriors of the eorles. His huscarles. And my father. I took a deep breath. The huscarles were highly skilled and had the best armour and weapons a blacksmith could make. *If it hadn't been for Stígandr's uncle, my father would be one of them now.*

Chapter 3

SEPTEMBER IN THE YEAR of OUR LORD 1066

On the early morning of the 20th of September in the Year of Our Lord 1066, Eorl Morkere and his brother led our army to Fuleforde near Eoforwic. On the plain between the river Use and the dyke with the wide marsh behind it, we waited for the wælwulfas. The two eorles had brought their huscarles and many sworn followers but also mercenaries hoping for rich rewards for their service. Their army was complemented by ðegnes like my father, who brought their own warriors to protect the north while the king was at the ready in the south.

While we were waiting, I helped my father put on his chain mail and helmet with nose guard, then gave him his sword, spear and the big round shield. In the light of the rising sun, he was a truly magnificent sight, a warrior who had proved himself a worthy fighter for his country in several battles. A mixture of pride and fear came over me. In a few years, it would be me sitting on a warhorse and going to war for Eorl Morkere and the king – if God so willed that I would become a warrior and that there would still be war then. For so long, Norþmenn and Englishmen had lived peacefully together, and suddenly, they would once again battle each other for a land they both called home.

On the other side of the plain, the Norse troops were gathering around their king. But only when the sun was almost highest in the sky had the waters of the Use receded enough for the battle to begin. Eorl Morkere led the first attack.

The roar of the warriors rushing towards each other was deafening. Soon, the first men fell, struck down by axes and pierced by swords. The two armies mingled into a uniform mass moving back and forth, and rising, wave-like, where warriors stepped over dead men.

Whenever the battle lines changed, we handed the exhausted warriors something to drink and, if necessary, new weapons before they plunged back into the fray. Together, with other youths, a few women with healing skills and a priest, we also took care of the wounded. Some of them, we were able to save, but with most, we were less lucky. They died as we were still pulling them to safety or succumbed to their injuries shortly afterwards. As I looked at one of the dying, I saw again the image of my father in his polished, shining armour. By now, it would be smeared all over with blood and bearing witness to the blows of the enemy's weapons through the broken chain links and dents in the metal. Nothing would be left of the splendid impression he had made before the battle. And yet that was what mattered to my father. *He who does not fight is worth nothing.*

A piercing sound made me hark. Was someone sounding the charge? One of the older warriors, who was taking a sip from a water bottle, paused. A dull rumble, followed by shouts and screams, approached on the flank where the eorl's brother was positioned with his men from Myrce. More and more men dragged themselves back to us from the thick of the fighting, badly wounded, but we only saw the reason for this when the first Norþmenn appeared in the midst of our army. Wielding their mighty two-handed axes, they drove a wedge between the English warriors, breaking them up and closing down on each group they had cut off from the rest. The hosts of the two eorles were separated, and while one part was able to hold off the Norþmenn in the narrow ford, the Norþmenn pushed Eorl Morkere and his army further and further back and northward, like a pack of wolves driving a flock of closely huddled sheep.

"Wiþertrod! Wiþertrod!" shouted a warrior running towards us.

I began to tremble. *Retreat?* Was this a ruse on our part, or were the Norþmenn really more than we could handle?

I stumbled a few steps while the fighters were swaying to and fro like waves. But just as the tide flows inexorably onto the beach, these waves too washed their load unerringly in only one direction – and that was the one in which we were standing. Where was my father?

Not far from us, I could hear the roar of the enemy hordes, through which Ulfgar's voice came to me as through a mist. "Teng recene, Oswulf! We must hurry back to the horses."

Reluctantly, I averted my eyes from the battlefield and ran after Ulfgar. "Have you seen my father?"

"How could I?"

True, it was impossible to make out a single man among the thousands of warriors. But how could I not see my father anywhere at all? As we were fleeing across the marshland and past the scattered weeping willows, I continued looking for him, but he was nowhere to be seen.

Unflinchingly, the Norþmenn pursued the retreating Englishmen, and whoever reached a horse, mounted and galloped off. Yet for the slow ones amongst us, there was no escape from the enemy axes.

Father's horse was prancing when we reached it. I yanked the reins loose and had trouble holding it.

"Father?" I asked myself rather than the men approaching. My heart was pounding. I saw the image of my father sitting proudly on his horse this morning, fading into the dreadful sight of the bloody, filthy, mutilated dying and dead scattered across the battlefield.

"There he is!" Ulfgar pointed to a cluster of men rushing towards us.

I recognised his brown shield with the four flaming stripes I had painted myself and breathed a sigh of relief. Father had come back! Alive. "Quick, Father!" I shouted unnecessarily.

We jumped into the saddles and spurred the horses on, just wanting to get away from the wælwulfas as quickly as possible. I was close to tears. This had been my first battle, and the English army had failed miserably. We were defeated and fleeing from an enemy who had crushed our forces and was now free to enter the gates of Eoforwic. Like rabbits, we ran away, eorles, huscarles, ðegnes and all their warriors – or at least those who had survived the slaughter. Being the son of a nobleman certainly may have sounded good to a peasant and undoubtedly had many advantages, but it also had its dirty sides, and this was one of them.

I prayed to God that word about our losses would not reach Ledlinghe. My mother and siblings would fear the worst. I didn't dare think about how Godgifu would receive the bad tidings. Should our happiness here on earth really have been so short-lived? At least, Ulfgar and I were still alive. But what was to happen next?

Disheartened and exhausted, I returned to our tents with Ulfgar and the rest of the warriors and helped tend to the wounded.

Our scouts reported that the Norse king had sent messengers to Eoforwic to give the scirgerefa the choice of surrendering the city with or without a fight. We were so close, but our army was scattered in all directions. For a long time, it looked as if neither of the eorles would be able to gather all the warriors together again. and that we would simply have to stand idly by as the Norþmenn took Eoforwic. But the Almighty had mercy on us and sent us a messenger from the south on the third day.

"I bring good tidings," said the messenger. "The king and his warriors left for the north two days ago and will reach Tatecastre tomorrow."

The warriors cheered. I leaned towards my father. "Where is Tatecastre?"

"Southwest of Eoforwic, less than half a day's walk or a couple of hours on horseback."

"Do you think the king will arrive in time to save Eoforwic from the Norþmenn?" The thought of another bloodbath made the hairs on my arms stand up.

"Hard to say. The Norse king will not wait forever for an answer from the scirgerefa."

Soon, scouts were on their way to look for the surviving stragglers of our army and tell them to gather in Tatecastre.

The next day, on the 24th of September in the Year of Our Lord 1066, I caught sight of the king and his huscarles arriving at Tatecastre with a sizable host of warriors. A messenger, who had told the scirgerefa of the king's arrival, reached us a few hours later.

"The scirgerefa has sent word to the Norse king that the inhabitants of Eoforwic will freely submit to him and that he, the scirgerefa, will hand over the city to him. They will meet with the Norse king and some warriors at Stanfordbrycge to decide who is to rule Eoforwic in the name of the Norse king."

King Harold listened carefully, then he rose, looked at his huscarles and said in a firm voice: "Six feet of English earth I will give him. Nay, seven feet he shall have, for they say he is a great man."

The men raised their fists in the air and cheered for the king. Everyone standing around us joined in the cheering, and Ulfgar and I also got carried away.

"Beo ðu hal, leof cyning!" I shouted, and the others joined in, repeating my words. At that moment, I understood again why I wanted to be a warrior, perhaps, no, most certainly a huscarl. Here was a brave, fearless king, determined to defeat our foe and restore peace to his land. That's what I wanted to fight for!

∼

IT WAS THE 25th of September in the Year of Our Lord 1066 when King Harold and his men marched through Eoforwic without the slightest resistance from a Norþmann. About a mile before the bridge over the Deorwente, beyond which the Norse were waiting, King Harold slowed down his men and ordered them to get ready for battle on this side of the river. The huscarles dismounted and handed the horses over to us youths.

My father handed me the reins of his horse. "It is time, Oswulf. Today, we must defend the honour of the king and this country. This day decides the fate of us all. Be proud to be here at this moment to support your king and your country. You are still young and inexperienced in war, so stay back. Beware of the Norþmenn! They fight without regard for their own lives, for their greatest glory is to die in battle and go to Valhǫll. If anyone stands in your way and challenges you to fight, fight like a man. You want to become a huscarl of the king one day, but only the bravest will reach that goal. I know that one day, you will be one of them. I've seen you fight. I know what you can do. Prove today that you are not only brave, but also wise!"

It will not be enough to defeat them. I will have to kill them if it comes to it.

I swallowed. "I will, Father."

"God þin feorg freoðie, min sunu." He turned and followed the other warriors who lined up behind the huscarles.

Not a word was spoken. When the men stopped advancing, I climbed a tree to see what was going on. Two men were riding towards each other: King Harold and a man from across the river. The latter carried only a sword – so he was neither a huscarl nor a Norþmann. King Harold greeted him and seemed to be talking to him. The other listened to the king's words without moving. In the end, he answered curtly, turned his horse and rode back across the bridge.

The time for words was over. The battle began. Our warriors set off with determined steps. My heart pounded as I followed them with Ulfgar. Once again, we were fighting Norþmenn, those men who had brought a shameful defeat on us four days ago. But this time, they were up against the king's finest warriors. This time, I was sure, the fortunes of war would be on our side.

My hands trembled with excitement while our warriors, after an initial halt, poured across the bridge to the other side of the river and attacked the shield wall of the Norþmenn. I stayed on the south side of the bridge with Ulfgar and with part of the army to guard the horses and look after the exhausted and wounded.

"What if the Norþmenn cross the bridge to our side?" I asked Ulfgar.

"That won't happen any time soon," he replied. "Did you see how they ran when they saw us? They were expecting a handful of harmless citizens of Eoforwic, and what do they get instead? A host of warriors in full battle dress. Archers, spearmen, swordsmen, huscarles – there is something for everyone. Most Norþmenn don't even wear armour or a shield."

"And if some do make it to us?" At Fuleforde, I had seen how the two-handed axe of the Norþmenn cuts through metal like a hot knife slices through butter. If one of them came straight at me and lashed out with his axe, my new chain mail would offer me no protection whatsoever.

"Then we have to fight." Ulfgar looked at me. "You and me. The two of us together."

I nodded. "For Englaland and for Godgifu." Thinking of my beloved gave me strength. When all this was over, I would return to her, and we would live in peace, get married and have children.

High in the sky, the sun burned down mercilessly on the warriors, already steaming with heat. While urging our men on, it paralysed the Norþmenn. Our entire army had made its way across the river, leaving behind a scene of destruction. The trampled grass had turned dark red where it was not covered with dozens of bodies of fallen warriors. The sight of all that blood turned my stomach. This was a hundred times worse than watching a pig being slaughtered and more gruesome than in Fuleforde, where we had only seen a small number of the slain as we retreated. Slashed or pierced bodies, severed heads and limbs covered the ground so densely that we were sometimes forced to take several steps on the dead to quickly get to any wounded or weakened fighters and pull them out of the fray and back to safety.

The enemy shield wall finally broke, exposing the remaining poorly protected foes.

A cry of triumph rang out that the Norse king had fallen, hit by an arrow from our archers. Our men pressed forward and heckled the remaining Norþmenn who were desperately trying to stand their ground. It looked like an easy victory for King Harold today.

Far and wide, I could see no more foes trying to sneak behind our battle lines or approaching Ulfgar and me to steal horses or weapons. I put the spear down for a moment, took a breath and wiped the sweat from my forehead. My clothes stuck to my skin, my hair was so wet, I could not shake it away, but had to wipe it out of my face.

Ulfgar joined me, his ochre curls hanging down limp and dark, his face bright red from the heat and exertion. "They're not as lucky this time as they were at Fuleforde."

"Thanks be to the king and his men." I looked at the fighting in front of us wearily and ridden with guilt, for I had long since lost sight of my father at whose side I should have been. But I was too exhausted and too disgusted by the horror that was unfolding before our eyes. "My father is in there somewhere." I swallowed, but the lump in my throat wouldn't budge. "Maybe alive. Maybe dead."

"Tell me, Oswulf," Ulfgar squinted southward. "Are we expecting any guests today?"

Dryhten min! Fewer than two miles from us, a host of warriors in full battle dress was advancing. "Someone must have sent word to their camp at Richale. How could those traitors escape our archers otherwise?"

Ulfgar raised the spear. "We'll think about that later. The guests are here, so we must take care of them." He eagerly beckoned those around us at the far end of our army. "We need more men! There are more Norþmenn coming!"

The battle lines split. A large number of English warriors swung sideways and pounced on the new arrivals. The noise of fighting swelled as the two armies clashed. My skull hummed from the crash of weapons and shields, the swings of axes, the whir of arrows seeking their target in the tumult from above. The screams of the dying mingled with the gasps of the exhausted fighters who had been standing their ground since this morning or thrown themselves into battle as soon as they arrived after a hasty march from Richale. My father had always said that I was tough, but this was only my second major battle. I was sixteen winters old and nowhere near ready for such sustained fighting. My arms and legs were heavy, my back ached, my throat was parched. All I wanted was to sit down and rest.

"Where are you going?" Ulfgar called to me as I walked towards a group of trees near the battlefield.

"I can barely hold the spear." After making sure that everything was safe, I sank down on the ground, exhausted, and my friend sat next to me. To my surprise, I noticed a person standing in a southerly direction, far away from the hustle and bustle, watching the events unfold. Something bothered me about the figure. I stood to get a better view.

"Don't tell me you see more Norþmenn!" said Ulfgar.

"Not *more*, just one in particular." I kept an eye on the battlefield as I cautiously took a few steps forwards.

"One in particular?" Like a stork in a swamp, Ulfgar stomped beside me over the bodies lying on the ground.

I kept glancing at the fighting next to us to make sure that no one attacked us by surprise.

From the looks of it, all the newly arrived Norþmenn were now involved in the fight, except for a few who stayed out of the battle and watched the noise and clamour from a safe distance – and one of them was the lonely figure I was approaching.

"Isn't that Stígandr?" I waved at the man, but he had his eyes firmly fixed on what was happening before him.

"I didn't know *he* was coming," Ulfgar said.

"What is the son of a shoemaker doing in the middle of a battlefield?" I waved again and quickened my pace.

Now, he turned his head in our direction, but instead of waving back or walking towards us, he looked around searchingly.

"He hasn't recognised us." By now, I was trotting as fast as my strength would still allow me. "Stígandr! It's us, Ulfgar and Oswulf!"

"Doesn't look like he wants to talk to us." Ulfgar panted beside me.

Our Norse friend stared at us as if the Fiend was approaching him personally. Then he took a few steps back before turning and running.

"What's he doing?" I asked. "He can't just run away. There may be more Norþmenn on their way here from Richale, and he's going to run right into them. Stígandr!"

"Perhaps he has secretly joined our host and is now afraid that he will be sent back to his father."

Ulfgar's breathing was heavy, and I was also finding it harder and harder to run.

"Why is he even here?"

"Maybe he wanted to find out if his uncle is still alive." Ulfgar groaned as much as his breath would let him. "I'm knackered. Why are we running after him anyway?"

"You're right." I stopped, aimed and threw my spear. It whirred into the air and landed some ten paces near Stígandr, who startled and stumbled. With all the strength I had left, I hurried to him and threw myself on top of him. "Stay here, Stígandr! It's too dangerous out there."

"Let go of me!" He tried to shake me off, but I wouldn't let go.

"Only if you keep still and don't try to run away."

He swung at me and tried to wriggle out of my grip. "Let me go, I said!"

A paw snapped at his wrist. "That's enough now!" Ulfgar pulled him to his feet and clasped him tightly until he held still. "There are enough men fighting on this battlefield already."

I struggled to my feet. The noise of battle roared behind me, so although we had stopped fighting physically, we continued shouting at each other. "What are you doing here?"

Stígandr's face was red with anger. "That's none of your business!"

"Why did you run away from us? How did you get here in the first place?"

61

"Are you afraid that I will rob you of your glory on the battlefield?" Stígandr's pointy chin beard quivered. "That I will tell at home how our highly praised eorles and their brave warriors ran for their lives at Fuleforde?"

I froze. "Who told you that?"

Stígandr hesitated a moment too long for me to believe his answer. "Rumours."

"You're lying!" I stepped closer. "You've been spying on our army, isn't that right?"

"So what? I don't see why it should matter to you."

"You have no business here. This is a battlefield for warriors."

"Then what are you doing here, Osfriðson? Neither do you."

"Not yet, but you never will."

"Good, so we've talked about everything you wanted to know." Stígandr looked up at Ulfgar and bared his teeth. "Now, perhaps you can leave me alone."

Ulfgar and I glanced at each other. He nodded and released his prisoner. Stígandr straightened up and ran his finger along the inside of the neckline of his tunic as if he needed to free himself from a collar that was too tight.

I picked up my spear and waved to the two. "Come, let's go back."

Ulfgar picked up his spear and wanted to follow, but Stígandr made no move.

"What is it?" I asked him.

"I'll stay here. I don't want to disturb you."

"Come on. We're all over there. Who can tell if more Norþmenn will show up here?" I paused. What had I just said?

Stígandr dismissed my worries. "You go ahead. I'll keep well away from the battlefield and walk along the river to the bridge."

Ulfgar and I exchanged a long look. Was he thinking the same as me?

"You're behaving very strangely, Stígandr," I said. "You appear on the battlefield out of nowhere, you won't tell us what you want and how you got here, you refuse to go back to our side with us. What's going on?"

"I don't see why this is strange at all." He looked at me in a decidedly innocent way.

"So, you also don't think it's strange that you're standing on the side from which the Norþmenn approached, do you?"

"I didn't want to get in your way."

"Really? Then what are you doing here? Did you happen to stroll by and think: 'Oh, there's a battle going on. I'm going to see who's fighting whom.' Are you trying to make a fool of me?"

Stígandr turned his gaze to the battlefield. "You don't know what you're talking about."

"You didn't happen to meet a Norþmann on your way to the battlefield, or perhaps several? In Richale, for example?"

"Leave him alone, Oswulf," Ulfgar said. "We have to go back."

I snorted. "I thought you were my friend, Stígandr. That you were one of us."

"Maybe we were once." Stígandr looked to the side as if none of this concerned him. "Until your father put it into your head that you must become a huscarl. Since then, I have just been the poor shoemaker's son to you, and you the soon-to-be master warrior. Suddenly, you were something better than me."

"That is not true. We are all part of a God-given order in which everyone plays their role. Mine is to fight. Yours is to make shoes."

63

"My uncle succeeded in breaking out of this rigid order. He has become a huscarl with land and property."

I pressed my lips together and took a deep breath, but I couldn't stop myself. "Because he cheated my father and stole from him. Your uncle does not deserve his rank. He is a liar and a thief."

"You cannot bear that others are better than you and your father. That is why you make up stories to stain other people's names and deeds."

How dare he! "At least I'm not sneaking around any Norþmenn." I dropped my spear and threw myself at him. "Out with it! There is no sensible reason why you should be here. So, what were you doing on the side of the enemy? Where have you been all this time? I haven't seen you in any of our tents."

Growling and barking like two dogs in a fight, we rolled across the ground, hitting each other.

"Get off me! I don't owe you an answer!"

That was enough. I drew my scramasax.

"Oswulf!" Ulfgar grabbed my arm just in time before I could put the knife to Stígandr's throat.

"Hlafordswica! You're lucky Ulfgar is holding me back, or your head would be rolling across this field right now, even though you're not taking part in the battle."

With widened eyes, Stígandr stared at the knife hovering over him. "Wait! I can explain. Don't let go of his arm, Ulfgar! Let me speak, Oswulf."

I looked at Ulfgar, who nodded briefly but did not let go of my arm, just to be sure. "I'm listening. But be quick, before Ulfgar gets bored and releases me."

Beads of sweat rolled down Stígandr's face. He looked frantically back and forth between Ulfgar and me. "They forced me."

"Who is 'they'?"

"The Norþmenn. They made me warn the men in their camp at Richale."

"When?"

"When they saw King Harold and his army."

"They didn't even know then that there was going to be a battle."

"They didn't want to wait for an attack."

"How could they force you to do this if you were not amongst them before? At no point have our warriors crossed the path of the Norþmenn."

Stígandr swallowed. "They... they caught me while we camped outside Eoforwic."

"Was that before the battle at Fuleforde or after?"

"After it. They cut me short."

"Why didn't they just kill you like everyone else who couldn't flee fast enough?"

"I begged for mercy."

"You're lying. They slaughtered everyone they could lay their hands on."

"They spared me."

"Probably because you have such a pretty face!"

"I offered them my services. In their language."

"You shamelessly offered to spy on us for our foe?"

"They would have killed me otherwise. What would you have done in my place?"

I pondered. "So you have been their watchman since the battle at Fuleforde?"

Stígandr nodded hurriedly. "Exactly. Because they made me do it."

"What did you tell the Norse king?"

"They threatened me to tell them everything. How many warriors King Harold has and where he will lead them, when they would get there, everything."

"You're a liar." I pushed my scramasax towards him, but Ulfgar held onto my arm.

"It's no use killing him, Oswulf," Ulfgar said. "We already have enough dead and injured to take care of."

"Can't you see that everything he says is a lie?" I asked. "He has not been caught and forced to spy on us at all."

"But it is true. Believe me."

"Well, let's assume it is as you say. So, after Fuleforde, you told the Norse king all about our army."

"Yes exactly, that's how it was." A few teeth appeared in Stígandr's lower jaw.

"You told him that the rest of our troops were waiting at Tatecastre for King Harold, who would then pass through Eoforwic with a large army of battle-ready warriors to attack the Norþmenn at Stanfordbrycge."

"He knew that through me, exactly." The whole row of teeth shone out at me from Stígandr's lower jaw.

"You seem proud of your betrayal."

The smile disappeared. More beads of sweat ran down Stígandr's forehead. "What? No, no, quite the opposite! I am so ashamed of what I have done because I betrayed my homeland. But now, you know why I am here and that I was forced into this and that we are both fighting on the same side."

"No, we don't."

Stígandr frowned. "I don't understand." He looked at Ulfgar as if for help.

"Then let me explain it to you, Stígandr. You're a miserable liar, and even when you have a knife at your throat, you lie."

"But I am telling the truth!"

"Really? Let's suppose King Harald knew indeed how large the English army was and that they were going to attack him and his men. Then why did he only bring a few of them here, and most importantly, why did he show up dressed only in a tunic and helmet instead of arming himself and his followers to the teeth? Perhaps because he knew nothing at all? Because someone who was caught at Fuleforde would have been unaware of the approaching English army? For we heard about it only on the day after the battle."

"Oswulf." Ulfgar's grip on my arm tightened.

"Let go of my arm, Ulfgar!" I tried to wrench my hand holding the scramasax free.

Stígandr squirmed to get rid of me and the blade flashing rather too close to his throat. "Don't do it, Oswulf! You would regret it."

"My only regret would be not cutting your throat right now, you wicked liar." I snorted and tugged at my arm, but there was no escape from Ulfgar's pincer grip. So instead, I tried to throttle Stígandr with my other hand.

He grabbed my hand and pushed it away. "No, Oswulf, wait! That's not all."

"Do you want to tell me more lies?" I wrestled and writhed as Ulfgar pulled me away. "Hlafordswica! You'll rue the day you came here instead of helping your father at home in the workshop."

"And you?" Stígandr's voice cracked. "Will rue the day you failed your father in battle. They will attack the huscarles. Kill them. Then the king and Eorl Morkere. And your father, too."

I froze. *My father!* I was wasting time with Stígandr while my father was possibly fighting for his life and desperately needed me. "I must find him." I jumped up and fastened the scramasax to my belt. "You're getting away today, but I'm not finished with you yet."

I grabbed my spear and ran like mad towards the battle. Ulfgar shouted after me, but I didn't listen nor look back, I dashed forward. Without a shield and armed only with a spear, I was completely unprotected, but I did not care at that moment.

It was late in the day, and there were more dead than living warriors on the battlefield. Not tripping over the bodies was more difficult than shunning an enemy weapon. I looked around in all directions and at last found my father. Holding the spear ready to stab, I picked my way between the few fighting men towards my father.

I was only twenty paces away from him when he stepped on a shield that had long since ceased to be of any use to its bearer. Flailing his arms, he stumbled sideways as his adversary's two-handed axe came down on him. "No!" I roared, pulling up the spear and throwing it at the Norþmann.

My father screamed and thumped backwards onto the ground. His adversary jerked and slumped down, my spear stuck in his back.

I rushed to my father and stared in horror at the huge pool of blood that formed where his shield hand had once been. The axe had severed it along with the shield. "Father! You have to hold on! I'll get help. I'll take you home."

Ulfgar appeared out of nowhere, cut a long strip off a dead man's tunic with his dagger, put it around my father's upper arm and pulled it as tight as he could before tying it with a knot. When I looked at him questioningly, he shrugged his shoulders. "I once saw a physician do it."

My father moaned and tried to sit up. Ulfgar reached under his shoulders and carefully lifted his upper body. "You must not move, Osfrið! You need a physician urgently. Oswulf will fetch your horse. Hurry!"

Afraid that my father would die in my friend's arms and before my eyes, I had stood there, petrified and listening to Ulfgar's words, until I awoke from my stupor. I set off running to fetch Father's horse, and all of a sudden, an eerie silence seemed to descend over the battlefield. The fighting noise died away. Instead of the clang and clank of weapons and armour, moans and shuffles filled the air. Dead bodies lay everywhere, spears, axes, helmets, severed limbs. Those who still had enough life in them stirred and cried out for help. Survivors wandered around, looking for brothers-in-arms, alive or dying, for rings or coins they could secretly put into their pouches, for swords and chainmail to replace their own that had been lost or damaged in battle. It reeked of sweat, blood and destruction. And in the middle of it all, my father lay with a mutilated arm, while his son was paralysed by the experience of his second battle. I didn't even know if we had won or lost. I grabbed the reins of our horse and galloped him to where Ulfgar was still holding my father in his arms.

We lifted him onto the back of the horse, holding onto him so that he didn't slip down again. I climbed into the saddle behind and held him tight. As we rode slowly past the fallen and surviving warriors, the royal standard with the dragon of the kings of Westseaxa swayed gently in the midst of a group of warriors.

"The king is alive." My voice trembled as tears welled in my eyes. "I see the king, Ulfgar. King Harold is alive. We have defeated the Norþmenn."

"I hope they have had enough now. I, for one, certainly have."

I took a deep breath. "Me too, Ulfgar, me too." On my left arm, I felt my father's heart beating faintly but distinctly. "Do you think he'll make it?"

Ulfgar regarded my father. "Osfrið has been through other things. Nothing will knock him off his feet so quickly. Especially not a Norþmann."

While some of our warriors chased the last few fleeing Norþmenn towards Richale and those who remained cheered our victory, my father groaned.

"He needs a physician, Ulfgar, or he will die."

I didn't know if Ulfgar had understood me over the noise around us, but he nodded and told me to wait. Then he weaved his way through the crowds.

I held my face close to my father's ear. "Father? Do you hear me?"

He showed no sign of life.

"Father? Father!" I began to sweat, even though the sun was low on the horizon and the air was cooling noticeably. "Can you hear me? You must not die. Not yet." A low humming in my ear made me look at my father's face. "Father?" I whispered.

His right eye opened a crack. His mouth twitched almost imperceptibly as if he were trying to smile.

"Father, you must hold on. Ulfgar is looking for a physician who will help you. Promise me you won't die!"

The eye closed again. Father's chin fell on his chest.

Terrified, I ran my hands all over his chest and held my breath. I felt a very gentle movement, a shallow but rhythmic lifting and lowering, accompanied by a throbbing that felt surprisingly strong. My father was alive. *Still.* I breathed a sigh of relief and looked impatiently around for Ulfgar.

A short time later, he returned with a horse in tow. "There is a place called Cattune not far from here, barely half an hour's walk south. They have no physician, but a very knowledgeable healer."

I hesitated. "But he needs a physician! Let's take him to Eoforwic. There's bound to be several of them there."

Ulfgar mounted his horse. "It will be dark by the time we get to Eoforwic. It's too far." He grinned and stroked his short beard. "Maybe the healer in Cattune is pretty?"

"She can be ugly as night for all I care, as long as she can nurse my father back to health. Come on, we have to go!"

We followed the old Roman road far too slowly, but more than a fast walk was not possible, given the state my father was in.

"Why did Stígandr lie to me?" I asked.

"Hard to say. Maybe because he wanted to get rid of your scramasax at his throat and therefore told you what you wanted to hear?"

"Do you think he really worked as a spy for the Norþmenn?"

"If so, he was not very successful."

"He must have lied. He probably wasn't even there in Fuleforde but heard about our defeat from a travelling minstrel or a messenger."

"You should not worry too much about it, Oswulf. It doesn't matter whether Stígandr lied or not. We won the battle, and hopefully, we have seen the last of the Norþmenn here in Englaland for a long time. Their king is dead, Eorl Morkere's brother too. The wolves and ravens will take care of their dead warriors at Stanfordbrycge. I don't know how many of them are still in Richale, but they will go home with far fewer ships than it took them to get here. It's over, Oswulf."

"At least we won this time, that's true. But at what price? Many warriors have lost their lives in these two battles." I felt for my father's heartbeat. The throbbing was weak but regular. "It will never be the same again when we return to Ledlinghe."

"Probably not, no."

"I wonder if Stígandr will return to Ledlinghe with our men?"

"I would think so. A shoemaker from Englaland is not what Vikings usually bring home from their raids."

I could not help a grim smile. They probably couldn't even sell Stígandr as a slave for a decent price, and I doubted that they were in need of shoemakers in Norweg. So most likely, we would all meet again in Ledlinghe. Just as before. Except that nothing would be as before. We had defeated the Norþmenn, but across the water, the French were waiting for the wind to shift so they could finally set sail for Englaland.

Chapter 4

After a short ride, we arrived in Cattune and rode to the manor. There, we were told that the herb woman actually lived in Wilburgfos, a small village within the manor and soke of Cattune, about half an hour to the southeast. In order to spare my father a further journey, I asked if there was someone here who could help him.

The seneschal sighed. "Your father has more than a few scratches from the battle, my boy." He pointed to the bloody stump on my father's arm. "We could treat something like that here, but it would be doomed from the start. If you want to save your father, you must ride on to Wilburgfos. If anyone can save him, it is Hild the healer at Kjetil's manor house. Hurry! It is already getting dark."

So we continued on our way as the sun slowly disappeared on the horizon. Shortly before nightfall, we reached Wilburgfos. It was indeed a small place, and we quickly found the manor house. As we rode into the yard in front of the great hall, a man about twice my age came towards us.

"Wel gesund, hlaford min," I said, bringing my horse to a stop. "We are looking for Hild the herb woman."

"At such a late hour?" The man raised his torch and gave me and my father a curious look. "What happened? Have you been set upon?"

"No. We come straight from the battlefield at Stanford-brycge, where King Harold defeated the Norse army. My father needs help urgently."

The man was talking to one of the youths who had run after him and sent him back to the great hall. Then he beckoned to us. "Take him to Hild's herb hut, just over there. He must be treated as soon as possible, otherwise it will be too late."

Too late. Like a lightning bolt, it struck me that my father might already be dead. But now was not the time to check his heartbeat and breathing. The sooner the healer looked at him and treated him, the better for him. *And for me.*

Ulfgar had jumped off his horse and gently pulled my father from the horse's back, while the other man reached for his legs to catch them before they slipped off.

A small group of people approached, led by the youth who had been sent into the great hall and a small, delicate woman who advanced with quick steps. After taking one look at my father, she waved the man and Ulfgar to her hut. "Carry him in there! Hurry up! I must look at him in the light. When did this happen?" She looked questioningly at Ulfgar as she walked beside him.

I suddenly realised that I was still sitting in the saddle, as if spellbound, instead of following my father into the hut. "About two hours," I shouted, jumping off and hurrying after them. "It was still light when we set out. A Norþmann cut off his hand with an axe. Are you Hild the healer?"

"That's me." She cleared a makeshift bed, on which Ulfgar and the other man laid my father after they had painstakingly removed his chainmail. Then she lit oil lamps and placed them near the bed.

The walls of the hut were full of wooden boards on which were lined up little jars, pots and all sorts of vessels containing powders, tinctures, leaves and other remedies I had never seen before. Bunches of herbs were tied on strings, hanging from the ceiling and giving off a strange mixture of smells: sweet, acrid, warming, mellow, bitter. There were rolls of linen, several knives and sickles, spoons of various sizes, smaller and larger pots and other utensils that a healer might need to do her work.

"He is weak, but he is still alive." Hild moved a stool next to the bed and began to examine my father's left arm. "Who tied off the arm?" she asked as she continued to look at the wound.

"Me," said Ulfgar.

"You did well." Hild looked at him and smiled mischievously. "Are you a physician?"

Ulfgar's chest swelled with pride. "No, but I once saw one treat a wound like that."

"You are a keen observer, hlaford min." She was still smiling, and Ulfgar lowered his gaze as if afraid to look at her any longer. I had heard of people saying that herb women were witches and that they could curse a man just by looking at him.

The man who had greeted us on our arrival reappeared in the hut, accompanied by a man with a large moustache and a young woman.

"Thank you, Cenhelm," the moustached man said in a low voice. "You can go to sleep now. I'll take care of the rest." He came closer and regarded my father, Ulfgar and me. "I regret that such a sad cause should bring you to my manor house. My servant, Cenhelm, told me that you rode here from Stanfordbrycge."

"That's right," I replied. "First, we went to Cattune, but there we were told that your healer was the only one who could save my father."

The man hummed in agreement. "Hild is indeed a very good healer. But tell me, your father fought in King Harold's army?"

I nodded. "He is a ðegn of Eorl Morkere, one of the best." *Who is dying right now.*

The man stroked his moustache as he regarded me and Ulfgar from head to toe. "A ðegn and his sons, huh? I don't often get such noble visitors here in Wilburgfos."

"I'm just a friend," Ulfgar said, then pointed at me. "This is Oswulf, son of Ðegn Osfrið. My name is Ulfgar, son of Godric the smith."

The man uttered a brief laugh. "Forgive me! I was so excited about having guests at such a time of night that I forgot to introduce myself. My name is Kjetil."

A Norþmann. The thought curdled my blood, only to make me wonder about myself. What had happened to the peaceful life together of Englishmen and Norþmenn? Until a few weeks ago, hadn't we shared fields and woods with our neighbours without mistrusting each other? Had we not supported and helped each other in times of need? Had those two battles not only destroyed lives, but also all that trust, that closeness? Perhaps we should not have visited Wilburgfos. Who could say which side this man was on?

"This is my wife, Edeva," the man continued, pointing to the woman at his side.

He is married to an Englishwoman. Maybe there is hope for us after all.

Edeva chastely cast down her eyes and bowed slightly. Even in the dim and flickering light in the hut, her skin shimmered silvery white like the light of the moon on a clear night. What a fine sight she must be in the daylight!

"Like Hild, she is an experienced healer and will assist her. Your father is in good hands. They will do everything to save him." Kjetil waved us towards the door. "Come, let the women do their work. They will let us know if there is any change in your father's condition. Until then, you can strengthen yourselves in the great hall. You must be hungry and thirsty after such a battle, although..." he glanced at me, "you look pretty young to be fighting in the king's army."

Outside, a lean man with a black robe and a dangling cross, accompanied by a boy with a bell and a lantern, hurried after a youth about my age.

"Ah, Father Leofric! Sorry for troubling you so late at night, but it is urgent."

"I am sure you will have a good reason for driving me all the way to you at this hour." Leofric stopped, panting, and jerked his Bible and robe into place.

"We have a seriously injured man in the hut there who may not live much longer. Hild and Edeva are with him right now to see if they can save him with what they know."

At the mention of the names, the priest winced and drew in air through his nose indignantly.

"It will be in the Church's best interests if he survives," Kjetil continued with a gleeful glint in his eye that could be seen, even in the moonlight. "He is a noble warrior of the English king. If the Lord holds his protecting hand over the wounded man at this moment, King Harold will certainly reward His earthly servants and their places of worship."

A smile twitched across Leofric's face, but he seemed anxious not to let his joy at Kjetil's words show. "I will do everything in my power to ask the Lord's blessing for your guest."

"I appreciate that, Father. I will have a little compensation for your trouble served up in the great hall."

The priest's face lit up before his smile disappeared when he saw me staring at him. "May God repay you, my son." With a subservient nod of his head, he made his way to the hut where my father lay.

"What an uncouth man," I muttered to Ulfgar as we continued on our way.

"For a man of God, he does not seem averse to earthly pleasures." Ulfgar looked around once more.

"Father Leofric is not a bad man," Kjetil said, "even if his flesh is sometimes weak. If you know this weakness, however, it is easy to... let's say... lead him."

We accompanied Kjetil into the great hall where a servant laid linen sheets and fresh clothes next to two buckets filled with warm water. She watched with wide eyes as we took off our dirty clothes, which she took from us with a smile.

After we had washed and put on clean clothes, we settled down with Kjetil at one of the long tables. A servant brought us food and a large cup of ale, which we greedily downed. While we ate, we had to tell Kjetil all about the battle and the victory.

Finally, he leaned back and interlaced his fingers. "You are young and strong; I could do with your help. I assume you will stay here until your father is well enough to make the journey home."

"You have great faith in your healer's abilities, Kjetil," I said. "I pray to God that you are right."

"Every person has something they are good at. With Hild and Edeva, it is the ability to heal people with their knowledge of herbs. What are you good at?"

Ulfgar and I looked at each other in surprise.

"Well," Ulfgar began hesitantly, "we are both familiar with working at a manor and will repay your hospitality by working for you."

Kjetil propped up his head on one hand and looked at my friend. "Hm. I don't think this is what you excel at, but so be it. For now, we will see what chores you can help with. I am sure we will soon find out what you are really good at and where you could be of more use to me." He stood up. "You should go to sleep now. You have had a hard and long day. A little rest will do you good."

"But my father? I have to go to him."

I rose and started to make for the door, yet Kjetil gently but firmly held me back. "For the moment, there is nothing else you can do for your father but pray, Oswulf. Believe me, Hild and Edeva know what they are doing and will do everything in their power to make sure you see your father alive tomorrow."

I looked to Ulfgar for help, but he sighed, "He is right. In your current state, you would be of no help to your father. But if he survives, he will be all the more grateful to see you alive and well."

"Come," Kjetil said and pointed to a corner in the great hall where Cenhelm had also made himself comfortable and was sleeping peacefully. "Lie down here and sleep. Tomorrow, I will show you around the manor, and we will see how your father is doing. Good night."

~

THE THOUGHTS of what had happened kept turning in my head. Images of the battles woke me from my sleep again and again. Even in the stillness of the night, the noise of screams, the dull thud of weapons on wooden shields and the clang of metal on metal rang in my ears. Only yesterday, we faced the Norþmenn as foes, now we were lying in one of their manor houses, trying to save my father's life. Perhaps he had died in the meantime, while I lay here, comfortable and rested. *I must send a messenger to Ledlinghe in the morning. They won't even know what has happened since we left the village. Perhaps none of the men we accompanied have survived the two battles. And Father might be losing his battle, too.*

I looked around in the dark. A faint hint of light fell through the small openings under the roof, enough for me to find my way to the door. Ulfgar was sleeping peacefully amidst the odd rhythmic snoring from elsewhere. I left the great hall and stepped outside. The night air was cool, but not yet frosty. The thin crescent of the moon bathed the yard in a dim light as I made my way to the herb hut. I absolutely had to see my father. To my surprise, something flickered in the window. Had someone left a light on? Was that the lantern that would tell me when my father had left this world? Or was there someone else with him? I knocked softly on the door and listened.

"Who is it?" asked a muffled female voice.

"Oswulf," I answered without further explanation. At that moment, it did not even occur to me that whoever was sitting in there might not know my name or who I was.

"Enter, Oswulf," said the voice.

I opened the door and peeked into the room. On the stool next to the makeshift bed sat Edeva, Kjetil's wife, sewing in the glow of the light. I glanced cautiously at my father.

"Come in and close the door."

I did as I was told and slowly walked towards the bed. My father lay there, motionless, peaceful, without making a sound. Was he still alive or was Edeva already holding the wake? *Which I, as his son, was supposed to be holding.* "Is he...?"

"He is still alive, but he is very weak." Edeva smiled wearily.

I had no idea what time it was and how long she had been sitting here, but surely, she had already spent several hours looking after my father. "Is there anything I can do?"

"I don't think so."

"Mm-hm." I wiped my upper lip.

"He lost a lot of blood, even though your friend tried to at least stem the bleeding. I washed out and cleaned the wound. Hild has swathed it with herbs to prevent it from rotting and to speed up the healing."

"Why are you still here?"

"I keep changing the cloth strips. As soon as they are soaked with pus and blood, I boil more herbs and wrap them around the wound."

"I owe you for what you have done, Lady Edeva."

"God has given me the gift of healing, so it would be a sin not to use it to help the sick and wounded. My husband gives me all the freedom I need to do this. He is a good man."

"He is indeed."

We were silent for a while until Lady Edeva rose and examined my father's arm. She looked at me with her fair eyes and smiled. "You should go back to sleep. Surely, you are exhausted from the fighting."

I fiddled with my tunic, looked from Edeva to my father and back again. "Yes, I suppose I should. Do you need anything else?"

"No, thank you. I have everything I need here."

I didn't know where to put my hands and finally stroked my tunic helplessly. "Very well, I will go then. Good night, Lady Edeva."

"Good night, Oswulf."

∼

IN THE MORNING, Kjetil showed us around the manor and the village. Wilburgfos was larger than Ledlinghe, with a handful of fields enclosed by woods. To the west of the manor, the Fors Bekkr meandered into the village, a small river that offered not only fresh fish but also a means for a mill to grind crops into flour.

Back at the manor house, Cenhelm and a messenger from the king were already waiting for us.

"King Harold has made the Norþmenn swear that they will never again enter our land to wage war on us," the messenger said proudly.

"Good tidings forsooth," Kjetil said. "Give the man a drink, Cenhelm. I'll be with you in a moment. As for you two, I have thought of something for you to do. If you fought in King Harold's army, you must know a lot about weapons, right?"

Ulfgar swung a strand of hair out of his face. "We wield them at least as well as we clean them, don't we, Oswulf?"

"As a ðegn, my father always made sure that his battle wear was clean and ready to use at all times," I said, not without pride. "I know how to get old, rusty chain mail shiny and supple again and how to quickly make even the dullest weapon as sharp as a shearing knife."

Kjetil rubbed his beardless chin. "That could be useful. King Harold may have banished the Norþmenn from our land forever, but our coasts will continue to attract the greed of others."

I snorted. "Who knows if these Niþingas from the north will keep their word?"

"Even Norþmenn have a sense of honour, Oswulf, when it comes to keeping their word, though not all of them. Do you think that I belong to the latter?"

"I meant the Vikings who invade our coasts." I made a sweeping gesture towards wherever I thought those were. "You're not a Viking. You live here and have your manor house here."

Kjetil folded his arms. "Yes and no. My great-grandfather was, in fact, one of those Vikings who invaded Englaland, but he settled here with his family. I have a Norse name, but deep down I feel like an Englishman, just like you, even though our ancestors come from different countries."

Just like Stígandr. Maybe I was wrong to suspect him. Surely, it just so happened that he appeared on the far side of the battlefield. "Do you know that the king has gathered the fyrd in the south because he fears that the French might attack any time?" I asked, trying to steer our thoughts in a different direction.

"The fyrd was disbanded a long time ago," Kjetil replied. "The men have been away from their homes for months and need to help with the harvest."

"That means the king's entire host of warriors is currently here in Norþhymbre."

"That's what it looks like, yes."

"Do you think the French will attack?"

"There's no doubt about that. That is why it will be good if you and your friend take care of the weapons and armour of all men who are able to fight. I think we must be prepared. Cenhelm will get you everything you need."

Edeva crossed our path and nodded in a silent greeting when she saw us.

"How is my father?"

"His condition is very serious. He absolutely needs rest."

"Can I see him?"

Edeva tilted her head as if she had to refuse a child a favour. "Don't worry, Oswulf. I will let you know as soon as anything changes – for better or worse." She turned hastily away and continued towards the herb hut.

"Come on, Oswulf!" I felt Ulfgar's warm paw on my shoulder. "Let's do some work. Standing around does no one any good, least of all you. Come on, it'll take your mind off things."

We carried rags, oil, wax, a bucket of ash and a bucket of sand to the yard in front of the great hall and got the pieces we were to clean that day. The sun was shining. It was warm, but rubbing down the rusted and dirty parts would not bring sweat to our foreheads. Since we had fought at Stanfordbrycge, autumn was bringing along shorter and cooler days.

I was wiping around on a sword while my thoughts wandered off to Kjetil and the herb women. Could we really trust them? "My father's condition hasn't changed," I murmured, scrubbing the individual grooves in the sword's hilt with the rag.

"That's good, isn't it?" asked Ulfgar. "At least he's still alive."

"Unlike the Norþmann who attacked him and who has hopefully been slowly eaten by the crows. Would that he had not died from a single thrust of my spear! He should have endured the same torment as my father."

"He's dead, Oswulf," Ulfgar said. "What more do you want? It wouldn't make your father any more alive."

"The Norþmann made my father, a strong and brave ðegn, weak as a newborn child – anything could kill him in this state. And we are in the manor house of a Norþmann."

Ulfgar looked at me and shook his head. "They say war changes people, and when I see what two battles have done to you, I believe it. Where has your sudden distrust of the Norþmenn come from? What have the people who have lived in this land for centuries done to you? Those who attacked us came from far away."

"But how do we know what Hild and Edeva are doing with my father? Everything is a big secret and—"

"Oswulf! Come to your senses! I know your father is badly injured, and what we saw on the battlefield was terrible. But I was there too, and I don't hate every Norþmann I meet because of it. Especially not those with whom we have always lived in peace. As for the herb women, they have powers and knowledge that we don't understand. Kjetil has confidence in their skills, and we have also been assured in Cattune and Stanfordbrycge that only Hild can save him."

"Maybe, but I still wonder if we shouldn't have gone to Eoforwic and taken him to a physician. After all, he is still alive, and by today, we would have reached the town long ago."

"How do you know if he would have survived the longer ride? There's no use in worrying about it now. We are here, and no matter who takes care of your father, it is in the hands of the Lord whether he remains in this world or goes to the next."

I sighed and turned the sword in the light of the sun to look for more dirty spots and damage. Out of the corner of my eye, I noticed someone approaching.

"You're the two who arrived at the manor last night, huh?"

"They've heard about us before we even meet them!" Ulfgar said with awe.

I looked at the youth standing there. It was the one who had gone to fetch Kjetil and the rest from the great hall.

"Fought in the king's army, didn't you?" The boy moved his arms about restlessly. "I want to fight for King Harold later, too." His eyes glowed with excitement.

After a sideways glance at Ulfgar, I looked up at the youth. "How old are you?"

"Sixteen winters. And I'm pretty good with a sword." He lunged to the side, bent one arm upwards and stretched the other arm straight out. With shouts to match his movements, he leapt forward a few times, swiftly slashing and thrusting.

Ulfgar burst into laughter. I shook my head and continued to polish the sword in my hands.

"What are you laughing at?" the boy grunted.

"We could have done with someone like you," Ulfgar said.

"Really?"

"Yes. Then the Norþmenn at Fuleforde and Stanfordbrycge would have died laughing."

The youth came up to us. "Oh, think this is funny, eh? If it's so funny, the way I fight, then let's fight. C'mon, I'll fight one of you, and then we'll see who dies laughing. Git hildlatan!"

His bragging was annoying me. Who did he think he was?

"Get us two thick sticks!" said Ulfgar. "Or twigs, if sticks are too heavy for you."

The youth sneered. "Ha! Sticks? Only children fight with 'em." He pointed to the weapons in front of us. "There's enough swords there. Why don't we use those?"

"Because you can't handle them," I snapped at him.

The boy stood wide-legged in front of me. "Think you're better than me 'cause you're the son of a ðegn, eh? If you can fight so well, then fight, you coward. Or don't you dare? You're so scared you'll wet your breeches, aren't you?"

I slowly looked up at him. "You're waving your arm in the air like you're chopping old vegetables with a dull kitchen knife."

The youth flared his nostrils in anger.

Ulfgar took the next helmet. "You're messing with the wrong man, my boy."

"We'll see about that." The would-be fighter grabbed one of the swords and took a few steps backwards. "Go on, grab a sword!"

I looked at Ulfgar, who shrugged his shoulders. "You don't want to look like a coward, Oswulf, do you?"

"You're wasting your time, boy. And most of all, you're wasting mine."

The youth shifted his weight onto one leg and put his free hand on his hip. "I see. Fighting with a peasant boy is not good enough for the noble lord." He raised the sword and pointed the tip towards me. "But I ain't just any peasant boy. I am Cenric, son of Cenhelm, and as of yet, I've not lost a single fight ever."

"A man of many honours, forsooth," Ulfgar murmured.

The tip of the sword was now almost touching my chest. I took a deep breath without looking up. What was this stripling thinking? "Take that sword away!"

"You afraid I'll thrust it into your cowardly belly?"

Cenric had not quite finished when I leaned back, threaded his sword with the one I was holding and knocked it out of his hand. I jumped to my feet, grabbed the second sword and held both sword tips to Cenric's throat. "Not really. What about you?"

With bared teeth and widened eyes, Cenric stared at the two swords and made no sound.

"I warned you," Ulfgar said with a sigh as he laid a spear to the side.

I threw the sword Cenric had chosen back onto the heap of weapons and sat down. After another wipe with a dry cloth, I put the sword I held to the side and picked up the next one.

Cenric cleared his throat and took a small step backwards, just in case. "You're pretty fast." When neither of us answered, he started kicking from one leg to the other. His hands swung back and forth, his fingers intertwined and unknotted again.

I looked at him grimly. "Why are you still standing there? Don't you have anything to do?"

"Who did you learn that from? Your father?"

"What, that I won't be accused of being a coward?"

"Nay, the thing with the sword. How did you do that?"

"I use a sword like a weapon, not like a kitchen knife."

"Can you teach me?"

"Me?"

"Aye. Why not?"

"The stripling fights miserably, but he's a lot better at thinking, Oswulf." Ulfgar nudged me. "The French could soon appear on our shores. We will need every man who can handle more than a pitchfork."

I should teach someone how to fight with a sword? "How am I meant to do this, Ulfgar? I fight without thinking about my movements beforehand."

"Then I'll attack you, and Cenric can watch what you do to fight me off. And then he does the same with me, and you watch us and tell him what he's doing wrong."

"Who has taught you so far?" I asked Cenric.

He looked around questioningly. "Who?"

"Well, you, the young men here in Wilburgfos. There must be someone to teach you how to wield a sword."

Cenric hunched his shoulders. "Nay, not really. Father showed us a bit what to do with a spear, an axe and a sword. But most of the folk in Wilburgfos are peasants. Their sons have to help in the fields. They've no time to learn how to fight."

"Think about it, Oswulf. It would help take your mind off worrying about your father. Kjetil will be grateful for someone who knows how to wield a weapon as well as you do. No lord will refuse to have skilled warriors defending his manor."

I stared at Ulfgar as if he were out of his mind. *At sixteen winters, I should turn village youths into swordsmen?* The thought was mad. On the other hand, spending more time fighting instead of cleaning weapons or handing them to other warriors in battle seemed tempting. Back home, practising with my father was part of the daily life of a ðegn's son – why should it be different elsewhere? *Above all, if I want to become a huscarl, I must not neglect daily practice, no matter where I am. I'm sure I could work my way into the army of Eorl Morkere and even King Harold if I pass on my knowledge here and bring on skilled warriors. Won't they tell others what an outstanding fighter I am and that I am worthy of becoming a huscarl? It would bring me one step closer to my goal, should my father...* I gritted my teeth.

"Well?" asked Cenric.

Ulfgar leaned towards me. "What do you think, Oswulf?"

I looked up. "I don't want to decide right away. I will think it over. God willing, I can speak to my father soon. Then I will ask him for advice."

❧

THE DAYS PASSED, and apart from the fact that King Harold had moved his warriors to Eoforwic after the battle at Stanfordbrycge to celebrate the victory, we had no further tidings about what the king was up to next or whether the French had landed in the south. I was also still unsure how my father was doing. Both Hild and Edeva failed to answer my questions in a way that put my mind to rest. He was still weak and shaken by fever, so they told me, but he was a tough fellow who clung to life with all his remaining strength, perhaps, because he was desperate to see his son once more. Whether that would bring him back to life or rather be the last thing he would do before he died of his injury was in God's hands.

On the first Sunday after the feast of Saint Michael, I sat with Ulfgar and the other people from the manor in the great hall to have the first meal of the day. "We're stuck here like a careless animal that has fallen into a deep well," I said, poking vigorously with my spoon at the greyish-brown barley mash we were fed as usual in the morning. "Does anyone amongst the king's warriors even know we're here? That we have not returned to Eoforwic with all the other survivors?"

"Hardly," Ulfgar replied. "They may have found that your father is missing in Eorl Morkere's army, but they will assume he was killed on the battlefield. Whether they searched for him among the fallen I doubt. There were just too many of them."

"So no one will let us know when the king's army moves on, but shouldn't we be there? Maybe Kjetil is deliberately keeping word from us."

"Why should he do that? He has kindly taken us in and offered us shelter and food. He even has two healers who are both looking after your father."

"Yes, but perhaps the herb women are delaying my father's healing on purpose so that we don't leave the manor."

"You're not yet a huscarl that the king could not do without, my dear Oswulf. You are one of several youths who pull the wounded from battle and provide them with drink and weapons."

"Don't you think it's strange that I'm not allowed to see my father at all?"

"I don't think he'll be happy to have guests in the state he's in yet – if he is able to notice them at all." Ulfgar shoved another spoonful of mash into his mouth.

"We've been here almost a week now, but I have not seen my father since we arrived. Every time I have gone to the herb hut and asked to be let in, I have been denied entry for some reason. I am being kept away from my own father."

"Your father is badly injured and needs rest. I'm sure it's for his own good."

"How can you tell? We don't even know these people."

Ulfgar scraped his bowl noisily with his spoon. "That's true. But do you think everyone would have recommended the herb woman to us if she was no good?"

"Maybe they just wanted to get rid of us in Cattune. After all, it was already late in the day when we arrived there. We may have told them about the seriously injured man just so we could sneak into their manor and then rob or kill them at night."

Ulfgar paused. "You should learn to play the harp. Then you could recite your gleoman's stories with music."

"Doesn't anything seem strange to you here?" I held my spoon over the bowl and watched closely as the barley slurry trickled off my spoon in a crumb-filled stream, swirling into the liquid in the bowl. It was strange, wasn't it, that we had been put to work, as if we had come here for this, while my father was locked away in a hut stacked with herbs. What was going on in there? What were those healers doing with my father?

"The only thing that seems strange to me at the moment is you." Ulfgar licked the spoon with relish.

"Think about it, Ulfgar, two youths arrive at your manor in the dark, claiming to bring a seriously injured man."

"You must be joking. A chopped-off hand is pretty hard to fake."

"Listen to me first! So, these two young men arrive and one of them says that his father is injured. How would the men at the manor know that it's really the father and not some injured person that the two had picked up on the battlefield or wherever? And then the youths say they want to see Hild the healer, who happens to live at this manor."

"She doesn't happen to live here. We asked for her, and anyone we asked specifically sent us to Wilburgfos."

"Yes, but the people here are unaware of that. Now, all of a sudden, the injured man disappears and no one is allowed to see him except this herb woman and the woman married to the hlaford, who, to make matters worse, is a Norþmann."

Ulfgar put the spoon in his bowl and, with his moustache smeared with barley mash, looked at me for a long time. "We had already been told in Stanfordbrycge that there was a herb woman named Hild nearby who can heal the sick. That's why we're here. I can also understand that she wants peace and quiet while she treats your father. You don't like people pacing around you or snooping behind you all the time when you're working either. And lastly, it is not the fault of the people in Stanfordbrycge, Cattune or Kjetil himself that Kjetil's forefathers were Vikings."

I looked around then leaned towards Ulfgar. "I don't trust these two healers. This Edeva is friendly, but there is something lordly about her friendliness. When she tells you to come in, what she really means is, go away and leave me alone!"

Ulfgar laughed out loud. "Oh, Oswulf, the barley mash doesn't agree with you, does it?"

"Why do they keep everything they do in that herb hut so secret?" I sucked in the air through my nose and looked at Ulfgar stiffly. "You know what they say about women who are skilled in the art of healing?"

Ulfgar grinned. "That their barley mash is spicier than other women's because they know their herbs?"

"Ulfgar! My father's life is at stake here. Maybe Hild and Edeva are not just herb women. They might also be skilled in the evil arts and doing all sorts of hellish things to my helpless father." The last words came out in a whisper as the thought choked me. I swallowed hard and looked at Ulfgar urgently. "The Norþmenn are probably behind all of this," I croaked. "And they also came up with the ruse with Cenric so they can use my fighting skills for their own purposes. I wouldn't be surprised if Stígandr also showed up soon."

Ulfgar wiped the barley crumbs from his beard and regarded me rather worriedly. "I'm beginning to think that maybe you should be treated, not your father. Or that you've been smelling the herb vials too much." He pushed his bowl away and rose.

"Where are you going?"

"Well, to the herb hut, of course."

"But no one is allowed in there."

Ulfgar ran his hand through his tousled wildcat mane. "Have faith in Ulfgar, your friend and helper."

I puffed out my cheeks and blew air through my lips. "You'll never make it into the hut! They didn't even let me, his own son, see him."

Ulfgar put his paw on my shoulder. "You really need to calm down. Now, come with me and learn from the master!"

I laughed. "Learn from the master! As if! But I'm not going to miss seeing how they show you the door. Just you wait! They'll chase you away just like they did with me."

"Ungeleafful." Ulfgar waved aside my words and headed for the door.

I followed him shaking my head. What made him think that Hild and Edeva would let him, of all people, into the hut? Why should they? And if they actually did, how would they justify it to me? As the son of the injured man, didn't I have much more of a right to see my father? At least, I might have the opportunity to take a look at him, should Ulfgar really succeed in gaining access to the herb hut. Perhaps I could accompany him in that case. Of course, it would hurt my honour that I myself hadn't been able to get to my father, but if I could finally see him, thanks to Ulfgar, I would be able to get over it. If only he was well and the suspicions that had been swirling around in my head and weighing me down for days turned out to be untrue. I wouldn't even be able to be angry with my friend if he did get me into the hut, though he would probably tease me even weeks later about how he had persuaded Hild and Edeva, while I had miserably failed to do so several times. Fortunately, I had more luck with weapons than women.

Ulfgar stalked up to the herb hut and peered through the small window. Then he winked at me and knocked on the door.

"Who is it?"

"I bring a sick man for you."

I looked around and whispered, "What sick man?"

"Forgive me, Oswulf!" Ulfgar stamped on my foot with such force that I cried out as if an ox had kicked me. "It's for a good cause."

The door opened, and Hild stuck her head out. "What happened?" she asked when she saw me moaning and hopping on one leg.

Ulfgar gently put his arm under my armpits to support me and smiled sweetly at me. "Something heavy fell on his foot. He can barely walk." He pointed into the hut. "I know you're busy, but could you perhaps…"

"Certainly, bring him in." Hild opened the door and stepped aside.

"We owe you a lot for your kindness, Hild." Ulfgar pulled me past her with a broad grin. I would have liked to strangle him at that moment, but the fact that I would finally see my father washed away my anger.

"Sit down here," Hild said, pulling up a stool for me. "I'm going to have a look at your foot."

While she opened my shoe and undid the cloth strip on my leg, I peered over to the bed. My father was lying on his back. His face was red and sweaty despite the coolness of the room.

Nevertheless, he had a peaceful expression on his face. Almost like that of a dead man whose soul had just flown to its maker.

Hild was running her hand over my foot. How could I ever have hoped that a woman as delicate and weak as Hild could save a man like my father? His wound required the skilled knowledge of a physician, not a woman dabbling in the art of healing by occasionally attending to scratches and bruises. Those disappeared after a few days even without secret herbal potions and spells. How could I have been so stupid! *Why did I listen to one man's rede at Stanfordbrycge and not ride to Eoforwic instead?* I buried my face in my hands. *How am I going to explain this to Mother?*

"Does that hurt?" Hild gently turned my foot.

Yes, it does. I wiped my face with my hands. "No. There's nothing wrong with my foot."

Hild rose and tossed her long hair over her shoulder. "Nothing is broken, but your foot will continue to swell and go blue. I'll put some arnica on it."

I waved it off and grabbed the cloth strip to put it back on. "Thank you, don't bother. We've already wasted enough time here. We should go."

"Would you want to see your father before you leave?"

"What for?" I scowled, rolling a length of cloth around my lower leg. "I will take him home as soon as possible. Did you at least call the priest in time, or did my father die without the last sacraments?"

Hild strode over to my father. "He is weak and feverish, but we were able to pour some soup into him."

The roll of cloth fell out of my hand. "Are you saying..." I stood up and walked cautiously towards the bed, "my father is alive?"

"Many would have died of less, but your father is a tough man. He holds onto his life."

He is holding on. He is still alive. Ðe ic herige, Drihten æl-mihtne, forðam þu bist swiðe rummod and swiðe mildheort! "Can... can I talk to him?"

Hild made a head movement towards my father. "Talk to him! Hearing his son's voice will hopefully give him the strength he needs to get through the fever."

My lips were as dry as a harvested wheat field on a hot summer's day. *Talk to him? What should I say?* I wiped my mouth and chin.

Ulfgar gave me a push. "Go on, Oswulf! You can't stand that long with your sore foot."

I drummed my fingers on my lips as if to tap out the words. *Say something...* I bent down carefully, almost fear-fully, to my father's ear. Maybe then the words would fall out, stuck somewhere in my throat. "Father?" I breathed. "It's me, Oswulf, your son. I don't know if you can hear me. You must get well, do you hear? Mother is waiting for us in Ledlinghe. King Harold is giving a great feast at Eoforwic. We have yet to drink to our victory over the Norþmenn. We must go to Eoforwic. You do want to make merry, don't you?"

As I spoke, my gaze had wandered along my father's body. He was covered with two thick, coarse blankets of dark wool, under which a light linen cloth with sweat stains peeked out. Under his red head and the strands of grey hair was a horn-coloured cloth on which had formed a damp circle, like a halo around the back of his head. Thick layers of cloth pro-truded from the slit left sleeve of his tunic, covering the place where, not a fortnight ago, there had been a healthy, strong hand, the one that had so faithfully carried Father's shield and protected him in all the battles. But perhaps there was no reason to be sad. After all, my father was still alive. Had not the god Tyr also lost a hand, bitten off by the monstrous wolf Fenrir? Even with one hand, Tyr was still the great Germanic god of war, no less revered after this misfortune than before.

My father's lips opened ever so slightly. They trembled as if he wanted to say something. No sound came out, but my father seemed to be forming a word.

I tilted my head forward in confusion. Nothing. I couldn't hear anything at all, but I could feel my father's breath escaping his mouth and tickling my ear. Smiling weakly, I straightened up again. "He... he wanted to say something. I felt his breath. He heard me. He's alive. He's alive, and he heard me!"

I jumped towards Hild and flung my arms around her. "You've saved him. You—" Hastily, I let go and averted my gaze, ashamed of letting myself get carried away. "Forgive me! I didn't mean to offend you. I was just..."

Hild smiled at me kindly, like a mother whose child is happy about a beautiful apple she had saved especially for him. "That's all right. But now, I must ask you to leave. Your father needs all the rest he can get."

"Sure, sure." I grabbed the cloth and my shoe and hopped through the door that Ulfgar was holding open.

"Are you sure your foot is all right?" asked Hild as we walked into the yard.

Ulfgar raised his hand. "Don't worry. I'll make sure he watches where he puts it."

I looked back at Hild once more. "I am deeply grateful for what you're doing for my father, Hild."

"I am happy to help if it is in my power. Now, go and pray that your father will survive the fever."

She closed the door and left us standing in the yard.

"You can put your clothes back on now." Ulfgar pointed at my bare foot and the cloth strip I was still holding.

I growled. "If you hadn't stood on my foot like an ox, I wouldn't have had to take them off." I slumped on the floor and began to wrap the strip around my lower leg.

Ulfgar raised his hands. "Have you seen your father or not?"

"Yes, but did you real—"

"There you go! The end justifies the means. You may now thank me."

"All right. You win."

"Is that all? I would have expected a little more."

I rolled my eyes and sighed. "Ulfgar is the very best. Is that enough?"

Ulfgar stroked his short beard thoughtfully. "That didn't really sound like it came from the heart."

I put on my shoe, lifted myself off the ground and shook the sand off. "Let's say I owe you one, all right?"

Ulfgar made a face as if he was considering my offer carefully. Then he slapped me on the shoulder. "All right, my friend. And should you need my help again..."

"Then I will first put my feet somewhere safe."

Both of us laughed. How long had it been since we had done that? *What would I ever do without you, Ulfgar?*

❧

IT WAS A grey morning when the tidings from the south reached us.

Only a few days ago, I had started to gather together all the youths and young men who could hold a sword in the yard to see what their fighting skills were like. Many a time it hurt my eyes to watch them almost twisting their arms while wielding the weapon. Some appeared only once and did not stay long when they saw that a youth like me wanted to teach them how to use weapons. Most, however, were quite curious and were happy to let me show them more skilful and effective ways to perform certain movements. In fact, ever since our memorable encounter while cleaning weapons, Cenric's pride had given way to a surprising eagerness to learn. Like a sponge, he absorbed everything I said and showed him. Even Ulfgar was amazed at how much the youth, whom I had recently mocked as a master of kitchen knives, had changed.

The other members of the manor did not mind us and went about their work as usual. Sometimes, Kjetil stood in the yard and watched us silently, but with an appreciative look, as we practised.

The aforesaid day was particularly busy, but we tried as best we could to go through the moves conscientiously. After all, a brief distraction could have terrible consequences in a real fight, as my father had experienced first-hand a few weeks ago. And there would not always be someone else around to step in and kill the opponent in time.

As I took a break from fighting, I noticed two riders in fine clothes appear in the yard. *The king's messengers*. I asked Ulfgar to take charge of the fighters and hurried over to the men, who were now joined by Kjetil.

"King Harold is on his way south with his huscarles," said one of the messengers. "He is calling on all lords to provide men for an army to follow him as soon as possible."

A cold shiver ran through my gut. I lowered the spear I still carried. "So, the French have landed on our shores." My heart wished for a denial, but somehow I knew that what we had feared for so long had come to pass. We had driven the Norþmenn out forever, but now their descendants from Normandig were invading Englaland like hungry wolves. This seemed to worry Kjetil as much as it did me. So maybe he was on our side after all, as Ulfgar never tired of pointing out.

"They have, forsooth," said the second messenger. "Their leader, Willelm of Normandig, landed at the bay of Pevenesel with his fleet the day before the feast of Saint Michael. They have been laying waste all the land along the coast and killing the inhabitants. Instead of riding north to Eoforwic, they are waiting for King Harold and his host of warriors to come down to them."

"He kills innocent people and destroys the land to lure the king down south? Niþing!"

"He certainly got exactly what he wanted," Kjetil said.

"King Harold aims to get there by the middle of the month to put an end to the destruction," said the first messenger. "The French army is said to be about three times the size of what King Harold is left with after the battles at Fuleforde and Stanfordbrycge. That's why he needs more men."

"But even his huscarles on their horses will be exhausted by the time they reach the south," I said. "And the rest of the surviving warriors? They have fought two long battles and will have to march for several days to get there."

"That may be true, but the king has no choice," said the second messenger. "He has no army in the south to defend the country against the invaders. All his men are here in the north."

"That's true." Kjetil nodded sadly. "He must not continue to leave the south unprotected but must get there as soon as possible before the French wreak further destruction."

My heart was burning. What was happening to my home? Torn to pieces like a sheep mauled by a pack of hungry wolves? And the shepherd who was meant to defend it looked like a sick man with old shepherd dogs who could do nothing against the wolves' ravenous appetites. Perhaps the wolves would finish them off, too. *What would happen then? What would become of Englaland, the king, its inhabitants? What about me? I wanted to be a huscarl to the king. The English king.* I was trembling.

Kjetil put his hand on my arm. "We shouldn't worry yet. No one knows what will happen when King Harold and the French face each other. There will be a battle, of that I am sure. But it is in the Lord's hands who wins it. May He have mercy on us and the destiny of this land."

I nodded weakly but was not convinced that the battle had not already been decided. If the king was able to delay fighting, they might have a chance to win. Taking on a horde of rested and battle-thirsty Frenchmen with exhausted warriors meant certain defeat.

Kjetil patted me on the back. "Cheer up, young friend. We will prepare as best we can for whatever may come. I watch you regularly during weapons practice. You really seem to know what you're doing. Who taught you that?"

"My father."

"He must be a very good teacher. I appreciate having the two of you on my manor. If the English in the king's army fight anywhere near as well as you do, I see no reason for Englaland to despair."

I stifled a smile. It felt good to be praised for the work I was doing, especially by someone I suspected of being allied with the Norþmenn. But Kjetil wasn't one of them. I had been wrong about him. He was not a foe, he felt the same as I did, and the Norse and French attacks on this land caused him as much pain as they did me. His name was Norse, but he was an Englishman at heart.

Thoughtfully, I strolled back to where Ulfgar was keeping the youths busy fighting. Others had also told me that they admired not only how I handled weapons, but also my ability to pass on that knowledge. Could it be that my destiny was not to become a huscarl, even though it was my father's wish? Perhaps, instead, I was born to teach others how to fight so that Englaland would always have strong and skilled warriors to take on any further assaults on their country?

❧

About four weeks after the battle at Stanfordbrycge, my father had, to my great relief, overcome the worst of what had befallen him after his injury on the battlefield. The cut looked gruesome with its scarred scab, but it was neatly stitched and healing well. My father would no longer be able to hold a shield as usual, so I made him one with a double loop that could be slid over his arm and then pulled tight. That way, he would be able to stand his ground in the thick of battle in spite of his missing left hand. After all, his right hand was intact and just as dangerous as ever. Of course, my father was still very weak after everything he had been through. The bones were shining through his skin, his movements were slow. He needed help to sit up or turn in bed. But he was aware of what was going on around him and regularly took a little soup and a warm herbal drink.

One day, as I was sitting at his bed, helping him spoon up the soup, Kjetil stepped into the room.

"You sent for me," he said. "I am glad to see you are getting better every day. Now, tell me what I can do for you."

"I should be the one asking that question, Kjetil," my father said in a low voice. "You were kind enough to host me, my son and his friend for many weeks without asking anything in return."

"Well, the two young men have made themselves very useful here. No one beats your son at fighting, and he seems to enjoy showing off his skills and passing them on to others. People have said many good words about him, not just his pupils."

I grinned. *My pupils? Am I a teacher then? At sixteen winters?*

"I am glad to hear that. After all, he is to follow in my footsteps one day and become a ðegn, perhaps even a huscarl of the king." He raised the stump of his arm. "It certainly looks like my days in the king's army are done."

Kjetil and I exchanged a look. No one had yet told my father that the French had landed in Englaland and that King Harold was on his way to battle with them. We did not want to put my father's recovery at risk unnecessarily. When we knew how the battle had ended, it would be early enough to tell him about it.

"Your healer has done wonders to bring me back to earth from the realm of the dead. At least most of me."

Kjetil cleared his throat. "You'd better not let Father Leofric hear you say that, or the salvation of your soul will cost you dearly."

"I would like to thank you for your kindness in welcoming us and for what you have done for me, Kjetil. I owe a lot to Hild and to your wife." He pointed with his right hand to a small, locked chest that stood under a shelf. "Oswulf, will you bring me the chest, please?"

He rummaged under the rolled-up sheet behind him, which served as a pillow and at the same time as a support when he sat, and pulled out a small key, which he held out to me. I sat down on the stool, put the chest on my thighs and unlocked it.

"I would like to give you something as a token of my gratitude," my father said.

I opened the chest and held it out to him.

He pulled out his scramasax, a short sword with an elaborately crafted hilt and protected by a richly decorated sheath of soft pigskin, and held it out to Kjetil, who spread his hands in amazement to receive the sword. "Take this as thanks for all you and the people of Wilburgfos have done for me and my son."

Kjetil examined the sword with wide eyes. "I cannot accept that, Osfrið. You should save the scramasax for your son."

My father shook his head. "I have decided that Oswulf will receive my longsword when I no longer need it. The scramasax, however, is due to you as a reward for your help, for without your healers I would not be alive now."

Kjetil took the short sword in his left hand and grasped my father's hand with his right. "I thank you for this precious gift, Osfrið. I will cherish it as befits the scramasax of a ðegn."

The door flew open and Cenric rushed in. "The king's dead, and everyone else too."

We stared at him as if a two-headed calf were standing in front of us.

Kjetil was the first to awake from his stupor. "What are you saying?"

"The French killed King Harold. And all those who fought with him."

They killed the whole army? All the fighters, the brave hus-carles, the ðegnes, all the men who had gone into battle with their lord? Everything was spinning around me. If I hadn't been sitting on the stool and holding the chest in my hands, I might have staggered like a drunken Viking.

"Who told you that?" Kjetil seemed to be the only one who could think clearly and not be overcome by his dismay and anger.

Cenric wiped the tears from his face, looking like an owl with dark circles around his eyes. "The messenger out there."

Kjetil glanced at my father and me and raised the short sword. "Looks like we could put this to good use soon. Your son should do the weapons practice more often from now on." He pulled Cenric along and closed the door. My father and I were left alone with a feeling of great emptiness.

"How could God let this happen?" I asked after a while.

My father slowly propped himself up on his bed. His face was still gaunt from the struggles of the last weeks, but in his eyes burned again the fire that befitted a warrior. "The Lord works in mysterious ways, Oswulf. But it is not for us mere mortals to question His decisions. Perhaps he wants to try us by shaking our world to the ground."

"An ordeal? But haven't we just driven the pagan Vikings out for good after so many centuries of plundering and pillaging? How many more trials by ordeal do we have to pass?"

"We have defeated the Norþmenn. We will also defeat their French descendants." He reached out and stroked my arm. "It will be a hard and long fight, but we won't give up that easily, will we, Oswulf?"

Time passed and the blood month came. Many animals were slaughtered to make food for the winter. The smell that spread through Wilburgfos in those days reminded me of the sausages and smoked meat hanging everywhere in Ledlinghe and so many other places in Englaland in those days.

We stayed another three days after the slaughtering. Getting to Ledlinghe needed less than half a day's walk, but only now was my father strong enough to ride back safely.

He did not yet have the strength he used to, being only able to take a few steps on foot if he was given a little support. His movements were still slow, and he would probably never recover his old nimbleness. For another battle, it would not be enough, but for life on the manor? Surely, he would need more help there, too.

How far this would affect my weapons practice and my becoming a huscarl, I could only guess. We would have to see how my father coped with only one hand.

"You've served us well here," Kjetil said, while Cenhelm helped me put my father on the horse with the aid of a small stool. "We'll miss you."

With a swing, we pushed my father up so that Ulfgar could get hold of his leg on the other side and pull it towards him.

With a groan, my father slid into the saddle and slowly straightened up. A smile crossed his face. Either he was glad to return home and see his wife and children that he'd left behind, or it did him good to finally be back in the saddle after spending the last few weeks mainly lying down.

"Our work is nothing compared to what your wife and Hild have done." I looked up at my father with satisfaction. "If you are ever in need, we will stand by you."

Kjetil took the hand I held out to him and put his other hand on top. "Wilburgfos will not forget you, young Oswulf. We would be glad to see you again one day."

I nodded and then got on the horse behind my father, while Ulfgar mounted his own. Cenhelm handed us the weapons we had rescued from the battlefield at Stanfordbrycge.

"What will happen now?" I asked as I picked up the reins.

Kjetil shrugged his shoulders. "We will have to wait and see. I heard that Eorl Morkere and his brother fled from Eoforwic with their surviving warriors after the battle at Fuleforde. Whether they are back at their manor houses or already in Lunden, no one could tell me."

"What do they want in Lunden?" my father asked.

"They are part of the witan, who already chose King Harold. It is rumoured that the witan met in Lunden after his death and decided that Eadgar Æðeling should be the next king."

"The ætheling?" my father asked in surprise. "He does have kings amongst his forefathers, but he is younger than Oswulf. How is he to rule a land over which the French descend like crows over a freshly sown field of grain?"

"It seems that he is supported by four powerful Englishmen who survived the French attack: Eorl Morkere and his brother as well as the Archbishops of Cantwarebyri and Eoforwic."

My father looked at Kjetil sorrowfully. "We lost many men to the Norþmenn near Eoforwic. The two eorles only just escaped the axes of the Norþmenn. Do you really think they'll be able to install an immature youth as heir to the throne against the French? Men who do not shy away from killing women and children and destroying everything as they please?" He shook his head. "I fear for Englaland and the difficult times ahead of us."

Kjetil held out his hand to him. "This country has survived other trials. It was on the brink of death when the Danes invaded many centuries ago and plundered and pillaged everything. But after every defeat, the English have risen again. Let us keep faith in ourselves and stand up to the French!" He grasped my father's hand. "Farewell, Osfrið. May God protect you and your family."

❧

Just as we reached the village in the early afternoon, a large, black, barking beast came running towards us.

"Bargest, old girl! Come to Ulfgar!" Sitting on the horse, my friend spread his arms as if waiting for the dog to throw herself into them. Instead, she bounced round the horses in huge leaps, wagging her tail excitedly.

The smell of smoke filled the air as we passed the first huts. The people of Ledlinghe were filling up their winter stocks with smoked meat, but the only sound was three children running after a flock of chattering geese.

Old Dunstan came towards us with his donkey, loaded with two sacks of grain. "Osfrið?" he asked incredulously, stopping. "You've been gone a long time."

"I'm afraid that was unavoidable, Dunstan," my father said.

"They say there were terrible battles near Eoforwic."

My father took a breath and gave me and Ulfgar a sideways glance. "It's true, Dunstan. Unfortunately, we do not bring good tidings. We did win against the Norþmenn, but while we were fighting at Stanfordbrycge, the French landed in the south. King Harold could not stop them." He lowered his eyes.

"Will there be a war?"

"It's already over, Dunstan. The French have defeated us. King Harold is dead and the English army destroyed. If my son had not saved me in my last battle, I too would be dead now."

Dunstan nodded appreciatively. "Your son is a good boy, Osfrið. You should be proud of him."

"I am, Dunstan. Very much so."

The old man pointed ahead. "I must go on to the mill. God bless you." He clicked his tongue once and trotted off with his donkey.

We slowly approached the blacksmith's hut, where we left Ulfgar. My gaze wandered over the wooden structure, which was framed by two large apple trees. It looked like we would need the blacksmith's services very soon.

"Don't you want to see Godgifu?" my father asked, as Ulfgar allowed Bargest to lick him enthusiastically.

The image of my beloved's adorable face appeared before me like a vision. How I would have loved to run to her, to take her in my arms after all these weeks and cover her in kisses. Instead, I shook my head. "It's been almost a month since I sent a message to mother. She should be the first to know that we've returned. Ulfgar will tell Godgifu that I am back and will visit her later."

Ulfgar nodded and went away with Bargest and his horse.

A muffled neighing sounded from the stable next to the smithy. A bleating voice made me sit up and take notice. I steered our horse closer to the stable.

"Where are you going, Oswulf?" my father asked.

"I want to greet an old friend." I brought the horse to a halt and peeked into the stable where Ulfgar's father was cutting the hooves of one of the horses. Apparently, it was to be re-shod, because he had all his tools ready, as well as four new horseshoes. Stígandr was leaning against the wall with his legs crossed and his arms folded, watching the blacksmith with drumming fingers. When his horse turned its head towards us and whinnied, Stígandr looked up.

"Eala, Osfrið, hlaford min." He approached us to a certain distance. "I understand you were badly wounded in battle. They already feared for your life." He made a large-framed gesture with his hands. "But to my great joy, I see that you are well. No doubt you owe it to the commendable efforts of your son, who never let you out of his sight."

A few insults came to mind that I wanted to hurl at him, but because I couldn't decide which would be most appropriate, my father beat me to it by speaking.

"Well, I'm fine again." He raised the stump of his arm. "But I had to leave part of me on the battlefield. My son saved my life, otherwise, the rest would be lying there now too."

Stígandr tugged at his chin beard. "Yes, your son is indeed a capable boy. And so eager when it comes to the good of the fatherland. Only, alas, a little hasty with his suspicions."

"At least I wasn't sneaking around on the Viking side of the battlefield."

The blacksmith hammered rhythmically on a red-hot iron, which he turned back and forth on his anvil with a pair of tongs.

"What are you talking about, Oswulf?" My father looked at me over his shoulder.

"Stígandr was also at Stanfordbrycge, Father."

"Was he?" My father frowned. "How come I didn't know about it?"

"I decided late that I should come along," put in Stígandr.

"He was standing off the battlefield on the path the Norþmenn took from Richale. Ulfgar and I beckoned him towards us, but he tried to flee."

"It is an unfortunate misunderstanding, Osfrið. I wasn't trying to flee. I just stumbled."

"Besides, he told me himself that the Norþmenn forced him to spy on us."

Stígandr placed a hand on his chest. "You threatened me with a sword. What was I supposed to do? I only told you what you wanted to hear."

"You lie as soon as you open your mouth."

"Would you have believed me if I had told you something else? If I had told you that I had personally offered King Harold to spy on the Norþmenn for him, would you have believed me? That I was to find out for our king how many Norþmenn had remained in Richale and that they were going to join the warriors already at Stanfordbrycge at some point anyway? That I was to find out when they were leaving to do so? Would you have believed me?"

I kept silent. Stígandr, of all people, as the king's spy? Had he really been on the side of the English all along? Indeed, he still knew the Norse language well enough to easily mingle with the Norþmenn, but wouldn't this disguise have been noticed at some point? Or had I actually done him wrong, just as I had initially misjudged Kjetil and the herb women?

There was a hiss as the blacksmith put one of the hot irons on the horse's hoof.

"What do you have to say to that, Oswulf?" my father asked. His voice sounded calm, but he clearly blamed me for having gone too far and threatened someone unjustly and with a sword. That was not proper for a future huscarl. *Nor for the son of a ðegn.*

Stígandr smiled and pushed his lower jaw forward so that his teeth showed. This goat smile had once been pitiful, but after the quarrel during our last hunt and since the events at Stanfordbrycge, it was like a slap in the face.

That was the day I began to hate my former friend. I wish I had cut his throat on the battlefield.

But then I wouldn't have got to my father in time.

I snorted. Was I supposed to be grateful to this liar because I wouldn't have been able to save my father if it hadn't been for him?

"Maybe I was wrong," I murmured.

Stígandr put his head to one side and held his hand behind one ear. "Sorry, but my hearing is not so good. What did you say?"

"I said I might have made a mistake." I squeezed the words through clenched teeth. *Ðu scealt gan libbende on helle.*

Stígandr opened his arms. "Well, that happens, young Osfriðson. You were wrong. We all make mistakes sometimes, don't we? I'm sure your father agrees with me."

My father nodded. "Man is flawed and fallible, Oswulf. The Lord has given him weaknesses but also the strength to forgive others for their weaknesses."

"Wise words, aren't they, Oswulf? You see, I am not at all angry with you for being wrong. You are a young warrior who wants to become a huscarl. You sometimes don't know what to do with your excess strength, and in the heat of battle, your judgement wanes. I am only a shoemaker, yet I can understand how difficult it can be to meet all expectations. That is your lot as the son of a ðegn. You were born to follow a higher calling and therefore have to learn much more than I, a simple shoemaker's son. But I am sure that one day, you too will acquire the wisdom and maturity of your father and become a worthy huscarl."

Another loud hiss of hot iron on horn as the last horse-shoe was placed on the animal's foot. If the anger that had just built up inside me could have escaped through my nose, it would have drowned out the sound completely.

Stígandr waved his hand. "Forgive me, but the blacksmith will soon be finished. God be with you."

I felt ashamed and didn't say another word until we arrived at our manor house. Only when we were greeted there by the rest of our family, beaming with joy, did I regain hope – hope that in the years to come, I would learn to master not only all sorts of weapons, but also my mind and my tongue, and that one day, Englaland would once again be a free country under an English king.

In December of the Year of Our Lord 1066, the Archbishop of Eoforwic crowned Willelm of Normandig King of Engla-land in the cathedral at Wincestre – where King Harold and all his predecessors had received the crown. We had lost the battle. But contrary to what my father said on our return to Ledlinghe, the war for Englaland was far from over, and not only in my heart.

Chapter 5

Almost three years had passed since the death of King Harold, and it seemed that our country was slowly calming down under the French rulers. Where travelling minstrels and merchants had previously talked about rebellions in Norþ-Walas, Eastengla and Norþhymbre, they now only mentioned the few people who continued to travel to Scotland or to the great ports to leave the land and seek their fortunes elsewhere, across the water. Even the last two great English eorles, Eorl Morkere and his brother, had submitted to the king shortly after the coronation and had been living at Willelm's court ever since – even if many doubted that this was by choice and that it would last.

An eerie calm settled over the land, and in Ledlinghe, too, life had fallen into its ordinary way. Stígandr had taken over the workshop after his father's death at the end of the winter and had hired two apprentices. Since he was constantly travelling to the ports and big markets to get leather, orders and tools, we rarely saw each other. I also saw Ulfgar less, even though we continued to hunt together while we still could.

115

The new king had started to ban hunting in many of the woods in the south, and those who were caught doing so faced harsh punishments.

For a year, I had been married to Godgifu, but the duties of a ðegn, which my father was slowly handing over to me, and the daily weapons practice to become a warrior, left me little time to spend with my sweet wife. I loved Godgifu, but after my failure at the battles of Fuleforde and Stanfordbrycge and my shameful judgements on Kjetil, the herb women and Stígandr, I had vowed to become an exemplary and brave warrior, excelling both on the battlefield and at the manor house – worthy to become a ðegn like my father and, eventually, a huscarl of Eorl Morkere or the king. For that continued to be my greatest wish, and my father encouraged me in it, probably because he noticed how his strength was increasingly failing him.

When he wasn't teaching me in matters other than physically fighting, I spent hours working on each and every skill I needed as a warrior: strength, endurance, speed, cunning fighting moves and ruses, but above all the handling of weapons of all kinds, whether spear, one-handed or two-handed axe, short or long sword, bow and arrow, dagger, even slings, clubs, sticks, fists and whatever else seemed usable as a weapon, I used everything and anything against very different opponents, and soon, there was no one near or far who could seriously threaten me. All my deeds and desires were guided by my hope for the one day that was sure to come at some point. It was only a matter of time before the wheel of fortune would turn for us. And it did, in the middle of the harvest season.

The peasants were in the fields, harvesting the crops before the rain and cold of the coming autumn could destroy them. A team of oxen with a cart rumbled along the road into the village, bringing the bundled sheaves of wheat. From the yard in front of the granary, the dull thudding of the threshing flails could be heard as the men beat the grains out of the ears. Women and children eagerly gathered the grains and sifted them into a bucket or threw them in the air to separate out the chaff. Two children held up a sack made of coarse cloth while two others poured in the buckets of sifted grains.

Ulfgar and I were returning with our catch from the nearby pond when the clatter of horses' hooves caught our attention. We barely had the time to move to the side before a group of riders in full battle dress trotted past us and headed for the front of the church.

"Earnest visitors, methinks," Ulfgar murmured, glancing after the riders with narrowed eyes.

"Come, let's hear what they have to say!"

We hurried to the small gathering that was forming around the riders. Mostly old men who took care of mending tools and equipment while the young ones worked in the fields or with the cattle came wandering over to hear the tidings.

"Greetings, men of Ledlinghe, from our lord, Gospatric, Eorl of Bernicia," called the foremost horseman, gazing over the crowd of old and young men, children, dogs, three pigs and a few chickens. "Englishmen, the day has come for us to take back our freedom. Willelm of Normandig, who wrongfully seized the crown of Englaland three years ago and bloodily crushed all resistance, has oppressed us long enough. Eadgar Æðeling, the last descendant of the kings of Westseaxa, the only one with a true claim to the English crown, fled from his captivity to Scotland a few months ago."

The elderly cheered cautiously. Eadgar Æðeling was younger than me, maybe eighteen winters old – far too young for someone who wanted to enforce his claim to the throne against a man of about forty winters who seemed determined to hold onto the English crown by any means necessary.

"He heard of the unrest in his beloved homeland, where brave men, whose king he is supposed to be, are fighting to shake off the French yoke. Eadgar Æðeling is determined to wrest his land from the greedy hands of the French."

The cheering got louder. I listened up. My heartbeat accelerated. *He wants to fight for his right?* Was this the opportunity I had been waiting for these past three years?

A blurry image shifted before my eyes, becoming clearer and clearer with each detail I saw. With King Harold's standard in his hand, Eadgar Æðeling stood on a pile of dead French horsemen, while the surviving ones fell on their knees before him, whimpering for mercy. From the right approached the English Archbishop of Cantwarebyri, the crown of Englaland in his hands. Eadgar Æðeling knelt down, and the archbishop solemnly placed the crown on his head. The crowned man rose to the cheer of his countrymen.

Tears came to my eyes. Had we passed the trial God had imposed on us through the French? Had the time finally come to chase them, too, from our land? My stomach was tingling. I could hardly wait to pack my weapons and go to war. At long last, I would be able to stand out in battle before the eyes of the future king.

"At Richale, on the banks of the river Humbre, lies a fleet of nearly three hundred ships which our future king has assembled with his allies in Scotland and Denmark to defeat the French together."

Some of the bystanders began to murmur with a worried look. The image of an English victory that I had just seen so clearly burst like a pig's bladder that had been filled with water and then pricked with a needle.

"Of all people, the Danes and the Scots are to save our country from the French?" I murmured to Ulfgar. "What happens if we win? How can Eadgar Æðeling be sure that they will actually put him on the throne and not one of themselves?"

"That would be nothing new," said Ulfgar. "We've already had two Norse kings, but I'm sure the Scots wouldn't mind either to rule over Englaland. It would save them from constantly pushing their border back and forth."

The foremost horseman continued. "The people of Norþhymbre also stand together behind their future king and have joined the revolt against the bastard from Normandig. Eorl Morkere and his brother, who have fled from Willelm's court, are leading their warriors to strengthen their ancient claims to Myrce and Norþhymbre. With a common army, united under Eadgar Æðeling, they have already surprised the French at Dunholm." The rider had to speak up, as the cheers got louder. "They have killed the new Eorl of Norþhymbre, the Frenchman Robert de Comines, and completely destroyed his entire following."

The shouts and clapping of the bystanders became so loud that the speaker had to pause. Fists were raised in the air. The fighting spirit was beginning to rise again in the men, and I too pushed my fists in the air and roared out my elation about this English victory.

"Not a single one of them survived to bring the tidings to the French bastard in Wincestre." The horseman almost shouted and raised his hand to continue speaking. "But he will hear from us, for Eadgar Æðeling and his army are on their way to Eoforwic to besiege the city and free it from its French rulers. I ask you, men of Ledlinghe, are you ready to go into battle with your future king against the French niþingas?"

An loud cry of approval went through the men. Hands, fists, brooms and other tools were waved aloft.

Ulfgar clenched his fist and roared, "Ða Frenciscan sculon deaþe sweltan!" Then he turned to me and grinned. "Eadgar Æðeling has learned well from the French."

"What do you mean?"

"The French army is in the south, so he stirs up trouble in the north to make it come to him – like the French did with King Harold, just the other way round. And we know who won there, don't we?"

Ulfgar was right. Except that the French had devastated whole swathes of land after their arrival. Eadgar Æðeling's men, on the other hand, only seemed to attack the French, but not to murder and plunder as they pleased. Their deeds were laudable forsooth, but would it be enough against warriors as ruthless as the French?

❧

So, Ulfgar and I were soon part of a large crowd of keen warriors eager to join their rebellious countrymen in the revolt against the foreign rulers. All hopes rested on the young shoulders of the only living descendant of the mighty Ælfred of Westseaxa. Just as that brave king had once snatched Englaland from the Viking hordes at the very last moment, so this time, Eadgar Æðeling was to free Englaland from the invaders and ensure that the land of the English fell back into English hands.

What a motley band of fighters we were, riding towards the largest city in the north of Englaland! In the two battles I had witnessed, at Fuleforde and Stanfordbrycge, an English army had battled against an army of Norþmenn. Today, we were on the same side, as if it had always been like that. And there were not only Englishmen and Norþmenn, but also the Scots, whom Eadgar Æðeling had brought with him. Three peoples who had been at war with each other for centuries were marching together to Eoforwic to...

"What do the Scots and the Norþmenn actually expect from driving the French out of the city?" I asked Ulfgar as we drifted along with the crowd.

"Perhaps they're hoping to extend their southern border into Englaland. If they help Eadgar Æðeling with his claim to the English crown, he might reward them generously with land in the north."

"Possibly, and what about the Danes? What do they get out of supporting him?"

Ulfgar shrugged his shoulders. "I don't know. Gold, honour, the chance for a bloody fight?"

"Why are they here anyway? Didn't King Harold drive the Norþmenn out of our land for good?"

"That was the Norþmenn. These are Danes."

"I have a bad feeling about this, Ulfgar. This is a huge army. There are enough warriors who will go into battle for Eadgar and his claim to the throne and who will keep the French warriors busy. The Danes have no reason to risk their lives for him. They will stuff their pouches while we are fighting and then sneak away rather than support us to the end against the French."

"You are still as suspicious of the Norþmenn as you were three years ago. Let them line their pockets if only they help us take Eoforwic as quickly as possible."

I swallowed the foul taste that formed in my mouth and tried to think of something else.

A little further ahead of me, riding with the experienced warriors, was my father, who did not want to miss this opportunity. He was convinced that this was one of the last chances to put an Englishman on the throne of Englaland again – and the last time for him as a ðegn to fight for an English king once more.

While I was indulging my thoughts in the rhythmic ups and downs of my striding horse, someone came to ride beside me. I glanced to my left and saw the bared lower teeth of an obviously good-humoured Stígandr.

"I see that you too have decided to support the pretender to the throne from the north."

I frowned. "Eadgar Æðeling is not from the north. He is one of us, a descendant of the great King Ælfred of Westseaxa."

"Oh, right, right. A blood relative of the learned Ælfred, who is known for his good relations with the Danes. Fortunately, the æðeling can count on the support of the Danish and Scottish armies," Stígandr strained in his seat to look around, "because he obviously hasn't been able to persuade many Englishmen to join him."

"How do you know how many there are? Besides, all that matters at the moment is to get Eoforwic back into English hands. For that, Eadgar Æðeling doesn't need to call together the entire fyrd and the army of huscarles and ðegnes."

Stígandr looked ahead, bored. "The latter would also be difficult. As far as I know, the huscarles and most of the nobles did not survive the battle at Hæstinga. The peasants don't care who they have to pay taxes and dues to anyway, be it to an Englishman, Norþmann or Frenchman."

"What are you trying to say, Stígandr? That Eadgar Æðeling does not deserve the crown? That the English are cowards who shy away from doing their duty?"

Stígandr clicked his tongue and looked at me pityingly. "Not at all! What are you thinking? I'm just observing and stating what I see."

I snorted. "I don't know why you're coming along at all if you think nothing of the æðeling's undertaking anyway."

Stígandr spread his fingers over his chest. "You know, I pondered for a long time whether I should really leave my workshop in Ledlinghe, but then I said to myself, Stígandr, do it! For the good of Ledlinghe and the glory of Englaland! As a dutiful and proud Englishman, you owe it to the rightful ruler of this land."

I frowned. Memories of the battle at Stanfordbrycge came back to me. Stígandr had suddenly appeared there too, without any real reason for his presence. I tried to push the thoughts away. My suspicions of that time had turned out to be wrong and unjust. I couldn't make the same mistake again.

Stígandr's face tensed, exposing a long row of teeth in his advanced lower jaw. "Are we not all English on this day? United in a single army with a single goal before our eyes: to take Eoforwic and destroy the French?"

There was a diabolical glow in his dark eyes that made me shiver, even in the warm summer air. What he said was all well, but how he said it made me think. Taking Eoforwic might have been the common goal, but did everyone want to achieve it for the same reason? What would happen if we really defeated the French and claimed Eoforwic? Would the city then belong to Eadgar Æðeling? Wouldn't the Danes and Scots want a reward? What would he give them in return? What if the

Danish king did not agree with Eadgar Æðeling or if he suddenly decided to claim the city for himself? What would Eadgar have to oppose him with? And last but not least, what would King Willelm do when he heard that Eoforwic had fallen?

As if he had read my thoughts, Stígandr continued, "Eoforwic now has two castles on a hill, each from which his men watch over the two rivers and the entire city. King Willelm ordered the second castle to be built after one of the French army leaders and many of his men were killed in the siege of the first castle in February. Since then, the governor of Eoforwic and the scirgerefa of Eoforwicscir have tried to keep the town quiet, but the townsfolk have never lost their will to fight against their French masters."

"How do you know?"

Stígandr looked at his fingernails. "You can find out a lot if you ask the right people."

So there were, in fact, two castles to be besieged? No wonder Eadgar Æðeling depended on a large army and support from foreign fighters! I had never seen a castle in my life and imagined that it would not be easy to attack and overcome the men within, but it was possible, apparently. After all, the people of Eoforwic had already killed a Frenchman once during a siege – although that didn't sound like much of a success, considering the effort involved in a siege. But it meant that even a castle on a hill had weaknesses, and perhaps we would be able to exploit them to our advantage.

Eoforwic sprawled over the plain like an endless, viscous wave dragging roofs, paths, carts, people and animals behind it. Between the Use and Foss rivers, the main castle was already waiting for our onslaught. French warriors, clad in full battle wear, lined the castle's mighty palisaded fence as far as the eye could see. Like an omen of what was to come, silent witnesses reminded us of the fierce battle that had taken place here only six months ago. Splintered wooden slats stuck out from abandoned houses like pikes lowered in defence. In trampled gardens, only a few neeps stuck their heads out of the ground, and small beanstalks searched in vain for a trellis to hold on to. The mutilated, charred remains of once magnificent fruit trees stood around like lepers, and on the east side of the city stretched a lake whose black water swallowed up everything that lay in its way, buildings, trees and shrubs. *Just like the new ruler of Englaland.*

When we reached the castle, our army split. One part went on to attack while the rest, me included, slowly pushed through to the bridge at the end of the great street called Micklegate. Only there could we cross the Use and then ride south again to the second castle.

Back when we had fought the Norþmenn at Fuleforde, we had caught a glimpse of Eoforwic as we passed it to the south on our way to the battlefield. At that time, I couldn't really gauge the size of the city. But now, after a restless night in the Danish camp in Richale, we were finally setting foot into it, and only then did I realise why it was called a city. Eoforwic was huge, much bigger than anything I had ever seen – but then again, what should I have seen, at only nineteen winters of age? However, as we soon discovered, even the streets of a large city were not designed for an entire army to pass through freely. How King Harold and his army had swiftly crossed its entirety to get to Stanfordbrycge as quickly as it did remained a mystery to me. Everywhere, it was teeming with houses, fences, stalls and wells. Stray pigs and geese were continuously running between one's legs, and we were constantly having to let through some cart or rider who was blocking our onward journey because they themselves were held up by some obstacle in front of them. Numerous wooden buildings and houses were huddled together – even around the castles there was only just enough space in the streets for two oxcarts to pass side by side. It was cramped and oppressive. High above us, the castles on the hills were guarding the banks of the rivers, watching us approach. I felt like a rabbit realising that a hungry bird of prey was circling above it, observing its next meal.

The rising heat of the day brought with it the stench of rotting waste, excrement and sweat, and the deafening noise of people, animals and other moving objects shouting, grunting, rattling, snarling and making a whole host of other sounds filled the air. Above it all, visible from afar and towering above the noise, crowds and smells, were the castles that Willelm the Bastard had built. Everyone knew by now that wherever he went, the new king built castles as a reminder of his power. When I saw the castles in Eoforwic, I knew why he did it and why the English hated him so much for it. Before the French came, the tallest buildings you could see from a distance were the churches or the manor houses with their great halls, where people would come together to eat, sleep, pray and live. Now, they were replaced by another symbol, far greater and higher, that of the French domination over the land and the people they suppressed.

"My neck is hurting from looking up." Ulfgar turned his head back and forth so that it cracked.

Pressed closely together, we were following the stream of countless men ahead of us. "I don't like any of this." I wrinkled my nose. "All those houses, all those people. And then those castles." My gaze slid upwards again.

"The king needs to keep an eye on his subjects somehow. Even more so when he is not particularly popular with them."

This reminded me of why we had actually come here. Eadgar Æðeling had sent three men to Eoforwic yesterday. They were to track down the leaders of the rebels and find out how people felt about a revolt before we began to besiege the castles as the Danish king had proposed.

"I've never besieged a castle before." Ulfgar looked at me frowning. "Must be a pretty tough undertaking."

"We will soon find out." I pressed my lips together and thought of my father, whom I had, again, long since lost in the host of warriors. I prayed to God that He protect my father and us in this battle and that we win.

Our leader, Gospatric, sounded the charge.

Ulfgar and I were standing too far back to do anything yet. So instead, we shouted our support to the men assaulting the castle. They formed a shield wall behind which they charged in waves with their spears and axes across the ditch and up the hill. Additional cover came from our archers, who shot their arrows at the French warriors behind the palisade fence of the outer bailey. Arrows hailed back from the Frenchmen, looking to find a hole in the shield wall and hit the unprotected archers. Having arrived at the fence, the attackers stabbed and slashed into the wood of the palisades while dodging the spear thrusts of the Frenchmen defending the wooden rampart. While we waited our turn for the assault on the castle, we pulled the injured down from the hill so that someone could tend to their wounds.

Some time later, as the battle continued to rage, we noticed trails of fire flying through the air.

"What was that?" I asked Ulfgar.

"They're shooting flaming arrows." Ulfgar scratched his beard. "It's about to get rather warm here, methinks."

"They're setting fire to the slats!" I shouted. "What an excellent idea! Why didn't they do it right away?"

"Maybe they forgot their tinder stones and had to buy some on the market first." Ulfgar watched the flight of the arrows carefully as the waves of attackers kept charging.

Owing to the heat of the last weeks, the wood of the palisades and of the tower in their midst was as dry as a withered leaf in the searing midday sun. A single arrow stuck in a gap in the wooden slats of the tower, and soon a small flame flickered at this spot. Our archers shot more fire arrows at the castle.

The Frenchmen on the palisades continued their defence. They seemed to have received support from other warriors because it was staking our men longer to get to the castle now. Maybe they had underestimated our army and had only put up a few men to defend the castle. Either that or the attackers were getting tired. In any case, more spears and arrows were raining down from the castle, and we had to take shelter behind the surrounding houses until it was our turn to attack.

Ulfgar and I had hastened behind a shed. I peered around the corner. "They're shooting back."

"Haven't they been doing this all along?"

"No, they're shooting with fire." I looked first at Ulfgar and then at the wooden buildings around us. "They want to set fire to the houses we are hiding behind."

"Then Gospatric had better end this siege as quickly as possible."

Ulfgar bent over to take a look at the castle, in which several fires were burning. The palisade fence had also caught fire, and behind their shields, two of our men were lighting more slats with torches. More fire would further weaken the defensive wall and also keep the Frenchmen busy with extinguishing them instead of defending the castle.

"I don't think the French can hold the castle much longer. A few more axe blows and there will be a hole in the fence. Look!" Ulfgar pointed to the spot where the fire was eating through the slats and two Danes were cutting huge cracks in the weakened fence with their mighty axes, "We're getting ready to break into the castle. Or to split the heads of the Frenchmen who want to prevent it."

The fire spread quickly. Large parts of the castle and the surrounding buildings were soon in flames, and broad clouds of smoke rose into the sky. But our army no longer needed the protection of the buildings. Like moths to a flame, we rushed to the beckoning gaps in the castle's wooden ramparts and pushed inside, where the last refuge of the Frenchmen was also ablaze. Surrounded by the embers of the crackling wooden beams, glowing dark red like a searing iron, the older warriors were already engaged in hand-to-hand combat with the Frenchmen in the outer bailey.

Now it was time to show what I had learned in the last few years and whether I deserved to become a huscarl. With my spear, I stabbed at a Frenchman who was fighting an Englishman and turned his back on me. The spear pierced his chain mail with a crunch. With a jerk, I pulled the metal tip out of the dying man, ready for the next.

We no longer had to fear an attack from the palisades, as most of the warriors had gathered in the outer bailey to try and fight off the invading hordes. Whatever guards were left, trying to slow down the onslaught outside the palisades with spears and bows and arrows, our archers took care of.

From the side, a Frenchman rushed at me with a spear and a huge shield. I hurled my spear at him, but he sidestepped behind two other fighters, and my spear got stuck in the ground instead of the enemy's chest. I took my axe and raised the shield. The Frenchman leapt out from behind the others and stabbed at my face. I jumped to the side. He thrust with his spear. With my shield in front, I threw myself forwards and against his spear, causing my foe to stumble backwards. I hacked into the handle of his spear with my axe. The wood splintered like a chicken bone. The Frenchman threw away the splintered spear shaft and reached for his sword. I aimed at his right side, but he warded off with his shield and swung the sword towards my neck. I ducked under the shield, lunged and slashed at his outstretched sword arm. A dull thud. The sound of shattering bones. Blood. The Frenchman cried out and dropped the sword. His forearm dangled uselessly from his upper arm. I looked him straight in the eye before slashing at his unprotected side. Just in time, he raised his shield, so I swung my axe above the ground at knee height, as if cutting ears of grain with a sickle. This time, the shield came too late. My axe slid through the Norman's lower leg. He groaned once more before he collapsed, bleeding and buried under his shield.

The blood rushed in my ears. My whole body shook with excitement. "Ða Frenciscan sculon deaþe sweltan!" I shouted Ulfgar's war cry and looked for the next enemy. I was no longer the inexperienced and frightened youth of Fuleforde and Stanfordbrycge. I had worked hard on my fighting skills and had been involved, a few times, in ambushing and killing the French tax collectors. I had experienced myself what French rule meant to us Englishmen. Had seen the streams of gaunt, exhausted people, old and young, fleeing from the French cruelty in the south and east. I also knew about the Welsh revolts. Yes, the resistance to the new rulers had died down, but it had never ceased completely, and if we stopped fighting now, it would be too late. We would have lost Englaland forever.

When all around us was fire, smoke and dead Frenchmen, Gospatric's voice rang through the castle, "The French are dead. Down with Willelm the Bastard! Long live our beloved King Eadgar Æðeling!"

The remains of the burning tower collapsed with a crash, interrupting the cheers that accompanied Gospatric's words.

"Follow me to the other castle!" our leader shouted, pointing his spear eastward.

We squeezed our way through the flames, which by now had left sprawling holes in the palisades, and gathered at the foot of the hill.

As we were walking past the burning houses to the bridge over the Use, Ulfgar pushed his way through to me. His ochre hair stood out as if a wildcat were bristling its fur, so he looked even bigger and wilder than usual. He grinned broadly. "The castle is on fire and all the little Frenchmen are being roasted like honey-glazed duck on a spit."

I wiped the sweat and sticky hair from my face with my sleeve. "May God help us in the fight at the other castle, too."

"He will." Ulfgar raised his blood-blackened axe and roared, "Down with the French!"

Our brothers-in-arms quickly picked up Ulfgar's battle cry, and so we continued our way to the bridge, chanting.

Beyond the river, there were also flames, but they were no longer confined to the great castle and its surroundings. Instead, they were spreading across the city. People ran coughing from burning buildings. Men with sticks chased after squealing pigs, trying to keep the animals together and drive them all in one direction. Cows, donkeys and horses were herded out of stables whose roofs had caught fire and were threatening to collapse. A mother dragged two crying toddlers behind her, while the older children carried the few belongings they were trying to save from the flames.

Is this really right what we are doing? I thought as I looked into their frightened faces. *We're not only killing the French, but also our own countrymen. We're destroying their homes and their lives. All in the name of a youth who is a stranger to his own land.*

People had formed lines to the river, using buckets, small barrels and bowls to try to put out the fire on the adjacent houses.

When we crossed the bridge, so many buildings were already on fire that the thick clouds of smoke burned my eyes. We turned right to go down the road that led south to the main castle, or what was left of it. The castle's tower was a stump that lit our way like a beacon. The palisades were a burning heap of rubble. A cheerful crowd of warriors emerged from the former castle, which looked like a large funeral pyre. At the foot of the castle hill, they joined the rest of the army, which was approaching us and seemed to be driving the fire forwards. Only a few houses remained unscathed, while the south-westerly wind blew the fire further north.

The two parts of our army met joyfully. We patted each other's backs, raised our fists and weapons and shouted our praises to the Danish king and Eadgar Æðeling.

A man pointed to a group of warriors in front of the castle and roared, "Those French turds will bleed even more.

We have captured their scirgerefa. If the king wants him and his family back alive, he'd better bring a huge money pouch."

The crowd jeered and sneered, and it took a while to hear the cries from the northern side of the city. But eventually, the shouts for help filtered through.

"The cathedral is on fire!"

"We need help!"

"Fear the wrath of God!"

The cathedral is on fire. A sudden pain cut through me. For sure, this was a sign from God. He was angry with us because in our bloodlust and thirst for revenge, we went murdering and pillaging through Eoforwic and did not spare the innocent. "We must help them!" I said first to Ulfgar and then louder to the others around us. "We've burned down the castles and killed the French, but we can't stand by and watch a place of worship go up in flames."

"Certainly we won't," one of the Danish warriors shouted, grinning broadly. "First we'll get the treasures out of there."

"Exactly," another bellowed. "The French won't need them anymore."

With that, a cluster of warriors rushed northwards.

I looked uneasily at the others around me. Feelings ran high in the summer heat and the smoking fires everywhere. I feared that not many would hesitate to loot other buildings along the way and attack the local population. My heart was pounding like a hammer on an anvil. "This is not what we wanted when we came to Eoforwic."

"You won't be able to stop the Danes on your own," said Ulfgar, who looked equally stunned at the greedy hordes who had just fought with us against the French, only to abandon us for gold and treasure shortly after victory.

This time, the uneasy feeling that had befallen me at the beginning had not deceived me, no matter how successful our fight against the French might have been, God would punish us for our deeds, that much was certain. "Where's the Danish king? Why doesn't he hold his people back?" I looked around frantically.

"He was probably the first to run off to the cathedral, and his men follow him blindly. No Viking ends a victory without taking home plenty of booty."

"What about Eadgar Æðeling? There must be someone to put an end to this killing and plundering!" I stood helplessly amidst all those running for help or for booty, unable to do a thing. Even years of hard practice to become a warrior had not prepared me for the unpredictability of others.

"I doubt if he can do much against the Danes with our small English army. There are just too many of them."

Pushing people aside, I hurried northwards. "Then at least we must try to appease God's wrath. Come! Perhaps we can still save the cathedral." I beckoned our fellow warriors. "Follow me! We will prove to God that we fight only the French, not the people of Eoforwic. We must put out the fire in the cathedral."

We hurried back up the road we had just come down. We had destroyed the castles and killed or captured the Frenchmen in them, but it was not yet over. Instead of celebrating the victory, we ran as fast as we could through a burning city whose inhabitants were losing their homes, animals and families because of us. We wanted to free the city from the French. Instead we razed it to the ground as the French had done with our settlements, including everyone and everything that stood in their way. What was happening right here and right now made

us no better than them, and I was sure that the people of Eoforwic were hurling all the curses of which they were capable at
every single one of our warriors, whether Danish, Scottish or
English. It was our fault that their homes were burning, and
we truly deserved their hate. But if we failed to save the cathedral from the fire, then very soon and above all, we would feel
God's punishment.

When we reached the vast place of worship, large parts of the
roof and the southern wall were already on fire. At the portal,
armed men were pushing their way out and in. Some of them
held golden goblets and statues decorated with precious
stones. On the western side, people were passing on buckets
to bring water from the Use. A couple of carts drawn by oxen
brought water in large barrels, which was then poured on the
blazing flames by two men. While Ulfgar, I and those who
had followed ran to help with the water buckets, the Danish
hordes used the confusion to also search the neighbouring
houses.

A priest stood close by, shaking his head and making the
sign of the cross as he looked around in despair. "If the archbishop had not died recently of a broken heart over all the
misfortune in Englaland, then surely today would have been
his last day on earth," he said.

The southern wall of the cathedral suddenly gave way to
the fire and collapsed with a loud crash. Shortly afterwards,
the roof of the nave on that side lowered, thundering onto
the rest of the southern wall and throwing a huge cloud of
dust into the air as it crumbled to the ground. I stared, spellbound and held my breath in horror. *What have we done?*
Like a brittle old shed, the rest of the roof finally came tumbling down. Anyone who was still in the cathedral looking for

booty now rushed out screaming or was buried forever by the falling stones and debris. Tears stood in my eyes. We had won the battle and yet we had failed. I felt empty and useless. What was the point of fighting if it brought misfortune and death to my countrymen? "There's nothing more we can do here," I said with a heavy heart. "Let us return to the main castle!" I beckoned the others to follow me.

The streets were still crowded, but now, it was the inhabitants who wandered helplessly and desperately through their destroyed home town, wailing loudly.

"Where are the Danish king and Eadgar Æðeling, anyway?" I asked Ulfgar as we moved forward through the smoky streets. "Shouldn't they gather their men and tell us what to do next?"

Ulfgar shrugged his shoulders and let his gaze wander over what had once been a proud and thriving city and was now being reduced to ruins. "I don't know where they are, nor have I seen Gospatric and the two eorles again. Very suspicious."

"It is, forsooth. Where have they all gone? And where is my father?" A sudden terror seized me. Where was he? He must have started fighting at the main castle, while we entered the town and rode on to the second castle with the rear part of the army.

When we reached the smoking heap of embers that, until a few hours ago, had been the awe-inspiring seat of the scirge-refa of Eoforwic and his troop of French warriors, several hundred men had gathered around Gospatric at the foot of the castle hill. While the others joined them, I searched for my father outside and inside the safe parts of the castle, but to no avail. Finally, I descended and spied a small group of Englishmen near the big water. "Father!" I shouted, dropping the axe and shield and running towards him.

My father turned around, just in time to catch me in his arms as I threw myself against him and hugged him tightly. "You're alive, Father. I was afraid they had killed you."

My father patted me on the back as if calming a child who had woken up from a bad dream. "Fear not, my son. As long as I can still stand, I will fight, even if it is the last thing I do."

He let go of me and pointed to the loops fastening his shield on his left forearm. "That was an excellent solution you came up with. It has served me well in battle. But now, tell me, my boy, how did you fare in your first real battle as a warrior?"

I struggled to smile. In my mind I saw not only the enemies I had defeated, but also the fearful faces of those I... we... had left without hope and home. "I think I fought well, but where have all our leaders gone? I see only Gospatric over there. Where are Eadgar Æðeling, the two eorles or the Danish king? Did the French—?"

"The Danish king ordered his men to retreat to Richale, to celebrate the victory over the French, I assume. The two eorles and Eadgar Æðeling have also left with their warriors. And rightly so because it's important to keep an eye on the Norþmenn. You know they are unpredictable and should never be trusted, even if they pretend to be on your side."

At least in this battle, Father's old grudge against his former friend had been confirmed. It was not enough for the Norþmenn to take the castles and kill their garrisons to bring the only French stronghold in the north back into English hands. They wanted gifts for their help, not just words of praise and a feast, and they had taken them without paying attention to the rest of the army and the leaders' next steps. Who knows what else crossed their minds? Their king was a cousin of King

Harold's. He might want to assert claims to the throne himself now that Eoforwic had fallen.

I looked at the burning city. Where once the castles towered above everything, there were only flames. Eoforwic was burning. Its castles, cathedral, houses, shops, sheds, stables. If the fire could not be quenched soon, hardly anything would be left.

"What happens now, Father? Will Eadgar Æðeling remain in Englaland to be crowned as the rightful king?"

"That will be difficult. The Archbishop of Eoforwic is dead, his city destroyed, and a successor is not yet in sight. Besides, Eadgar Æðeling would have to travel to Wincestre for that, and that is still firmly in the hands of the Frenchmen."

"Will he move south with his army?"

Father shook his head. "Eadgar Æðeling's army is made up of men from the north, from Norþhymbre and Scotland. They will hardly venture so far south."

"I would go with him and fight for him."

My father laughed and put his hand on my shoulder. "You would, my son, I know. A king couldn't wish for a better huscarl than you."

"What's going on?" shouted one of the Englishmen who had gathered in front of the castle ruins. All heads turned towards the far end of the road, where people came running out of the city, shouting. Most of them were men in battle wear, possibly those who had lingered on to sweeten the day's success in one way or another. But now, they were running from something and were heading straight towards us.

"Out of the way!" one of the runners yelled, jostling two men who were blocking his way to the bridge over the River Foss.

"The French are coming!" shouted another, trying to run as fast as he could without losing one of the four silver cups he was carrying.

We looked at each other in amazement.

"What French?" asked someone, as men hurried past him.

"We didn't leave anyone alive," shouted another. "How can that be?"

"They probably came back to life when you stole their cups."

More people came hurrying along the road and over the bridge, though we still couldn't make out why. My stomach was in knots. "We should take shelter somewhere," I said and ran to the castle hill where I had dropped my axe and shield.

"Run! The French are after us!"

That was the last cry we heard before we realised what was driving people away. There, at the northern end of the road, a whole host of mounted and heavily armed French warriors thundered along the street.

Where did they come from? We killed all the Frenchmen in the castles.

The French leader gave the order to attack the enemy warriors at the foot of the castle, who took to their heels and rushed off across the bridge to the other side of the river. Some jumped on the horses left there to escape to Richale or some other safe place. Others hurried into the nearby woods, probably hoping that the horsemen would give up the chase there.

As the leader rode past the hill, he looked up at me without slowing his horse. An icy shiver ran through me. The rider turned away again and charged towards the men fleeing from him and his warriors.

To my relief, I found that my father, together with the others who had been standing with him on the bank of the river, was not one of them, but had escaped behind the hill. Meanwhile, the French were stabbing the first runaways with their spears. Whether they would pursue them all the way to Richale or wherever they had gone, I doubted. Sooner or later they would come back looking for us. Then they would take bloody revenge on us. Not for what we had done to the people of Eoforwic, but for rebelling against their king, for destroying the symbols of French domination here in the north, wiping out their entire army and capturing their scirgerefa and family. King Willelm had yet to let any of the revolts go unpunished. One day, he would make us pay for what we had done.

We hid in the woods until the French gave up looking for us and rode back to the city. At dusk, we set off for Richale, where most of the army had retreated before the French horsemen arrived.

"These were the warriors that King Willelm had sent to Dunholm to put down the rebellion there," one of the men explained. "They say that Saint Cuthbert sent a mist to stop the French."

"As if the French would let that stop them!" sneered another. "More likely King Willelm found out that a large host was on its way to Eoforwic. He knew that the few Frenchmen in Eoforwic wouldn't hold the castles, so he ordered his men back ahead of Dunholm to support his warriors in Eoforwic."

"Ha! How miserably he failed in that."

"We lost a lot of men while fleeing from Eoforwic," said my father, who had been walking silently beside me until then. "Knowing King Willelm, more will follow."

"Why don't we go to Eoforwic again tomorrow?" I asked. "This second French army only consists of a small number of horsemen. They are no match for our entire army. Besides, they have no more castles to protect them. We could wipe them out, too."

"We would have to act soon for that," my father said. "Those castles can be rebuilt quickly. The hills are still there, and they can get wood nearby. In just a few days, they could erect new defences."

"So what? We'll set fire to them again."

"There is not much left to burn in Eoforwic, my son. Remember, too, that the people will not put up with another inferno. At worst, they will turn on us and join the French in defending their city. Or at least what's left of it."

Ulfgar pushed a thick branch out of his way and squeezed through between two trees. "The Danes have already plundered the town today. Why would they go back into a city with nothing left but a fresh lot of Frenchmen?"

"You mean the Danes will sit in their tents and see what King Willelm does?"

"They have captured his scirgerefa and can afford to sit and wait," my father said. "I don't think they will leave Engla-land until King Willelm has paid them for his release – and paid them well."

"Unless they are satisfied with what they have snatched from Eoforwic, in which case, they will simply kill him and go home," said Ulfgar, as if it were the most trivial thing in the world. "Then we have a problem because the Danes make up the bulk of our army."

I stroked my downy moustache, but whichever way I turned it, the chances of winning in the end were indeed slim. We had won this battle, but no one seemed to know where to go from here. Had the Danish king and Eadgar Æðeling decided what they would do with Eoforwic now? I could only hope that the two of them agreed on something, because otherwise, our victory, however good it felt, would have been utterly useless – just like all the other revolts that had taken place in the last three years since Willelm the Bastard became king. None of them had seriously troubled him. He ruled with an iron fist and would never let the crown he had once seized be taken away. Perhaps we would find out more in the Danish camp, whose lights showed us the way as night fell.

Over the fires that brightly lit the faces of those sitting around them, pieces of meat were being brushed and turned until they were roasted evenly and crispy brown. Men were sitting on wooden stumps, stools or on the ground, raising their brim-full clay cups, laughing loudly and waving roasted goose legs in their fists, which shone with fat in the light of the fire. At one fire, someone was playing a harp and singing a song that everyone joined in with, even though some of them were already too drunk to sing in tune. At another fire, the men listened intently to a storyteller who told a tale with words, hands and face.

There was, however, no trace of the Danish king, Eadgar Æðeling nor the two eorles.

"Where are our leaders?" I asked anxiously as we pushed our way through the crowd and I shook hands with some Englishmen who had fought with us at the second castle.

One of them wiped his mouth with his sleeve and pointed to one of the tents. "In there, talking about important things."

"What happens now? Do we fight again tomorrow?"

The other man shrugged his shoulders. "They'll tell us in the morning." He waved his hand towards the fire. "Get something to eat. Ale's over there."

We pushed further into the camp until we found a place where we could lay down our weapons.

Ulfgar stretched his arms. "At last! Now, I really need something to eat. Sieges make you hungry." Without further delay, he made his way to one of the spits, from which a suckling pig gave off its delicious smell.

Only when my stomach growled did I realise how hungry I was. I followed the trail Ulfgar had left on his way and got myself a cup of ale and a piece of meat.

Just as I was chewing the first bite, I heard a familiar voice next to me.

"Will you drink with me to our triumph, Osfriðson?"

Out of the corner of my eye, I saw someone hold out a cup to me. My gaze wandered from the hand along the arm to the hunched shoulders, past the pointy chin beard to the dark eyes sparkling in the firelight. "Stígandr! I should have known you would come. I didn't see you anywhere in Eoforwic, but you are here in time to celebrate."

"But, Oswulf, why so grim on this day of victory against the French?" He made a sweeping gesture over the men sitting around the fires. "Look at them celebrating and rejoicing. This has been a great day for Englaland and the resistance against the French conquerors. Wæs hal!" He raised his cup and took a big gulp.

I didn't feel like raising my cup. We had won, but it was a bitter victory. It had not been a battle on an open field, far from settlements and people living quietly. We had waged a bloody war on the French rulers of Eoforwic, but the ones who ended up paying for it were the townsfolk, whose lives we had jeopardised and destroyed for no reason. I took another bite and looked at Stígandr, chewing. "Where did you fight?" I asked, though I doubted he had fought at all. I suspected he had just sneaked into the camp a moment ago.

"At the main castle, of course."

Of course!

"The Danish troops showed the French rather quickly that they had the better army. As for yourselves, you took a little longer, but you did quite well in the end."

As if he had heard Stígandr, a man next to us laughed out loud.

"Quite well?" I didn't know what spoiled the taste in my mouth more at that moment, Stígandr's disparaging remark or the man's laughter. "The castle went up in flames, and we killed all the French."

"Well, that was the easier of the two tasks for which the Danish king's army came here. At the main castle, we had to be more skilful. After all, we needed the scirgerefa and his family alive."

"We could have done that just as well. Besides, you had four experienced leaders and their armies with you. We had only one."

Stígandr laughed, shaking his head. "Experienced! You sound like you almost believe it yourself. Your confidence in your leaders honours you, Osfriðson, but of all four, only the Danish king has the necessary experience."

If only Ulfgar would come back! Was I the only one whose efforts Stígandr was going to keep on slandering? "I know nothing about the Danish king and his achievements on the battlefield, but Eorl Morkere and his brother are experienced warriors."

Stígandr twirled the tip of his chin beard between his thumb and forefinger. "Yes, I forget. We saw that in the battle of Fuleforde. No, wait! That was a complete failure. The army destroyed, the leaders fled into the woods. But the battle at Stanfordbrycge? No, they didn't take part in that at all because they had no men left. But the battle at Senlac Hill... no, they didn't take part in that either. Oh well, even with the eorles and their troops, the English would have lost anyway."

I had lowered my eyes and remained defiantly silent while the other men's jeering and laughter surged over me like waves. Indeed, the reputation of the two eorles had not been particularly good in recent years. They had repeatedly appeared and disappeared. Moreover, they had submitted to the foreign king a long time ago then fled and were now fighting against him. But for how long? Would they disappear again and submit to Willelm the Bastard?

"And as for your English pretender to the throne, Eadgar Æðeling, what shall I say? He is a youth who has barely set foot on English soil his entire life. Now, he brings a host of fierce foreign warriors from Scotland to Eoforwic, believing the time is ripe for him to finally claim the English throne. But he is neither chosen to inherit the throne nor experienced as a commander."

I thoughtfully gnawed the rest of the meat off the bone and then threw it on the ground, where a dog greedily snatched it and ran off. What Stígandr said was true, as much as it pained me to admit it. The assault on Eoforwic had been a well-intentioned venture, but it had run into nothing. There was no common goal that united the different peoples who only a few hours ago, had brought down the castles of Eoforwic together. There were no common further steps that the leaders wanted to take. Their intentions were far too different for that. The only thing we had achieved was that a city – and with it, the livelihood of many people – had been almost completely destroyed, that we had exposed innocent people to the looting and murder of hordes, drunk with victory, and that it was only a matter of time before we felt King Willelm's wrath for this outrageous rebellion against his rule. The attack by the French riders brought down from Dunholm was only a small taste of what we had to expect.

"I don't really know what you're trying to say." My gaze found Ulfgar with two men who had been fighting with us, wildly waving a large piece of meat so that the fat flew through the air before all three burst out laughing. I tried to wash down my thoughts with several sips of ale. Let Stígandr say what he wanted to! We had defeated the French and destroyed their castles. Our English king, whom the witan had proclaimed as King Harold's successor, was alive and could count on the support of fighters from Scotland and Norþhymbre if it came down to defending his right.

Stígandr twirled the tip of his beard again. "Well, I think everyone will soon have to decide which master they want to serve, the one who is destined to perish from the start, or the one who sooner or later turns out to be the stronger one."

"Oh, is that so?"

Stígandr raised an eyebrow but said nothing.

"How do you know who will lose and who will win? For King Ælfred, too, it looked as if all English kingdoms would disappear as he made his last stand against the invading Vikings. And yet he pushed back the Danes and united his country."

Stígandr turned his gaze to the cloudy night sky. "King Ælfred. Now that was a king who knew how to unite several peoples under his leadership." His gaze became serious. He looked me in the eye. "Those days are gone, Oswulf. King

Ælfred's Englaland is no more. Kings change, and Englaland's glory and splendour fades away, while other countries rise to wealth and prosperity under their rulers. What do the English still have to offer? Most of the nobles have been killed in the great battles. Those who remain submit to Willelm the Bastard to save their skins and their lands before the French take them. Some fickle ones, like Eorl Morkere and his brother, pledge allegiance to the king, only to break their oath afterwards and side with the English again. Just you wait, soon, they'll be grovelling at the king's feet again, begging him for mercy because they have realised that their rebellion was futile. Eadgar Æðeling will hide in Scotland, hoping that his arch-enemies will continue to provide him with an army. They probably will, but not because they want to see him on the English throne but because they themselves have their eye on the north of Englaland and want to expand their kingdom southwards." He drew in a meaningful breath and straightened up as far as his hunched shoulders would allow. "Times are changing, Oswulf. Perhaps you should consider, too, who you will fight for in the future."

I stared at Stígandr. He openly invited me to commit high treason against the future English king, suggested that I bury my country and my hopes and that I throw myself at the feet of a foreign usurper who neither spoke my language nor had any legitimate reason to be my king?

"Do you actually know what you're saying?" I breathed, because I could hardly get a sound out of my throat from sheer horror. I drank most of the ale in my cup in one big gulp. Maybe this was all a dream because I was tired from the fight, with the flickering of the fires and the noise in the camp dancing in my head and clouding my mind.

"Don't wait too long, or it may be too late. The Danish king has already sent a messenger to King Willelm to let him know that they've caught the scirgerefa. I don't think the king will think long and hard about what he's going to do. He cares little for the life of a scirgerefa, never mind the life of anyone else. But the fact that his castles are in ruins and the entire French garrison of Eoforwic has been wiped out is not something he will let go unpunished. You'd better ask yourself now whether you want to face this punishment or not." He raised his cup once more and left me standing.

Stunned, I watched him go. Didn't my father once say that everyone had their name for a reason and that Stígandr would also live up to his name, "wanderer", at some point? Was he following the dangerous path towards our foe, the enemy from Normandig? Or had he already chosen to do so a long time ago, although he made me feel ashamed that I had misjudged him?

"Well, if that wasn't our old friend from Ledlinghe!" Ulfgar approached, chewing and glancing after Stígandr. "Did you enjoy chatting with him?"

"Stígandr is mad."

"I know. But why did it take him so long to explain that?"

"He wants me to betray Eadgar Æðeling and sell myself to the French bastard."

Ulfgar pursed his lips. "Rather daring, our Norþmann. So? Did you agree?"

"Of course not! But surely many will. Like a rat catcher, he will lead them straight into the mouth of the hungry monster from Normandig in return for a comely reward."

↔

In the morning of the following day, we were told that we were no longer needed. Eadgar Æðeling would travel back to Scotland with his army, while the Danes wanted to stay until King Willelm had paid them the money for the scirgerefa and his family. Only then – perhaps sooner if supplies ran low or winter came earlier than expected – would they return home to Denmark. At least, for the time being, they would not return to Eoforwic. There was nothing left there to tempt them. Besides, they feared that the French horsemen that had chased us out of the city would not idly watch them plunder and pillage the city again in such a short time. That left only the men of Norþhymbre, who had placed themselves under Eorl Morkere's command, even though they were not at all averse to Eadgar Æðeling's cause and expected more from an English king than from Willelm of Normandig. But neither Eorl Morkere nor his brother intended to wait here in Richale for an answer, let alone the king's appearance in person. Instead, they announced that they would retire to their shires and take their followers with them.

So, we packed up the few things we had taken with us, mounted the horses we had left in Richale before entering Eoforwic and headed home to Ledlinghe. With us went the uneasy feeling that King Willelm would not simply accept our storming of Eoforwic, as he had made clear earlier in the year after the revolts in Dunholm and Eoforwic. But for many weeks, nothing happened. Some saw this as a sign of hope that the king was slowly giving up on subduing the rebellious north. Others painted the king's revenge in pictures that surpassed everything we had ever heard of in terms of cruelty and horror. Only a few believed these gloomy predictions, for on the Day of Judgement, God would also judge King Willelm for his deeds, and over the past years, he had already burdened his soul with enough guilt.

The only thing we could be sure of at that time was that the Danes had indeed left Englaland without paying Eoforwic a second visit. Our scouts reported that the camp had been abandoned and not a single ship had been left. Whether they had received the ransom they wanted for the city's scirgerefa, or whether King Willelm did not care about him and therefore had not yielded to their demand, we did not know. But what did we care? The Danes were gone, which seemed to somehow answer the question of whether the Danish king would try to assert his own claim to the throne of Englaland after the victory at Eoforwic.

We did not hear much from Eadgar Æðeling during this time, only that his sister was to marry the King of Scotland to strengthen the bonds between the allies. True, Stígandr's words concerning the æðeling had made me waver, but if the latter went openly to war against King Willelm, I would fight on the English side. As long as there was that one glimmer of hope, I had no intention of submitting to the French dog, like so many others had done.

"If he hadn't become King of Englaland, Willelm would have made it pretty far as a castle-builder in Normandig," Ulfgar whispered to me, while a travelling minstrel in the great hall of Ledlinghe told us about the king's latest deeds. These consisted namely of two more castles built in Waruuic and Snotingeham, while he was on his way north, to see for himself what had become of Eoforwic. No sooner had the king reached the city, the minstrel sang, than he gave orders to rebuild the destroyed castles there. This time, however, the French used stone to prevent the castles from catching fire so easily, should intruders or even the rebellious inhabitants of the city themselves ever think of setting them alight again.

"I'm surprised that he suffers the humiliation so meekly," I said. "He is rebuilding the castles as if nothing had happened. He let the Danes leave peacefully, and not a word has been said about whether the two eorles or even Eadgar Æðeling have to fear any punishment."

"He'll probably think about it while he's ripping out the legs and cutting the chest of his yule fowl."

"Eoforwic must be a desolate place at this time." I couldn't help thinking of the misery of the people whose homes we had destroyed and who had been victims of the looting and violence that followed. I sighed deeply. "I wonder if the king thinks that his presence during the festive season will lift the spirits of the people and give them hope."

Ulfgar looked at me with raised eyebrows. "I don't want to doubt King Willelm's Christian disposition, but I rather think he celebrates the feast of the Lord in Eoforwic because he can keep a better eye on his northern subjects from there – and because he can strike back much more quickly if there is another English riot."

"He will not let the assault on Eoforwic go unpunished."

Ulfgar sighed, nodding thoughtfully. "There's a good reason why the Danes, Scots and the two eorles left so quickly."

"Which leaves only one part of the army that attacked the city and whose homeland is easily accessible from there."

"Norþhymbre."

Chapter 6

FEBRUARY IN THE YEAR of OUR LORD 1070

It was in the week after Candlemas when it all began.

Snow covered the landscape, glittering in the crispy winter air, but at least no new snow had fallen for a week. In January, we had spent a lot of time repairing damaged houses and sheds that had only received a makeshift mending after the storms and frosts last year. With no battles or skirmishes looming, there were at last enough men that the necessary work could be done.

The peasants had also begun to prepare the ploughs to break up the hard soil for sowing.

The children were running from barn to barn, filling their buckets with the dung of pigs, horses and cows, which would be used to fertilise the fields.

My elder sisters were both to marry in the spring and move in with their husbands, and Godgifu was grateful for the help she received from them on our manor. As the daughter of a blacksmith, albeit a wealthy one, she had yet to learn how to run a ðegn's household. Besides managing the manor, she spent a lot of time doing needlework and weaving or helping with the animals as we had not found a new servant to replace the one who had died.

"Are you happy, Godgifu?" I asked her one day.

She looked up from her handiwork in surprise. "Of course I am, Oswulf! A woman couldn't ask for a better husband than you."

I squatted down next to her and stroked her hand. "Sometimes, it seems to me that you are sad without me knowing why. Is it the dark season that weighs you down? Don't you have enough help here at the manor?"

"Oh no, no, Oswulf. It's nothing like that. It's just..."

"Tell me, deorling! I don't want you to be sad. If it is in my power, I will do everything to make you happy."

She looked at me for a long time, then put her hand on her belly and lowered her gaze. "We will have been married for two years in summer, but we seem to have angered the Lord..."

So that was what was troubling her. I pressed my lips together. There was indeed no sign yet that Godgifu was carrying a child under her heart. I clasped her hands and squeezed them gently. "Be patient and trust in the Lord! I am sure you will be with child soon."

I kissed her on the forehead and went to the stable where I wanted to repair a brittle wall with Ulfgar. Had I spent too little time with Godgifu and too much with other people's children whom I was teaching how to make arrows and handle weapons? Was I paying too much attention to my weapons practice and my goal of becoming a huscarl, caring too little for my family and the people of Ledlinghe for whom I was responsible as my father's son? Was I not loved and respected by others, whether as a teacher or a warrior, even in the neighbouring villages? Was the absence of a child God's punishment for the injustice and death I had caused in recent years among innocent people?

Ulfgar beckoned me to cut a piece of wood to the right length when Bargest rose with her ears pricked up. She barked and ran a few steps forward.

"Riders," I said in surprise to Ulfgar, who was watching Bargest.

Two horses trotted into the village. Bargest ran towards them and jumped around them, barking. The rider writhed in the saddle and weakly tried to rein in his horse. The second horse had a saddle but no rider.

Old Dunstan hurried over and brought the horse to a halt. Bargest barked once more and then sat, panting next to the old man.

"Frenchmen," the rider gasped, pressing his forearm hard against his stomach as he squirmed in the saddle, his face contorted in pain, "they kill everyone." His breath rattled. Blood dripped from his mouth. "Help us. Help…"

His head fell forward, pulling him down. Dunstan tried to stop him, but he was too weak to hold him.

Ulfgar ran to catch the rider, but before he reached him, the young man tumbled to the ground like a sack of flour and moved no more.

Bargest sniffed at him and whimpered. Ulfgar knelt beside him and felt for his heartbeat.

I stepped closer and peered over Ulfgar's shoulder. "Is he dead?" The huge dark red bloodstain on the rider's back gave me the answer before Ulfgar confirmed my suspicions with a snort.

"Dead. He's only a cnæpling! Doesn't even have a beard." He stood up with a groan and patted the neck of the horse that stood beside him, panting and still hot from the ride. "You couldn't save him, my friend."

I grabbed the reins of the second horse. "Should we look for the second rider? Maybe he is not far from here and still alive."

Old Dunstan nodded. "Perhaps you should. It would be good to know where they came from."

Ulfgar helped Dunstan carry the dead boy into a shed so that he wouldn't lure the greedy crows. Then we rode off, accompanied by Bargest, who shot through the air like an oversized black arrow. We followed the way the horses had come, watching for their hoofprints in the snow. With one eye on the ground and the other on everything that moved around us, we rode for a while until Bargest started barking and hurried towards something dark lying in the snow at the edge of a grove.

"I think we found him." I spurred my horse forward, jumped off and knelt down.

It was indeed another young man, with a huge gash on his thigh. Bargest circled us, whimpering as if looking for a way to help.

Carefully, I turned the injured youth around. "Can you hear me?"

He moaned softly. Bargest sniffed his face and licked his cheek. He moved his head. Then he opened his eyes and looked alternately at me and Bargest.

"Come here, Bargest," said Ulfgar. Bargest whimpered and trotted to her master, not without throwing a few more worried looks at the injured man.

"You fell off your horse when you were fleeing from the French with your friend. Can you ride?"

"Where is he?" groaned the young man.

Ulfgar and I glanced at each other. "He... made it to our manor," I replied. "Can you ride?"

He smiled tentatively. "Ðe ic herige, Drihten ælmihtne."

I beckoned Ulfgar for help, and we took hold of him and straightened him up. He groaned but allowed himself to be lifted onto my horse, grasping the horse's mane so as not to topple straight back down. After looking around again to make sure no one had seen us or was following, we made our way back to Ledlinghe.

"What is your name?"

After a long pause, he replied, "Cynewin."

I felt him slide to the side in front of me and tightened my arm to support him. "Your friend told us that the French attacked you. Where was that?"

"He's not my friend," Cynewin murmured as he slowly slumped backwards in my arms. "He's my brother."

"Can you remember where you were attacked, Cynewin? Was it far from here?"

He shook his head. "I don't know."

"Why did the French attack you?"

Cynewin growled.

"It's important, Cynewin. Think! If there is a band of French horsemen around here somewhere, they may still be nearby, and then our home would also be in danger. We must know where they attacked you and why."

"There were so many. They kill people and animals. They burn and destroy everything. My brother and I had just ridden out hunting when we heard the noise. We rushed back to the village. Father shouted at us to ride for our lives. A Frenchman killed him with a spear. Cynewulf and I turned round.

They stabbed at us with their spears, but we were able to flee." Cynewin sat up a little and tried to turn his head towards me. He groaned. "How is Cynewulf?"

"He... your brother is safe. But tell me, Cynewin, where did this happen?"

"In Huson."

"That's only an hour's walk from Ledlinghe." I looked at Ulfgar. "We need to get back as soon as possible."

My father sent out scouts in all directions to learn more about these French raids and to warn the ðegnes of the surrounding villages, provided they had not already become victims of the raids themselves. The fact that the king continued to stay in Eoforwic instead of returning to his seat in Lunden worried many men, but the tidings brought by the two brothers particularly troubled them. We knew that the French were not squeamish with their enemies, but the brutality and ruthlessness they displayed this time surpassed anything we had known or heard so far.

After a few days, some of our scouts returned, and what they told us made even seasoned and war-experienced men gasp.

"It seems King Willelm has split his army in two," one of the scouts told us with a worried expression. "One half moves north from Eoforwic along the old Roman road that leads to Scotland; the other half moves south towards Snotingeham. Then they split up into smaller groups that roam the whole country eastward. They destroy the fields and meadows, they pillage, they murder, they rob, they plunder, they lay waste everything in their path. No tree, no shrub, no house, neither man nor animal they leave untouched." He paused, propped himself up on the table and took a deep breath. "North of

Eoforwic, the raids destroy the holdings of Eorl Morkere, to the south, those of his brother. I assume this is King Willelm's revenge on them for their treachery and the attack on his castles in Eoforwic."

"This foul king does not shy away from the most unchristian deeds," said a second scout. "He must have sent out his men shortly after the feast of the Lord to take revenge on the people of Norþhymbre. The few survivors told me that whole regions have been laid waste, with famines looming the likes of which we have never seen before. People have lost all their supplies, and the land is unusable. Those who are not dead when the Frenchmen leave will die of hunger or pestilences soon after. The wolves and crows will have a richly laid table to feat on."

"Where are the troops now?" my father asked after a long silence.

"They seem to be moving back from the east towards Eoforwic. Some have sighted French horsemen at Escumetorp, south of the Humbre. Others report them in the area around Chileburne, north of Eoforwic."

"Chileburne is northwest of Ledlinghe." My father let his gaze wander over those gathered. "Maybe they are just beginning to ride eastward."

"Then we must prepare for an attack," said one of the ðegnes.

My father nodded. "We need to make sure our armour and weapons are ready. Ask everyone to put some supplies together and bury or hide them in the woods so that the French cannot find or destroy them. We will also build a stable in the woods and hide some of the animals there."

In the following days, Ledlinghe was bustling with activity as everyone prepared for a possible French raid. I was helping the other youths put up a fence in the middle of the woods when I walked too close to the pile of old slats, caught a nail sticking out and tripped. A big hole was gaping on the outside of my leather shoes.

"What's wrong?" someone asked, turning to me with a hammer in his hand.

"I tore my shoe. What fool stacked the slats with the nail sticking out?" I examined the hole, which would have to be patched soon if I didn't want a shoe full of snow.

"Stígandr will be pleased to see you." Ulfgar grinned as he lifted a wooden slat.

I groaned. "He'll probably tell me again how much work he has and that it takes longer or costs more if it's urgent."

"He must be busy," said the one with the hammer, hitting the nail between his fingers. "I haven't seen him for some days now."

I glanced at Ulfgar. Stígandr had attended the meetings with the scouts but disappeared afterwards. So it looked like he had indeed decided whom he wanted to fight for in the future. *Treacherous niþing!* "I'll quickly ask the shoemaker when he can mend my shoe. I'll be right back." *For I hardly think I will find him in his workshop.*

At Stígandr's home, I glanced through the windows and saw his apprentices, but their master was nowhere to be seen. I knocked and entered.

The oldest of the boys jumped up. "Wel gesund, hlaford min. Good to see you. What can I do for you, hlaford min?"

"I want to see Master Stígandr."

"He's not here, hlaford min."

"When can I speak to him?" I pointed to the hole in my shoe. "My shoe needs mending urgently."

The boy knelt in front of my shoe and looked at the hole from all sides. "Master Stígandr is away for a few days. But I can patch the hole for you. I'm pretty good at it."

"So he's off somewhere. Did he say where?"

The boy rose, shaking his head. "No, hlaford min. He said it was important for his work."

I stroked my little moustache. "I think so, too."

"Would you care to leave me your shoe? I'll mend it for you right away."

"That would be good." I took off the shoe and handed it to the boy, who immediately set to work.

Where was Stígandr? This time, if I caught him, no flimsy explanations would save him from his just punishment. He had tried several times to make common cause with our enemies, but the threats had been far from home. Now, however, the French were assaulting our neighbours. They could appear in Ledlinghe at any time, and I had to prevent it.

❧

DURING MORNING SERVICE at church, I looked out for Erik and Wulfnoð, who were regular scouts and messengers for us. As we left the church, I approached them and told them about my fears. "Did you get any hints as to the whereabouts of the shoemaker while you were out travelling?"

Erik squinted one eye and tapped his lips with his index finger as if he were thinking.

Wulfnoð, meanwhile, waved it off. "You worry too much, Oswulf. You always have. Stígandr has been moving about a lot these last few years. No one really knows where he goes and what he does there." He shielded his mouth with his hand and muffled his voice. "Maybe he's meeting up with a pretty cowherdess somewhere to buy leather for his shoes." He nudged me with his elbow, grinning. "For a decent fee, of course."

I rolled my eyes. Wulfnoð was a fool. "I don't think Stígandr is looking for cowhides to make cheap shoes. He wants more. He never wanted a life as a shoemaker in Ledlinghe. He thinks the Lord has chosen him for a higher calling. I have seen him on the side of our enemies several times and thought for a long time that I suspected him wrongly. But since I spoke to him in Richale, it is clear to me that he has found a way to finally achieve what he has long wanted. He will not miss the opportunity that the king and his warriors are still in Eoforwic. Willelm will continue to try and take control of Englaland and will not rest until he has devastated all the land and killed anything alive up here. Stígandr will help him find all the settlements in northern Englaland and make sure that he does not spare Ledlinghe. If we do not find him first, he will betray us all to the French." *And that's probably my fault. He hates me because I am the son of a ðegn and he is only the son of a shoemaker. He hates my father because he calls his uncle a thief and has never got over the fact that his uncle became a huscarl. He hates me because he sees that I can become a huscarl while he will remain a shoemaker forever.*

"You know, Oswulf," said Erik, still squinting one eye as if it helped him remember more clearly, "if I remember correctly, one of the scouts we met further north mentioned a man travelling on horseback with some heavily armed Frenchmen, himself without battle wear but with a round shield like an Englishman or a Norþmann. I don't think he had any shackles or injuries, so he didn't look like a prisoner."

"Eala! Where was that, and when did they see him?"

"This was maybe a week ago, near Aluertune. The riders were on their way to Chileburne then east towards Renliton and then back southwest towards Eoforwic."

I thought about where the places were that Erik had mentioned. "It seems like they are laying waste all the habitable land that lies outside the moors in the northeast of Eoforwicscir."

Erik nodded. "As far as we know, they are mainly destroying the regions where the rebel eorles have lands so that even if they decide to revolt again, they will hardly have any men left to support them."

"It takes about three days to ride to Aluertune. They must ride slowly for their attacks to be successful on such a scale. They also have to rest somewhere. So, they burn and pillage all the land they pass through and then spend the night in one of the unscathed settlements ahead of them. Deserted places offering little or no resistance." Like an approaching thunderstorm, black clouds gathered in my mind and darkened my thoughts. "They are leaving a swath of destruction wherever they go."

"When they return to Eoforwic, most of the land in Norþhymbre and in Myrce will resemble a black, barren nothingness. They spare very few places, only those that are too far off their path or that lie in rough terrain."

"Like the moors in the northeast."

"Exactly. Many have fled there because they know the French dare not enter. The terrain is treacherous and can prove fatal very quickly for anyone who doesn't know their way around."

"The moors are rough, but the distance from Renliton back to Eoforwic is easy to cover for a group of experienced riders – in a day if they do not stop to murder and destroy." I swallowed. Ledlinghe was right in the middle of the two places. If the French left Renliton, they could reach Ledlinghe in half a day. "Do you know where the French troops are now?"

Wulfnoð shrugged his shoulders. "We'd have to go back to find them again."

"I'll take care of that. Maybe I'll find our shoemaker at the same time." *And God help him if I do.*

At home, I packed food and drink, took my scramasax and got a warm cloak that would also serve as a blanket when sleeping, if necessary.

My father appeared in the doorway of the shed. "I've been looking all over for you, Oswulf. Your mother said you were getting ready to leave. Where are you going?"

"I've spoken with Erik and Wulfnoð. They told me that the French troops are on their way to us."

My father took a quick look outside and then entered. "The French are coming to Ledlinghe?"

"They can't be far. Erik said they were spied near Aluertune about a week ago and that they were riding in a south-easterly direction."

"Then we have to be ready for an attack."

I put on my weapon belt and adjusted the short sword. "I will find out where they are."

"That's too dangerous. Erik and Wulfnoð are experienced scouts. I will send them out again."

"Father, I am almost twenty winters old. Don't you think I know by now how to sneak up on someone?"

"That's not the point." He put his hand on my shoulder. "We need you here when the French come. You're our best fighter. Even a Frenchman will have a hard time against you. You must stay here. For Godgifu, for your family and for Ledlinghe."

I looked at my father for a long time. "They saw a horseman without battle dress and weapons accompanying the Frenchmen."

"That means little or nothing. No one wears their full equipment unless they are about to go into battle."

"He's the only one. All the others wear chain mail, helmet, spear and the huge French shield."

My father shook his head. "I'm sure there's an explanation for that. Maybe it's a healer or a priest. They wouldn't wear armour or have weapons other than a mace."

"Or it is someone who has allied himself with them because he wants to enrich himself. Stígandr, for example."

"Our shoemaker?" My father laughed in exasperation. "Do you not think you're going a bit far with your suspicions?"

"He admitted on the battlefield at Stanfordbrycge that he had negotiated with the Norþmenn, and at Richale, he urged me to betray Eadgar Æðeling and fight on the side of the French. Even now, he claims to be travelling again to look for leather and tools. He's a liar. Why do you think he keeps disappearing and no one knows where he is? He's a Norþmann, just like those who accompanied and betrayed us in Eoforwic. He's looking for an opportunity to enrich himself, and he has found it in the French fight against us."

The smile disappeared from my father's face. "Do you know what you're saying? You've been wrong about him more than once, haven't you?"

"Father, he told me in his own words when I put the scramasax to his throat. He's a traitor and will take every chance to betray us if it is for his own good. You say yourself: 'Never trust a Viking!'"

"He admitted his treason?"

I nodded.

"What will you do if I let you go? A scout should not be guided by the desire for revenge if he wants to do his duty properly. He must be able to observe and assess a situation impartially and with clear thoughts."

"I know that, Father. Let me go and I will prove to you that I can."

"Beware of hasty revenge! Are you sure you will keep your feelings in check?"

Could I? Stígandr had already escaped from me several times. Should he fall into my hands now, what would happen? Would I be able to restrain myself if he did indeed lead the French to our houses? "I will ask Ulfgar to accompany me so that at least one of us will be able to ride home and alert you if an attack is imminent."

"Should I really not send Erik and Wulfnoð instead? We need you here, Oswulf."

"If the French have really advanced as far as I suspect, we will not have to ride far to find them. Let me go, Father!"

My father tugged at his moustache and regarded me for a long time. "So be it. But promise me to turn back immediately if you see the French approaching. You're an excellent fighter, but even you cannot defeat a French army all by yourself."

"Thank you, Father. I promise."

So, Ulfgar and I rode north to Maltun. The French were bound to pass by on their way to Renliton. Shortly before Nortone, we heard screams and spurred our horses on. When we reached the place, four riders were setting fire to a barn, while others cornered a horde of pigs, stabbing them one by one.

"Frenciscan," I whispered.

"Niþingas!" Ulfgar snorted.

"We have to help the people." I stared at the slaughter before our eyes.

"There are too many for us, Oswulf."

I thought hard how we could intervene in the fight and looked around. Away from the action, a man was leaning against a tree next to a horse and seemed to be watching the whole thing calmly. "I knew I'd find him here!"

"Who?"

"Stígandr. Over there, by the tree."

"You're beginning to give me the creeps, Oswulf. Wherever you go, Stígandr appears."

"Ulfgar, you ride on to Maltun and try to find out where the rest of the French riders are. In the meantime, I will see what Stígandr has to tell me."

We separated and rode off in opposite directions. In front of Stígandr, I jumped off my horse and walked towards him.

Stígandr raised an eyebrow but otherwise did not move. "Young Osfriðson! Have you finally decided to fight on the right side?"

I drew the scramasax. "This time, you will not escape your fate."

"Isn't that what you said the last time we met at Stanford-brycge?" The teeth in his lower jaw showed. "As you can see, I'm still alive."

"Not for long if you don't draw your short sword soon. Come on! Let's get this over with."

Stígandr clicked his tongue. "Always in a hurry, those young ones!" He held out a water pouch to me. "Would you like a sip? The French have brought some very good wine to strengthen themselves before battle." He lifted the pouch and glanced at me diabolically. "Maybe that's why they always win against the English." He calmly took a sip and closed the pouch.

I was only three paces away from him. "Draw your sword, Stígandr!"

He just looked at me. "We should talk, not fight. Imagine the honour you could achieve in the French army! You're a unique fighter. Everyone in Ledlinghe knows that – nay, your reputation goes far beyond our little village. I'm sure King Willelm would love to have a warrior like you in his army."

"I don't give a damn what the foreign king would like. Just as he doesn't care about me and my countrymen."

"The French are highly accomplished warriors, unbeatable on their horses and even on foot, very difficult to oppose. The king likes to have an army of excellent warriors, whom he rewards richly for their victories."

"With the money he has previously taken from the English. He's a thief and a usurper. Do you really think I want to fight for such a king?"

"Well, you may be content with your miserable life in Ledlinghe. Perhaps you no longer want recognition for what you are capable of. Was it not once your greatest dream to become a huscarl to the king? A model warrior with the best equipment and a noble warhorse, fighting for your country and your king and richly rewarded with gifts, money, goods and lands? Or am I confusing you with someone else? Perhaps you have also come to realise that you are not good enough and would rather become a swineherd in Ledlinghe."

Stígandr's words echoed in my head. Fighting was what I did best, but there was little need for it in Ledlinghe. It was a small place, made up mainly of peasants. They needed men who could handle the plough and the scythe, not the sword. Of course, I would be able to work there, like my father and grandfather before me. But what I was really good at, the handling of weapons that I had practised for years, would never be of any use to me there. The Lord must have chosen another destiny for me, otherwise He would not have given me this special gift. It was my task, my duty, to use this gift to please God.

"It's a good opportunity for you, Osfriðson," Stígandr said with a luring undertone. "Do not waste your fighting skills in Ledlinghe. Think what you could achieve in the army of the French. Perhaps the king would give you the command of one of his cavalry troops. You would build your own castle – just imagine – not a small manor, but a mighty castle befitting a great warrior! You would rule as a baron over your lands assigned by the king, with dozens, maybe even hundreds of vassals and servants. And if you did your job well, you might become one of the king's greatest vassals. You would finally reach your goal, even if it had a different name: tenant in chief instead of huscarl."

Was Stígandr right? Could an Englishman really make it that far in the army of the foreign king? I knew of a few English nobles and bishops whom he had left in office or appointed himself. But he would hardly tolerate an Englishman in his army. Besides, the French fought on horseback, not on foot. I would still have to learn that. I looked at Stígandr closely. Why was he trying to persuade me to switch sides? There had to be a catch. Was he trying to capture me as a hostage for the

French? What for? If they were going to raid our village, they could catch me themselves, even though I had never heard of the French taking prisoners. Only dead enemies meant victory in battle. Besides, the king could raise taxes at will. And he had an army to enforce all his demands. He didn't need prisoners or a young Englishman from a small, insignificant village in the middle of the rebellious north. But perhaps I could persuade the French horsemen to spare Ledlinghe if I entered their service. My life for the lives of the villagers. Would they accept it? If so, how could I be sure that they would indeed spare Ledlinghe or that another part of their army would not attack the village despite our agreement? If they didn't accept, however, it would be my death sentence. They would kill me first and then raze the village to the ground. "What if I accept your proposal?"

A smile flitted across Stígandr's face, flashing the teeth in his lower jaw. "Then all options are open to you."

"Including that the French slay me even before they have heard me out."

"Now, now! The French are not barbarians. In everything they do, they have a certain style that I find quite attractive."

"Like slaughtering innocent villagers because their king wants to prove his power?"

"You are unfair, Oswulf. Other kings do the same. A king sometimes has to make decisions that don't please everyone. It has always been that way, and it will always be."

It pained me to admit that Stígandr did have a point there. At least, to some extent. I knew that from my father, when he himself had to make decisions in Ledlinghe and could not always satisfy everybody. But he had to do what he thought was best for the community, and everyone had to follow suit. The

169

king was in a similar position, only his decisions were much more far-reaching. But was the total destruction that King Willelm had chosen in the north really what was best for the community? Perhaps for the French, for it was them who would benefit most from crushing all resistance in the rebellious north. "The king's hatred for the people of Norþhymbre is what makes his troops roam the land murdering and pillaging. Who could serve him with a clear conscience when the blood of so many Englishmen is on his hands?"

Stígandr raised his already hunched shoulders so that they almost touched his ears, and it looked as if he were retracting his head. "It's your choice, Osfriðson. You can either live and make the circumstances work in your favour, or you can do as your countrymen did, who revolted against the king and have been dead for a long time or will die in the coming days and weeks."

I nodded thoughtfully as I pondered his words. "The foreign king leaves no doubt about that. But I will not be able to save them by siding with him. The only one I could save would be me. And even in that case, I am not sure the French would let me live." I pointed my scramasax at Stígandr and walked towards him. "Until I have that certainty, I will fight for my own and my family's life and kill those who attack us or who betray us for their own gain – like you, ðu wyrma gifl!" I leapt forward and stabbed at Stígandr's belly with my sword.

The Norþmann skipped to the side. He unsheathed his short sword and glanced left and right. "You're making a mistake, Oswulf."

"The only mistake I make is to let you live. You have escaped too often." I urged him backwards with several sword strokes.

I did not want to kill him yet. First, he had to tell me where the French were.

Stígandr jumped alternately to the left and right. "The French will be back soon."

I aimed at Stígandr's neck. "You'll be dead on the ground first, you traitor! I wonder why the French haven't killed you already."

Stígandr continued to back away, but he smiled. "I offer them valuable news."

"What news?" I gave him a tap on the shoulder, which he narrowly escaped.

He hissed.

I took a step back. My sword had only grazed his shoulder. The wound was not deep. "What did you tell them?" I gasped.

With his mouth gaping, Stígandr looked from his wound to me. One corner of his mouth twitched upwards. "I know my way around up here."

"Just tell me what you told them!" I pointed the sword at him and took a step forward.

Stígandr acted as if he had all the time in the world. I listened and looked around to make sure that the French horsemen Stígandr had spoken of did not suddenly appear.

"Well, they mainly asked where the big settlements were and where there were only smaller settlements."

"Why should they care if they destroy everything anyway?"

"Large places need many warriors, small places only a few. Simple."

If I hadn't known better, I would have said Stígandr was drunk. Was the cut deeper than it looked? "What are you talking about?"

A sneer spread across the goat face.

My chest was tingling. Something was not right here.

"You disappoint me. Have you learned nothing about war tactics?"

I quickly went through everything my father had taught me in this field, but my thoughts were buzzing like a swarm of excited bees whose hive had just been destroyed.

"I have told the French where the larger places are on their, shall we say, journey. So, that's where they went with a large army to punish the rebels."

"There are no rebels where they go. Only innocent people who have to die."

"If there are only small villages in the region which they cross, they can split up."

"That means they can attack in several places at once." My heart beat faster. I felt like I was going to retch.

"Indeed. They don't need the whole army for a small place. They split up and do a much faster and better job. You could learn a lot about tactical and efficient warfare from the French, young Osfriðson. Think about it."

"There are many small places around here." I stared at him as his smile widened with each word I said. "So, the French have split up and are moving around in small groups – and Ledlinghe is not far."

"That's right." The teeth in Stígandr's lower jaw flashed like small razor-sharp daggers just waiting to pierce through flesh. "Better make up your mind quickly."

My heartbeat was pounding in my ears.

The French in Ledlinghe!

"God sceal forlætan þe to ðam ecan forwyrde. You've known all along, and you've lured me here and detained me with idle chat."

"I knew you would come sooner or later. The scouts told us that two young, nosey Englishmen were riding through the woods."

"You saw us? What have you done with Ulfgar?"

Stígandr pursed his lips innocently. "Well, you'll have to find out for yourself how your friend is. And your family."

My family. Father warned me. He knew they would need me in Ledlinghe, but I rode off. Now, the French are riding to Ledlinghe, and no one there knows it. I must go back. Quickly.

I ran to my horse and jumped into the saddle.

"Good luck!" Stígandr called after me, and although I did not look back while spurring my stallion on like a madman, I could feel the goat grin in my back following me.

I chased past bushes and trees. My horse's hooves thundered over the hard ground, but they could not drown out the ominous, bleating laughter in my head. I prayed that I was not too late. At the same time, my thoughts wandered to Ulfgar. Had they caught him? Had he fallen into a trap they had set for us and which I had only escaped because I wanted to take revenge on Stígandr? Or was this the very trap they had set? My horse galloped as if the Fiend was chasing us, but I spurred it on relentlessly. "Faster, faster!"

Was it the cold wind that brought tears to my eyes? The despair that grew inside me the closer I got to the familiar surroundings of my home? I slowed my horse and glanced over my shoulder. Smoke was rising in the southeast over the woods and fields near Redrestorp. I was too late. From where I saw the plumes of smoke, it was less than an hour's walk to reach Ledlinghe. A rider with a fast horse would cover the distance in much less than half an hour. My body stiffened so that my horse fell into an unsteady trot. I screamed out my pain. The stallion leapt to the side and pranced around in confusion. I heard my scream echo, as if the woods were throwing it back at me. I screamed again. So did the woods. I listened up. It was not an echo. Someone was calling my name. Someone whose voice I knew well. I looked around and saw a single horse approaching from the distance. On its back sat a big rider who raised his round shield as if to give me a sign. I wiped my cheek and turned my horse. "Ulfgar! You're alive!"

"They left Maltun this morning in a southeasterly direction," he shouted.

The happiness of seeing my friend alive gave way to fear for my family. Ulfgar spurred his horse on, and I chased after him.

As Ledlinghe came into view, the band of French horsemen stormed towards huts and villagers. We heard the first cries and the roar of cattle. Women and children rushed around frantically between the buildings and the deadly horsemen. Some fled into the woods, while their men fought the invaders with axes, pikes and pitchforks or threw stones at them. The French simply charged past them, piercing them with their spears, or knocked them down with their mighty warhorses, trampling them to death.

I went for a French warrior who seemed to be keeping an eye on the outskirts of the village and had slit open his horse's flank before he even noticed me. The animal reared up with a cry of pain. I drove my scramasax into the rider's unprotected neck and pushed the sword forward until he slid out of the saddle, gurgling. A kick of mine into the horse's belly made it jump to the side, squealing. It stumbled over the rider and thumped down beside him. I spat on the man. "You were the first and you will not be the last."

I put the bloody sword back in its sheath and grabbed an axe. While I was looking for my next opponent, Ulfgar was crouching behind a hut and beckoned me over. I took aim and threw the axe. Another Frenchman toppled from his horse. I shooed the horse in front of me for protection, pulled the axe from the dead rider and ran crouching to Ulfgar. "Have you seen my father?"

Ulfgar had got himself some spears and lifted one of them over his shoulder. "No, but surely the French army is already a few warriors short because of him."

The spear whizzed off and hit a rider in the back just as he was stabbing a peasant with his sword. I stood behind Ulfgar and backed him up while he took down more opponents with more spears.

A bunch of children ran past us, pushed forward by one of the peasant's wives who lived not far from us. "Run, children, run! Hurry up!"

The hair on my skin stood on end when I recognised my three younger siblings. My brothers Wigstan and Oswine had not even reached the age to be taught how to fight with weapons, even less so against a horseman. My little sister Eda was completely defenceless.

Holding up her ankle-length tunic with one hand, the peasant's wife urged the children on with the other, all the while looking over her shoulder.

My youngest brother looked around, bewildered, then caught sight of me. "There you are, Oswulf!"

"Run, children!" the woman shouted before her face contorted.

A spear crunched through her body and came out of her chest. A French horseman pushed her aside, drew his sword and lunged at the children, who stood spellbound between horror and despair.

I jumped up and let the axe slice through the horse's hind leg. The animal let out a shrill squeal. Its hind legs slumped away. The rider was thrown backwards, flailing his shield and sword to keep his balance. I hooked the axe into the shield and pulled as hard as I could. The shield swung to the side. The Frenchman crashed down, his helmet toppling off his head. I lashed out and split his skull. The children hissed and screwed up their faces.

"What sort of people are you that kill even children?" I looked around. There was no French warrior anywhere near. "Run and hide in the woods, children. Quick! Run!"

The children hesitated.

I nudged the tallest one. "Wigstan, you're the oldest. Lead them into the woods, make haste!"

I shooed them away like a flock of chickens, hoping the French wouldn't notice their escape.

One by one, they disappeared behind the bushes and finally, into the nearby woods.

I pulled the axe out of the dead warrior and looked around the corner of the house. Ulfgar had used up all the spears. "Come! We must find my father."

We took shields and an axe each and weaved our way between small and large bodies, trying to save those who could be saved and kill those who attacked our village and wanted to destroy it.

Suddenly, Ulfgar stopped. "Bargest." He ran to a massive black carcass, its fur blood-red. "Bargest!"

I followed him, keeping an eye on our surroundings so that Ulfgar did not run blindly to his doom. He fell to his knees next to Bargest and put his hand on her bloody chest. Finally, his head sank down onto her neck.

"There's nothing more we can do for her, Ulfgar." I shifted from one leg to the other. "Come!"

Ulfgar rose. "The French will pay dearly for this."

We made our way to my father's manor. Behind us, the first flames flickered on the roofs of the houses. The snorting and neighing of the horses, the cows bellowing in agony, the squealing pigs, the crying children, the shrieking women and the groans of the mortally wounded men mixed into an unbearable thunderhead of noise. When we reached the manor, my father was lying in the garden, cruelly mauled.

While Ulfgar attacked a French warrior in front of the great hall, I fell on my knees beside my father. "Forgive me, Father! I am too late. You knew I would be needed here, but I went away. God has punished you for my disobedience. What have I done?" I gritted my teeth and tried to suppress the tears.

"Oswulf!" cried Ulfgar.

Ulfgar! I jumped up, but Ulfgar had defeated his opponent and pointed to the great hall from which screams were coming. Women's screams.

Godgifu! My mother and my sisters!

We rushed through the door, following the cries. Mother and Æðelflæd were lying just beyond the entrance. Their bodies were twisted, Æðelflæd's dress pushed up, the light linen shirt underneath soaked in blood and smeared with dirt. My hand clenched the handle of my axe. I gritted my teeth so hard it hurt and hurried on. Where were Godgifu and Wassa?

In the great hall, two servants and our groom lay dead under the tables, the benches stood at angles or had been overturned, the floor in front of the kitchen was strewn with shards of pottery. A Frenchman was just going for our cook in the kitchen, two more were lunging at Ulfgar. Further back, I heard the screams of my beloved wife, who was being assaulted by another French warrior.

"Godgifu!" I threw my axe at one of Ulfgar's opponents, drew my short sword while running and went for the Frenchman. Out of the corner of my eye, I saw Wassa's body sprawled backwards over a table, staring blankly at the ceiling. I snorted like a wild bull and sped up. Just before I reached the man on Godgifu, he drew his sword and plunged it into her belly.

She let out a shriek.

"Godgifu!" I gave her tormentor no time to pull his sword out again. He had no protection whatsoever, so I rammed my shield into his face. He stumbled backwards. I hacked at him like a madman, face, neck, arms, belly. As he writhed on the ground, badly wounded, I turned him onto his back with my sword. He groaned and looked at me defiantly from moist eyes. "Ðu scealt gan libbende on helle." I put the point of the sword to his throat, at the unprotected spot just under his chin, where his chain mail would do him no good. Slowly, I began to run the sword point along his skin, with very little pressure, just enough for the metal to nick his skin. A thin line of blood began to flow. "I'm not going to kill you. Not right away. I want you to die slowly, as punishment for what you have done to my wife and for the pain and suffering you have caused my family and Ledlinghe." I raised my sword and struck his right wrist. The Frenchman grunted. His wounds quickly sucked the life out of him. "You will never raise a sword against an Englishman again."

Seeing Godgifu's body covered in blood caused me more pain than any weapon ever could. Loath to leave the detested sword as a widely visible sign of the French victory, I pulled it from my beloved one's body. One last time I kissed her raspberry lips with trembling jaws and swallowed the tears that began to blur my vision. I had long escaped God's punishment, but now it was catching up with me with full force.

Ulfgar had in the meantime finished off the first opponent and was engaged in another fight when two more Frenchmen with spears appeared in the doorway to the great hall. "We have to get out of here!" he shouted at me and took a mighty swing with his axe. "Otherwise, we'll be trapped."

His foe was doomed. The blade landed with a crash on his shield, which burst in two like a nutshell. Ulfgar pushed the axe forward with all his weight. The Frenchman crashed against the wall, gasping for breath as Ulfgar reached for the scramasax. He struck at Ulfgar with his sword, but it only grazed the shield. The impact of his sword strike was drowned out by a gurgle. Ulfgar pulled the short sword from the Frenchman's belly and slipped it back into the leather sheath on his weapon belt.

Meanwhile, the other two Frenchmen made their way from the entrance door through the benches and tables and pointed their spears forwards to skewer us like pigs. We had nothing with which to stop them from a distance.

Except maybe…

"The knives in the kitchen," I murmured to Ulfgar, as the four of us eyed each other intently. "Can you hold them off a while?"

"With pleasure." Ulfgar grabbed the ale jug that was on the table in front of him and hurled it at the Frenchmen.

The jug spun around as it dispersed its liquid contents in a low-flying wave through the air. While the Frenchman in front ducked behind his shield, the one further back swerved to avoid the wet projectile.

I pulled an axe from the back of a dead Frenchman, threw open the door to the kitchen and rushed in. Reluctantly, I laid the axe on the hearth – I would have preferred to keep it, but I needed a free hand. I quickly rammed as many knives as I could find into the inside of my shield and took an extra handful. Then I pushed open the window, jumped back to the door and peered around the corner.

Ulfgar was battling both attackers, using a spear that he must have somehow seized from his opponents to keep them at a distance.

I placed the knives from my hand on the table in front of me and began to hurl them at the unprotected parts of the distracted Frenchmen. Only when a knife flew a hair's breadth past his face did the one with the spear notice me. With an incomprehensible exclamation, he turned to me and pointed the spearhead at me. I continued to hurl knives at him as I backed away. The Frenchman easily dodged and bounced the blades off his large shield. He came closer. I aimed for his face and threw. He ducked and raised his shield at the same time. With a leap, I fled into the kitchen, grabbed the axe, pressed myself into the corner next to the door and held my breath.

A spearhead pushed its way into the room, first at an angle, then straight. By now, my enemy was bound to have seen the open window. Another foreign exclamation followed. The Frenchman stomped towards the window and looked outside. I jumped behind him and took a swing. He spun around and ducked behind the shield. The axe crashed onto the wood.

My foe tore the shield aside, ripping the weapon from my hand. He threw away the spear and drew his sword. I took a step back, pulled out one of the knives still stuck in my shield and threw it at his foot. He cried out. I grabbed the spear and pointed it forward while retreating. I thrust a few times, but even wounded, the Frenchman moved faster than many an opponent I had fought so far.

"Are you two finished?" a voice barked behind me. "We have to get out of here before more of them come."

I stabbed at the Frenchman once more and hurried out of the kitchen, slamming the door behind me. "Run!"

We rushed towards the door of the great hall.

Behind us, my wounded foe smashed the kitchen door against the wall and limped after us with his sword drawn.

We ran outside and hastily looked around for shelter.

Cries for help came through the crackling and cracking of the burning huts. They came from a shed whose gate three French horsemen were just breaking down.

Ulfgar and I ran behind a hut as we considered how we could attack them.

The injured Frenchman shouted something from the door of the great hall and pointed in my direction.

I followed his gaze, which went to a rider watching the murderous activity of his men, seemingly unperturbed. Even though I couldn't see much under his helmet, I felt his eyes resting on me, and I was sure that I had seen the expressionless face of this man before, whose eyes had pierced me from afar. A bad memory welled up inside me like pus in a wound. *Eoforwic. The leader of the French horsemen who pursued the fleeing English and Danes and cut them down one by one.* Back then, I stood high up on the castle hill, far away from him. Now, he was less than a short spear-throw away from me here in Ledlinghe.

"Come on, Oswulf!" Ulfgar sneaked around the hut, picked up some large stones and fired them at one of the riders.

Like a clapper in a bell, a stone hit the Norman's helmet. The man's upper body swung backwards before it snapped back again, and the rider turned to face us.

Ulfgar hurled another stone in his face before he took the axe and stood with his legs wide apart. "Come here if you dare!" he called to him and took a few steps backwards.

Pressing my lips together, I got the spear ready. The pounding of my heart resounded in my head.

The Frenchman spurred the horse on and pointed the spear at Ulfgar. I felt my heartbeat trying to keep up with the thundering of the hooves. My breathing was shallow as if someone were pressing a heavy slab of stone against my chest.

I peered round the corner, spear in hand and eyeing the rider who was approaching at breakneck speed. When the horse was only thirty paces away from me, I took aim and threw the spear at the rider.

The tip grazed his chain mail without hurting him and shot across the horse's rump. The horse lunged to the side and trotted on in confusion before the rider spurred it on again about fifteen paces away, ready to impale me with his spear. Out of the corner of my eye, I saw Ulfgar run up from the right and swing his axe. I raised my shield and prepared to leap to the side. Suddenly, the horse squealed, stumbled and fell forward. Ulfgar's axe was stuck in his side. The rider fell, rolled onto his back and held the shield protectively over him as he writhed back and forth. His leg was trapped under the horse's body.

Before we could finish him off, the two other Frenchmen who had attacked the shed with him came riding up. The shed was still standing, even though the door was badly damaged.

We rushed behind the hut. There was no hiding place or anything that would offer protection against their horses and spears, at least, not for very long. Ulfgar and I looked at each other. Exhausted from the battle, we both gasped for breath. But we could not rest now. We had to keep fighting.

"Let's take them to hell!" I said, and Ulfgar nodded. "Come! Into the hut!"

We hurried inside and locked the door behind us. We wouldn't have time to catch our breath in here either. They would probably set the hut on fire and roast us like suckling pigs. We had to think of something quickly. I put the scramasax back on my belt and searched the hut for flints, tinder and a rope.

"They circle the hut like a pack of wolves surrounding its prey and cutting off any escape route," Ulfgar growled. Just in time, he jumped behind the door as a spear flew through the small window only a few inches from him. A second spear whizzed past right by my shoulder. Someone shouted something in their language, followed by an indignant neighing. Ulfgar picked up a spear and dared a quick glance through the window. "They've brought some friends." He smirked. "Two of them aren't enough to handle us."

I lit a makeshift torch I had crafted out of the leg of a stool, some cloth and a piece of rope and handed it to Ulfgar. "If this doesn't work, we'll either be skewered or smoked." I sighed.

"Then we have to fight." Ulfgar looked at me. "You and me. The two of us together."

I nodded. "For Englaland and for Godgifu."

"For Englaland and Bargest."

I lit the strips of cloth I had stuffed into a small bucket and watched the fire slowly spread. Then I picked up the rope and lifted the bucket. "You open the door and throw the torch outside. I run out and try to keep them away from the door until you are outside. Then God help us. Ready?"

"Ready."

I looked at my friend one last time. We had known each other for so many years now. On the battlefield, we could trust each other blindly. Each knew the other's movements, strengths and weaknesses. We were a tried-and-tested team of two. How often had a last glance at Ulfgar before a fight given me the certainty that we could do it? But this time, I looked in vain for the confidence in his gaze. "Whatever happens out there, Ulfgar, I want you to know that you've always been more to me than just my friend and brother-in-arms. You are like a blood brother to me, and I will fight to protect at least this last remnant of my family from the hands of the bloodthirsty French."

"I know, Oswulf." Ulfgar took a deep breath. "May God be with us."

I glanced at the burning bucket. Then I nodded to Ulfgar. He flung the door open, roared at the top of his lungs and hurled the torch between two riders in front of the hut. The horses neighed, bolting. I ran out screaming and began to wave the burning bucket in the air. The horses backed away and neighed nervously as they pranced away from the flying fire. With another cry, Ulfgar rushed out of the hut behind me and stabbed the nearest Frenchman with his spear. The horse reared, squealing. Ulfgar followed him, screaming and thrusting. The rider struggled to steady his horse in front of this loud and swirling monster. Meanwhile, I swung the burning bucket above my head as far as I could with the shield in my left hand and tried to hit our opponents with it. With a hiss, the bucket seared the shoulder of a horse. The horse reared up, threw the rider off and took off. I aimed at another rider, but he backed away before I could hit him. The bucket swung past the fallen rider and set fire to his tunic. The man screamed and rolled around to put out the fire. Hurling the bucket beside me, I ran towards the nearest horse.

Through the neighing and snorting of the horses, the French shouted scraps of words. Were they conferring aloud about how to quickly get rid of these two mad Englishmen, perhaps the last of Ledlinghe, before losing even more men?

I looked around suspiciously. The riders suddenly seemed unusually restrained. They shouted something to each other, but no one attacked. I glanced at Ulfgar. He too stood crouched behind the shield, watching the enemies around us. Nothing happened. What were these dogs up to?

Behind the three men who looked down at us from their horses, more riders appeared. This meant that they were no longer needed elsewhere. They had completed their task of destroying all life in Ledlinghe and could now join forces to deal with Ulfgar and me. Against four, we could have won. Against six, seven, eight or however many more came, no. One by one, they turned their spears on us.

There are too many of them. We will neither escape their bloodstained lances nor the ravenous fires with which they burn down our houses and villages.

Chapter 7

In my head, I see images of horsemen rushing towards me. Men in armour on huge warhorses, slaughtering everything in their path with spears and swords. I feel the heat of the flames that devour the wooden roofs and walls of the huts. I hear the death-cries of the men trying to stop the invaders, the shrieks of the women and the squeals of the children as the hordes kill them indiscriminately, the screams of the dying as they sink to the ground, pierced by the weapons. It smells of sweat, smoke, blood and decay. I try to swallow the metallic taste on my tongue. "I destroyed all of that."

"You have sinned grievously, Oswulf, but the Lord had mercy on you. He saved you and brought you to Wilburgfos to repent of your sins and save your soul from eternal damnation. Your thoughts and deeds were driven by pride, anger and envy. You bore false witness against others and violated the commandment of Christian charity. You must repent of your sins and turn to God again if the eternal kingdom of heaven is not to be closed to you."

186

I fold my hands hastily. "I repent of my sins and vow to do penance for them, Father. Tell me how I can regain divine grace."

"Under my authority as a member of the Holy Church, I hereby absolve you of your sins. In order that your soul may also be purified, you will fast for three days and keep vigil in the chapel while you say your prayers to God. May the Lord hear you and have mercy on your soul. Amen."

"Amen." Relieved and yet with a heavy heart, I step out of the chapel and walk aimlessly across the yard while trying to think clearly.

"Oswulf?"

The young voice that called my name brings back memories. I feel as if I have heard it long ago. I stop in the middle of the yard.

An awkwardly tall and thin young man comes stomping up to me from the side, English by the look of his chin-length light brown hair.

"Oswulf, son of Osfrið?" He tucks his thumbs into his belt, grins broadly and nods. "Well, who would've thought we'd meet again! Looking good, my friend."

"Cenric?"

"You remember my name?" Cenric utters a brief laugh. "I don't believe it! The master of the battlefield himself remembers Cenric, the insignificant Englishman from Wilburgfos." He makes an exuberant bow. "I am honoured, eala ðu wundorwiga!"

I look around in embarrassment. Suddenly, I'm almost grateful that the French don't speak our language and can't understand the swollen nonsense Cenric utters.

Cenric nudges me on the shoulder. "Tell me, what brings you to our manor house? Didn't see you arrive. How on earth did you get past all those Frenchmen?" His smile disappears. Before he continues, he looks around then says in a lowered voice, "Things've changed here in the last two years. Our new master is an unpleasant fellow, quite different from Kjetil. Sent him off to meet his maker, just like other good folk, when they raided the manor then claimed it for themselves. Supposedly, given to Lord Geoffrey as a reward for his services in fighting the English by some lord in Cattune." He spits out. "Niþingas! Think they can just stumble in here and take over the manors. Our Lady Edeva, poor woman, even had to marry the new lord. He wanted a French priest for the wedding but had to make do with Father Leofric. Serves him right! His wealhstod never left his side, translated every single word so that he wouldn't miss anything. Seen the host of servants this fellow's brought with him? Unbelievable! Whoever they didn't kill of us English now gets to do the dirty work. They made my father a servant. His work got taken over by two Frenchmen, a friendly one and another with woolly dark hair. Yfel gesiþ, if you ask me."

I step from one foot to the other. Thibault must be waiting on the battleground to introduce me to his pupils.

"Oh, yes, he also brought his two children and their wet nurse with him. Lady Edeva's desperate to get rid of her. Always looking at her husband in a strange way. I wouldn't be surprised if he secretly went after her. Wouldn't be the first time he's had his way with other women. When Lady Edeva was pregnant with little Hroðgar – Hroðgar, huh? The French call him *Raw-jaire*. Doesn't that sound ridiculous? Anyway, Hild – our herb lady, you remember her, don't you? – well, she had to look after Edeva quite a lot because the lady wasn't well for a long time. We even feared she wouldn't make it and that she and the child would die. So, in the meantime, Lord Geoffrey got his marital dues elsewhere. Was probably famished after the long absence from the manor. He still went on many campaigns during that time and could be away for months. What an animal!" Cenric shakes his head and snorts.

Did he even take a breath in all that stream of words? Before I start pondering the question, I take the chance, while Cenric has shut up for a moment, to point towards the battleground. "The master of arms is waiting for me, Cenric, but it was nice to meet you. Any additional Englishman in this manor house will make my life here more bearable."

Cenric pats me on the shoulder. "Oh, that's all right. We English stick together." His look becomes thoughtful. He furrows his brow. "Well, most of us, anyway."

"Most?"

"There's this one guy who showed up here with the French at some point. Not as a prisoner. He seemed to be part of them. He's not often here because they're always sending him off, some kind of messenger. I don't know why, but I can't stand him. Maybe it's just because of his silly little beard or his strange attitude. But he speaks English fluently and is polite and—"

"What's the name of this messenger?" A sneaking suspicion germinates in me.

Cenric waves it off. "Oh, he has one of those Danish names – you know, with that unpronounceable ending."

Stígandr.

Cenric leans towards me and shields his mouth with his hand. "The guy's name is Stígandr. Watch out for him! He may pretend to be English and work for us at the manor house, but I don't trust him. Nor should you!"

189

He straightens up with a weighty expression on his face and puts his fists on his hips.

I nod thoughtfully. "I will heed your advice, Cenric. It's unfortunate that I don't understand a word of French. I'm sure there would be some conversations to eavesdrop on."

Cenric puts his hand on my arm. "Fear not, my friend! Cenric will initiate you into the secrets of the foreign language."

"You speak French?"

"Indeed. And not bad, as some Frenchmen have grudgingly confirmed to me. Learned it from Frederic."

"Frederic?"

"Aye, the seneschal who looks after the manor house when Lord Geoffrey is away. He's really nice – for a Frenchman! You'll like him."

Well, well, well. A Frenchman teaching an Englishman his language. I could achieve much more if I understood and spoke French. I wouldn't always have to rely on Walchelin, who might not translate everything into English. Besides, I could speak to the French myself or listen in on their conversations. They would no longer be able to simply talk over me in my presence. I could learn many important details about their intentions and plans. "Cenric, we'll start first thing in the morning!"

Cenric pauses, then smiles incredulously. "Agreed."

"See you tomorrow, Cenric." I hurry to the battleground before Cenric might try to fling his arms around my neck in gratitude.

Two youths are already engaged in a fight with wooden spear and shield. Three others are standing on the edge of the arena, watching the fighters attentively. Thibault beckons me to him. Walchelin is standing next to him, frowning at the young fighters' movements. I sigh. It will take me a while to find my way around without the wealhstod. He is more to me than just a language mediator who converts foreign words into something I can understand. He provides access to the new world in which I will live. Most of the faces are unfamiliar to me, their way of life and customs different from those I am used to from my father's manor or which I experienced during my first stay at Wilburgfos. Without Walchelin, I would probably be rather lost here.

As I stand next to Thibault, the three youths regard me warily. One points at me and chuckles behind his hand. He whispers something to his neighbour while pretending to throw long hair back over his shoulder. His neighbour starts laughing, but Thibault calls them both to order in a sharp tone. Their laughter dies down, but they continue to eye me. The third one looks around questioningly and then turns to Thibault. From the tone of his voice, I gather that he must have asked a question. Thibault answers the boy before raising his voice and addressing the other youths as well. I listen to the strange singsong as I let my gaze wander over the five squires. I hear my name in Thibault's foreign speech.

So these are my pupils whom I am supposed to show how to fight with various weapons. I see small injuries on most of their faces, which probably testify to their inexperience with the shearing knife rather than a spear or sword. Apart from the sleepy little one standing right next to Walchelin, they are almost my age. Wiry, tall lads with silly bowl cuts. *I will not have an easy time with them, and they will do everything they can to make it as difficult as possible for me.*

Before I can start to wonder what is going on in the boys' minds, Thibault assigns me to my very first fight. At a quick summons, the blonde fighter leaves his battle companion, strips off his shield and holds it out to me, along with the wooden spear and a cocky grin. I accept the weapons while he joins the other two observers, who once again, cannot help whispering.

I get ready to fight and examine my opponent. A strong, red-haired guy with wide jawbones and deep-set eyes. One, maybe two years younger than me. His muscles stand out under his loose tunic. *Surely, a good axe fighter.*

With one leap, my opponent comes at me with his wooden spear. I jump to the side and aim at his shoulder. He pulls up his shield and swings my spear around with it. It almost slips from my hand, so I fasten my grip and duck. His thrust whizzes over my head into the void. From my crouched position, I ram the blunt end of my wooden spear onto his unprotected foot. He grunts. Before I can fully rise, he slams the shield across my back. I groan and have to brace myself on the ground with my weapon hand. In the background, I hear enthusiastic hooting and shouting. I throw myself forward and jostle his legs with my shield and shoulder. He flails his arms, stumbles backwards two steps and hits the ground. I stab him again, but he pulls up his legs, rolls to the side under the shield and is already back on his feet, his shield in front of him. Yet he has not quite regained his balance, and I kick against his shield and follow up with a thrust at his neck. He tries to dodge my spear and falls on his backside. A moment too long, his shield is on the ground, so I press the wooden stick down onto his chest. He throws up his hands and shouts something. Thibault's voice rings out too, but I don't dare turn around. My opponent smiles appreciatively, gestures for me to take the weapon away and stands up. He clamps his shield arm over the wooden spear and holds out his hand to me, accompanied by some unintelligible words. I frown at the others. Thibault grins with obvious satisfaction. The mouths of the four other pupils are open. Even the whisperers are speechless.

Walchelin nods at me. "Go ahead! Shake hands with him! This is Jehan, Thibault's best squire. You have just proved that you know very well how to fight. No other squire beats Jehan."

I look into Jehan's eyes and hold out my hand to him. *What would Father say if he could see me like this? I shake the enemy's hand as if we were allies.* I feel ashamed, but deep inside, pride fills my gut. Pride in my victory and its swiftness, which, judging by the faces of the youths, must have been daunting. *But they are young. They still have a lot to learn before they earn the rank of knight in the king's army. Getting the squires to respect me will not be difficult on this battleground. But what will their fathers say about me? Will it be enough for them if I excel in teaching their sons? Only yesterday, I was fighting them as an enemy, and today, barely a day later, I am supposed to look after their sons and live in the same manor house as them?*

The wealhstod points to each of the other pupils. "These are Jeannot, the youngest of the group, Roul, Eudo and Eustace – all sons of French nobles from neighbouring manors who are here to become riddan or chevalers, as we call them."

I look into their expressionless faces. I had suspected that they would not welcome me wholeheartedly, but they seem confused rather than annoyed by my presence and my task. *Except perhaps, Roul.*

The blonde's sardonic grin has given way to an upturned chin and downturned corners of the mouth.

Sure, he would like to look down on me, but he is shorter than me and for that reason alone, has to look up to me.

The other two next to him are whispering once again. The last of the group, Jeannot, looks at me dreamily. I assume he hasn't been with the weapons practice for long. He looks clumsy and thin. I doubt if you can even get a quick movement out of him. But perhaps he will surprise me with other skills.

The rest of the fighting lesson passes without incident. Everyone has to fight me once before Thibault continues with general exercises for the whole group. As I feared, Jeannot is slow, but he aims very accurately. Eudo and Eustace fight decently, but Eudo is too hasty and Eustace neglects the shield arm. Roul is a fanatical, unbridled fighter. He is constantly grunting or shouting. His movements are random and imprecise. He lashes out wildly and charges forward, hoping to catch his opponent off guard. In a battle, he would not survive long. *If Thibault has so far not been able to steer him in the right direction, how can I?*

When we take the practice weapons away together after the lesson, everyone except Jehan keeps a safe distance from me. He walks next to me and keeps glancing over. If we spoke each other's language, he would surely exchange a few words with me. But he doesn't speak English, and I don't speak French, so I limit myself to smiling briefly at him, which he answers with a nod.

As I enter the armoury, Roul appears in the doorway. He hisses a few unintelligible words, jostles me on purpose and stomps off. Jehan and I exchange a glance. Jehan shakes his head and indicates for me to go inside. Eudo and Eustace give me a wide berth and push their way through the door. Jeannot talks to me in his language and looks at me with wide eyes. Jehan makes a remark, whereupon Jeannot exchanges a few puzzled sentences with him. Then he looks at me, points at himself and the door, and makes a bow, taking his leave. Jehan must have told him that I don't speak their language. *Not yet. But that will change soon if I work hard enough on it with Cenric.*

❧

IT IS DARK in the great hall. Only a little light squeezes through the narrow openings under the roof, even though the days are getting longer now that spring is here. Outside, the birds are chirping. It must be just before sunrise. None of the other sleepers are stirring yet, but I am wide awake. Thoughts are circling in my head.

Those who were at Lady Edeva's manor house when I brought my father here are not angry with me. They know my past and the reasons that have brought me back. To them, it is clear that I did not enter the service of the French oppressors of my own free will, but that it was under duress and threats – just as they had no choice when the manor house was taken over by Lord Geoffrey and his men. The French have led the English people to believe that our manor houses were rightfully handed over by the king and his tenants-in-chief to their vassals, but that is not what the English have seen and experienced. The people of Wilburgfos too have been prisoners of their own situation.

But those others, new to the manor house to replace the dead, and the people outside the manor, the peasants, the slaves, the women who come to the manor house with their services, tributes and goods, they see only the English stranger who is neither servant nor serf like them, but who sits at the same table as their masters, takes part in their conversations and ensures that the enemy offspring practise the wielding of weapons with which they continue to oppress Englaland. Their looks speak for themselves. They despise me, avoid me where they can, spit on me or insult me when I cross their path.

If it were God's will that their wishes come true, he would have summoned me a long time ago. But He seems to have determined that I should not succumb to the revilement of my own people. I have survived two great battles and the fight for my home village against experienced warriors. Should I now fail because simple peasants hate me?

A sound makes me hark. A steady, muffled rustling in the rushes. Rats? The noise sounds too heavy for that. I sit up and try to make out something in the darkness. In the dim light of a candle, I glimpse several figures approaching.

"Who a—?"

Someone grabs me and stuffs a gag in my mouth. I try to scream and throw myself back and forth. A blow hits me in the face. I moan. The pain paralyses me for a moment. They drag me out of the great hall. I wriggle and grumble. A fist drives into my stomach. The gag almost suffocates me as I gasp for air. I retch and cough, which only takes my breath away more. They are pulling me somewhere, but I am too busy trying to shake off my drowsiness whilst not choking on the gag and somehow keeping up with my captors. After a while, the sandy ground beneath my helplessly stumbling feet becomes uneven and grassy. I blink and can only dimly make out bushes and trees appearing around me. My captors finally throw me to the ground. I groan. Before I can take the gag out of my mouth, they grab my arms, pull them onto my back and tie them together. With his foot, one of them turns me onto my side. I struggle to look up. In the weak light of the rising sun, the outlines of three men begin to show. My stomach is burning with pain. My nose is blocked. Something is oozing along my moustache.

The middle figure, holding the candle, speaks to me. In French. I try to place the accent, but it is only a whisper and difficult to tell who is talking to me. The large hoods hide their faces, especially as they are turned away from the emerging light. I regard the figures, looking for anything distinctive that might tell me who has abducted me. I recognise some of the words, but not enough to tell me why I am here, and with the gag in my mouth, I cannot ask – though I am not sure they would even understand me.

A kick in the stomach brings tears to my eyes. I writhe in pain. The gag clogs my throat and robs me of air. I desperately suck in air through my nostrils, making a whistling sound. The Frenchman laughs and keeps talking. I know his way of speaking. That sharp, cutting, hissing tone. I try to put a face to the voice, but in my head, there is only the tangled sing-song of the many French voices at the manor house. Impossible to filter out a single voice. Everything sounds strange and threatening. My head is pounding.

One of the henchmen is working on my hands. Out of the corner of my eye, I see a long rope in his hand. *They're going to hang me.* I close my eyes and pray to God to save me from such a miserable death. One last time, I hear the men talking, then they fall silent. Footsteps fade away.

The gag clogs my throat. I try to swallow, but I can't. I choke. I clench my jaws angrily, as if that could force the gag out of my mouth. But it sticks like resin to a tree. What time might it be? I blink again. The sun must have risen by now, and it will be bright enough for the first servants at the manor house to begin their day. *And still dark enough for the hunters of the woods, who hungrily roam the thicket in search of prey.* A cold shiver runs through me. Lying alone in the forest at this time of day, without weapons and with my hands tied behind my back, is not something anyone in their right mind would do.

I struggle to my feet. My stomach and face hurt, but I eventually stand up. I stagger forward until I feel a tug on my hands. As I turn round, my gaze follows the rope stretching from my hands to one of the branches on the tree in front of me. *They tied me up like an animal. Well, at least it's better than dangling from a branch with my head in a noose, but I have to get away from here as quickly as possible. Where am I, anyway?*

Between the trees, I recognise the outline of the manor. The rays of the rising sun show me the way there, but I can't follow them. I tug at the rope, but it won't tear or loosen. The branch is thicker than Ulfgar's upper arm. Maybe it would break if I hung onto the rope, but my hands are tied so tightly together that I will never get them in front of my body. *I'm more likely to dislocate both shoulders than have the branch give way under my weight. If only I had a knife! Why did I take off my belt with the scramasax last night before going to sleep?*

I look at the knot of the rope then feverishly search the ground around me. Only grass, herbs, moss and a few early blossoms as far as I can see. I stumble around the tree, hoping to find something somewhere. The rope winds up so far that I am barely three feet from the tree trunk. Nothing. I groan with disappointment and exhaustion as I walk back in the other direction to unwind the rope. *Will the three come back? Tonight, so the cowards can continue to hide their faces in the darkness? If I get hold of one of them during the day, then... But I have to get out of here first. There must be something I can use to cut this wretched rope. Anything. A sharp stone, animal bones, maybe the sharp edge of a tree stump. Anything.*

Under one of the bushes, I spy something grey – a stone! Not very sharp, but maybe it will do. I rush forward, but about two steps before I reach it, the rope tightens and pulls my hands up. I keep moving slowly as my arms go up and my shoulders press forward. One more step. I lean against the rope, stretching my foot out as far as I can. An ell from the stone, my toes tap into emptiness. I twist and turn, trying to close the gap between me and the stone in every possible position. My shoulders grind softly, my forehead is drenched in sweat, I pull hard through my nose to fill my lungs. The gag makes breathing a torture. Another hand span, a finger length. There! My toe touches the stone. Groaning, I stretch a little more, trying to ignore the pain in my shoulders. Slowly, I place my toe on the stone and try to pull it towards me. I slip off. The stone rocks back to its original position. I try again and again. I lift the stone a little, but just as I am about to tip it towards me, I lose my balance. With a loud crack in my left shoulder, I crash to the ground, closing my eyes just in time before my face lands in a pile of acorn caps.

Shaking my head, I struggle to my feet one more time. *A stick. I need a long stick.* Once more, I walk around the tree. With the twigs of the small bushes near me, the most I can do is knock away a pebble. My gaze switches between the rope, the stone and the surroundings of the tree. With a loud grunt,

I kick the trunk with all my might. Once, twice. I gasp, turn my back to the trunk and slide down it. The gnarled bark scrapes along my back. *The bark!* I jump up, pull the rope tight and rub it in quick movements over a particularly hard part of the bark. *It will take a while, but it might work.* I rub and rub, but all I achieve is a few mossy greenish patches on the rope. Not the slightest tear in the fibres. I tug the rope back and forth faster and faster. Nothing. It just won't break.

Screaming, I rub the rope over the gag in my mouth as if I could bite through it. The rope holds, and there is nothing I can do about it. I lean against the tree and sink down, exhausted and sobbing.

In my dreams, I see Godgifu before me. She waves at me, calls my name, runs towards me with her arms outstretched. I hold my arms out towards her and embrace her. But I feel only the warmth of my own body and the beating of my own heart. My arms hold the air in front of my chest, not the tender, soft body of my sweet young wife who had to die because of me. Godgifu's image fades until she disappears completely in the mist that spreads over the ground she had just walked across. Slowly, the mist lifts, but there is nothing to see except trees and bushes. I hear birds chirping softly. They greet the morning sun, whose rays fall here and there through the dense canopy of treetops.

In the distance, a few branches rustle and crack.

I startle, look around and listen. I hear faint footsteps. Someone is approaching. *Or something.* I'm shaking. It's either several or something big and strong. I circle the tree and try to locate the sounds. In my mind, I go through all the animals in the forest whose size would match the sound of the footsteps.

Maybe it's not an animal at all. Maybe it's people approaching, robbers perhaps. But what would they take from me? I have nothing of value to them. A hunter possibly? He could cut me loose. Or it could be the Frenchmen from this morning – if they dare do it, now that it's light and I could recognise their faces. But what danger is there for them? I don't even know if I'll ever get out of this alive. And even if I did, who would believe me at the manor house? One Englishman against three Frenchmen. I wonder if the weapons practice has begun yet. What will Thibault think of me if I do not show up? Will he send for me? Has anyone even noticed that I was not in the great hall this morning? Does anyone care? Would they come looking for me? Why go to so much trouble for an Englishman? There are enough of them, after all.

The steps get louder. They seem to be aimed in one direction, unlike those of a wild animal wandering between trees and bushes in search of food.

Maybe they are looking for me. Or they know exactly where I am because they tied me up there themselves this morning.

I clench my hands into fists and watch the direction from which whatever it may be is moving towards me. Someone shouts. I listen up. My three tormentors would hardly roam the woods roaring. I stand in front of the tree and listen.

Someone is calling my name!

As loud as I can with the gag in my mouth, I call back. It is more a muffled hum than a shout, but it's the best I can do. Now, I hear the voice clearly. An English voice. I scream at the top of my lungs.

What if they don't hear me? If they walk past me? I start to sweat. *This must not happen.*

I scream until my dry throat burns painfully.

Suddenly, there is a loud crack to the side. A French warrior is coming towards me. He shouts something, approaches and draws his sword. I stare at the blade and back away.

He will kill me. I shake my head. *No. No. No!*

He is only twenty paces away, talking to me. He knows my name.

I press myself against the tree, although I know it is useless. *He will thrust the sword into the trunk and skewer me like a fish for roasting.* I feel sick. My legs give way. I slide down the trunk. Someone catches me before I fall. I blink and look into the Frenchman's face. *Has he already put the sword through my belly?* I feel a dull pain there, but that's all. *Maybe I'm dying right now. Or am I already dead?*

"Oswulf! Praise the Lord that we have found you!"

I struggle to lift my head. Two faces appear behind the Frenchman. He leans me against the tree and pulls out my gag. My jaws clench. My chewing muscles ache. I shift my numbed lower jaw sideways.

Someone pushes me forward and grabs the rope around my hands. A cut. The shackles loosen. I breathe a sigh of relief, move my arms stiffly forward and rub my sore wrists. "Thank you," I croak, look up and see my saviour. Cenhelm.

He puts the knife back on his belt and hands me a water pouch. "Who did this, Oswulf?"

The cool water runs down my parched throat like a downpour on a dry riverbed. Only after several large gulps do I put it down. "Three men snatched me from the great hall before dawn and brought me here."

"Did you know them?"

"They were wearing hooded cloaks. It was still dark."

"So you don't know who did it?"

"One of them spoke French."

Cenhelm exchanges a glance with his two companions.

The man next to me helps me up. My whole upper body hurts, but I try to stand as straight as possible and keep my posture.

"Come," says Cenhelm. "We will take you back. Hild will tend to your wounds."

I rub my moustache. A few reddish-brown crumbs fall onto my hand. "How did you know I didn't just flee? I could have run away after all."

Cenhelm tilts his head. "Without your weapon belt, most of your clothing and on foot? It seems to me they did more harm to you than what I can see on the outside. Anyway, the master of arms insisted on it."

"Thibault?"

Cenhelm nods. "The fact that you did not arrive on time at the battleground seemed to worry him. He immediately sent two men to me so that we could go in search of you."

"How did you know I was here?"

Cenhelm taps his nose. "Old Cenhelm is a pretty good tracker, Oswulf. So far, no animal I've tracked has escaped me."

I frown and look at him. "Will they do it again, Cenhelm?"

He presses his lips together.

"No one at the manor house will do anything about it, will they?"

A thick lump forms in my throat, as if I have a gag in my mouth again.

"You should be prepared for anything. Whoever assaults a man in the dark, beats him up in the woods and leaves him to the wolves is capable of anything. Even of doing it again. Be on your guard, Oswulf!"

No one pays attention to us as we walk through the village towards the manor. The people have seen injured men all too often in recent years. They have stopped taking notice of it.

At the manor, Cenhelm sends our French companions to Thibault and Hild to let them know that we have returned. Then he beckons me to the herb hut where Hild once saved my father from certain death.

How strange it will be to be in the room that Father, Ulfgar and I left so full of hope, believing that the English would win over the French. Back then...

"Go on!" Cenhelm pushes me through the door.

The pots and pans still adorn the shelves of the small room. In front of me are the bed where my father fought for his life and the stool where Lady Edeva kept vigil. Weighed down by my memories, I enter slowly.

Cenhelm points to the bed. "Sit down there!"

Obediently I follow his command and lower myself onto the wide wooden frame.

"Hild will be with you in a moment," Cenhelm says and opens the door. "I'll get you some food and a cup of ale. You need it."

He closes the door.

Silence surrounds me. I look at my wrists. Deep rope burns run across the scraped skin. *They'll pay for this, those nipingas. But how do I find out who the three were who dragged me into the woods?* I close my eyes and try to remember our arrival in the woods, to hear once more the voice of the man I assume to be the leader. *Most French, and many English too, were not pleased when I came here, but is this a reason to kill me?* I laugh briefly. *What are you thinking, Oswulf? People have been killed for lesser reasons. Because their rulers wanted it that way. Because they were unlucky enough to be at the bottom of the wheel of fortune.*

I shake my head and have to smile at my own stupidity. A soft creaking noise makes me jump up. The door opens and in comes... I blink several times, but what I see is not a delusion of my mind. In the doorway, there is not the delicate and small figure of Hild the healer, but a much larger outline. My visitor turns around and speaks to someone. Two curious faces appear in the doorway, but quickly disappear again to talk excitedly in French outside. My visitor nods and closes the door. I am alone again.

How does Roul know I'm here? Does he have anything to do with all this? Did the leader send him here to see how I was doing? What condition I am in? Who told them that I survived? They must have either watched us arrive at the manor or heard from Cenhelm's companions that the troublesome Englishman was found alive in the woods. They will probably think of a better hiding place for me next time so that even Cenhelm won't be able to track me down.

Wondering about who would have reason enough to get rid of me, I come up with quite a number of nameless Frenchmen who are hostile to me. But why should they go to the trouble of snatching me away from the manor at night, instead of just killing me right here? Lord Geoffrey runs this manor house with all the severity for which the French are notorious. One dead Englishman more or less would hardly cause an outcry, let alone a retaliation.

Who would cry out for retribution anyway if something happened to me? My father is dead, and whoever was not killed with him in Ledlinghe now lives in another French manor house far away from here. Should my younger siblings perhaps demand justice for me? If they ever find out that something has happened to their brother.

The door creaks again, and once more, there are three visitors, but this time, they enter to take a closer look at me. Hild the healer, still as delicate and fragile as she was almost four years ago, draws in an audible breath when she sees me.

"Dryhten min! If I didn't know better, I'd say you were involved in a melee." She pulls the stool up to the bed and sits down. "Let me see."

Behind her, Thibault and Frederic the seneschal enter the small hut. Thibault looks at me anxiously. Frederic frowns. In a soft voice and looking at me, he speaks to Thibault. He too seems surprised at my condition. Meanwhile, Hild examines my nose as well as the wounds on my face, hands and the rest of my body.

Thibault and Frederic seem to have seen enough. They disappear through the door. Outside, I hear another voice speaking in French. After a few scraps of words, the door opens and Walchelin comes in. When he sees me, he raises an eyebrow. "Sire Geoffrey was not pleased that you did not turn up for your weapons lesson."

"Surely you don't expect me to beg his forgiveness."

"Where have you been?"

"Did Cenhelm not tell you?"

"I asked *you*, Oswulf, not Cenhelm."

I growl. *Always ready to command, those Frenchmen.* "Three men dragged me away early in the morning, beat me up and tied me to a tree."

"Did you recognise them?"

"No. It was too dark. But one of them, probably their leader, spoke French."

"Do you know why they did that?"

"No."

"You've only been here a little over a month, Oswulf. Sire Geoffrey is not known for his generosity. He offers you his hospitality because his master of arms asked him to. He expects you to fulfil your part of the bargain, too. You must prove that there is a good reason why you, of all people, teach the squires how to fight. Not showing up for the weapons practice without excuse is something Sire Geoffrey will not tolerate in the long run."

I jump up. "It wasn't my decision to get tied up in the woods!"

"Sit down and hold still!" Hild pushes me back onto the bed. She picks up the cloth she had started to put around my wrist and continues her work.

"Do you have any idea who it may have been?"

"Dryhten min, why are you asking me all this? Even if I recognised the men or knew why they did it, what difference would it make? Do you want to put them on trial for snatching an Englishman from a manor house? What's all this for, Walchelin? You act as if I am the most important man on the manor, the one whose health and wholeness lies at everyone's heart and who must be guarded and protected like a relic. This is ridiculous. To you, I am just a servant, one of many whose loss is easy to bear and for whom you can quickly find a replacement. Leave me in peace. I'll be on time for the next weapons practice. And if not, do not send out people to search for me again. Thibault will be fine without me, just as he was a month ago."

I hang my head. *First, they despise me and suddenly, everyone is concerned about my welfare.*

After a long silence, Walchelin clears his throat. "You disappoint me, Oswulf. I had expected more sense of honour from the son of a ðegn."

I stare at the floor so as not to have to look into Walchelin's face. The door creaks softly and closes. Walchelin is gone.

"The master of arms and the wealhstod are well disposed towards you, Oswulf," Hild murmurs as she gathers her remedies. "You should be kinder to them."

"I know." I shake my head in disbelief. *Why couldn't I keep my big mouth shut?* "They dragged me away like cattle for slaughter and tied me up. It's so... so shameful."

"There were three of them, Oswulf. You were alone and unarmed. Do not forget this!"

I look Hild in the eye. *Ledlinghe is burning. My wife is dead. My parents, my sisters too. They have captured my siblings and me and distributed us to their manors as servants.* "No, I do not forget. Nothing the French did to me I will ever forget."

"Don't do anything you will regret later, Oswulf. You got off lightly. Next time, it might be different." The herb woman puts her hand on my arm and leans towards me. "Use the trust of the two Frenchmen. Lord Geoffrey respects them greatly. It would be foolish of you to jeopardise their protection for the sake of a rash revenge. Be careful, Oswulf, and act wisely!"

"I will, Hild."

She empties the bowl outside and places it back on one of the shelves. I look at the poultice around my wrists, feel over my face. The wounds burn, but it's nothing I can't bear. In a few days, only the uneasy feeling in my stomach will remind me of the wounds.

"Thank you for everything you've done, Hild."

"I'm glad nothing worse has happened to you." And yet, she frowns.

I want to leave, but something is holding me back. Hild bites her lower lip as if she wants to say something but doesn't dare. My heart is pounding. I awkwardly wipe my hands on my tunic.

"Your father..." Hild begins.

No need to finish the sentence. Our faces speak volumes.

"Ulfgar?" Her question is just a breath of wind.

A word from the leader. A thrust with the spear. A gurgling sound. Ulfgar's heavy body collapses.

I shake my head. Hild nods silently. She must have expected the answer.

The door opens. Cenhelm appears with a cup of ale and a piece of bread in his hand. "Forgive me for coming only now. One of our messengers has arrived. I had to take care of him first as he brings important tidings for Lord Geoffrey. Here, drink!" He holds out the cup to me. "I see Hild has already finished her work. Perhaps you should come with me to the great hall then. There is much to discuss."

I hastily drink a few sips, bite into the piece of coarse bread and shuffle after Cenhelm. *Why should I attend a gathering of the barons when I can hardly understand a word of it anyway. Or is it about this morning's incident? Why do they make such a fuss about it? Why do they want to know everything in detail?*

Although there is no fire burning in the great hall, it feels comfortably warm against the fresh wind outside, which ruffles the young spring green of the trees and bushes. The dark wooden beams all but swallow the faint light that falls through the narrow openings under the roof. In the dim hall, tables and benches have been prepared, as if waiting to be set for the next meal. Two candles burn on the table around which Lord Geoffrey and his vassals sit. Some turn their heads towards us as we approach.

I hastily swallow the last piece of bread and empty the cup. Cenhelm directs me to a bench on the side. While the Frenchmen watch with suspicious glances, I sit down, put the cup on the table and turn to them in silence. I don't want them to think that I'm afraid of them and can't withstand their gaze.

Some of them have their backs turned to me, and others are hidden behind those in the front, so I cannot see all of their faces. Instead, I look at their hair as if I were determining trees by their shape and their leaves. The liege lord, Lord Geoffrey, sits at the head of the table to keep an eye on all the men. With his fair reddish-blonde hair, he shines like a torch in the night, even in this semi-darkness. To his right, at the very head of the long side of the table, blazes the wild hair of Hugues de Borre, his most trusted vassal, as Walchelin explained to me. Opposite Hugues, to the left of Lord Geoffrey, I recognise, even without looking at the hair, the slender figure of the seneschal, Frederic de Lisieues. On the other side of the table, the dark brown curls of the master of arms, Thibault, and the dark blonde hair of the wealhstod almost disappear in the faint light. The other men also seem familiar, albeit I don't deal with them on a daily basis. All of their singsong still sounds the same to me, yet I know that one of them has a lisp, another one a limp and a third has numerous scars on his face. So I may not immediately remember their names, but I know who I am dealing with.

What they say, however, remains a mystery to me. Their language makes my hair stand on end, but sooner or later I will have to learn it.

Poor Cenric. It is difficult for me to keep a straight face when he says sentences in French. How powerful and masculine English sounds compared to the unbearable twang and puckered-up sounds of that foreign language!

I listen to this very singsong at the table nearby, where lips are eagerly pursed and the already wild hair is tousled. To my surprise, I actually pick up some words from the conversation. The men look tense, even worried. Admittedly, that is often the case with the French. Except, perhaps, for the seneschal, the only one who occasionally puts on a friendly face. Hugues de Borre always looks like a dog whose bone has been taken away. He watches everything and everyone with his mean little eyes as if he suspects a danger to himself and the French rule everywhere. *Surely, he makes no exception with me.*

It becomes quiet in the hall. Walchelin stands up and beckons to me. "Come here, Oswulf. I have something to tell you."

Apprehensively, I rise and walk over to him. All eyes follow me as if to make sure that I'm not hiding a knife somewhere with which I will spring on them as soon as I am close enough. Walchelin tells me to stand at the end of the table, exactly opposite Lord Geoffrey, who is eyeing me warily with folded hands and a piercing gaze.

"One of our messengers returned today," says Walchelin. "He reports disturbing events in the southeast of the country. There are rumours of a possible Norse invasion. A growing number of Danish warriors and traders have been observed in the ports."

"What does this have to do with me?"

"In light of these tidings, your disappearance this morning seems suspicious to some members of the manor house."

"What am I suspected of?"

"You wanted to ambush the messenger and prevent him from reaching the manor house."

"Me? How was I to know that a messenger was on his way? You also seem to forget that three men dragged me out of the great hall this morning."

"Everyone knew that we were waiting for a messenger to return."

"Perhaps you French did. I, for one, knew nothing about it!"

"Some of us beg to differ. They think that even the English at the manor house were aware that the messenger would return at some point. After all, he had been away for several weeks."

"Oh, and I probably realised from the flight of the birds that today would be the day the messenger reached the manor. Is that what you want to say?"

Walchelin raises his hands apologetically. "I am only passing on what I have been instructed to pass on to you."

If I didn't know better, I'd say they're all drunk and don't know what they're talking about. *They're actually accusing me of working against them and trying to kill the messenger so they wouldn't get the news?* "Why would I do that?"

"Because you think you might benefit from it."

"You cannot be serious." I look at Lord Geoffrey. "Three of your men drag me from my sleeping place at night, punch me in the face and belly and tie me to a tree in the woods. If Cenhelm hadn't found me, I'd still be lying there, if the wolves hadn't devoured me by now."

Walchelin translates my words to Lord Geoffrey. The liege lord does not take his eyes off me. His advisors look alternately at the wealhstod, Lord Geoffrey and me. They exchange a few words before Walchelin takes a deep breath and turns to me again. "Can you prove it?"

"Can I prove what?"

"That you were taken away against your will."

"Why don't you ask Cenhelm? The tracks make it quite obvious that I didn't go into the woods by myself."

"The tracks only tell us that you were not alone. How do we know you were led away by force? Maybe you and your companions just wanted to set some traps. Or to ambush the messenger."

I'm beginning to sweat, feeling like a defendant before judge and jury, proven guilty for something he didn't do and for which he will hang. "Just look at me! They beat me. Ask the others who were also sleeping in the great hall when the three men came for me. There must be someone who noticed. And tell me, Walchelin, would you go into the woods without your weapon belt? I don't think so, but I wasn't wearing mine when Cenhelm found me. It was still lying in the great hall."

Walchelin strokes his chin. Hugues de Borre presses him with words. He is probably dying to know how the fish in the net is still trying to jump back into the water. After a short exchange of words, the wealhstod looks at me almost pityingly. "Perhaps your companions didn't at first know what you were up to. When you told them you were going to intercept the messenger, they didn't agree. You threatened them. A fight broke out. The other three shackled you, took off your weapon belt and tied you to the tree because they were afraid of being seen with you when they returned to the manor."

"This is simply not true! You want to accuse me of a deed I did not commit. Because you are afraid that there is a traitor amongst you. One of the men who kidnapped me spoke French. It was one of you. Perhaps he got rid of me because *he* wanted to ambush the messenger and have the suspicion fall on me. He didn't catch the messenger, but the rest worked out well for him. You suspect me because I'm English. Who would I go into the woods with? I've only been at the manor house for a month. The French avoid me because I am English, and many Englishmen avoid me because I teach your sons to wield weapons. Who would willingly go into the woods with me before sunrise? Have you also considered why we would need four men to intercept one single messenger? Perhaps you Frenchmen need a whole army for that. We Englishmen need only one man who knows how to use a bow. One well-aimed shot and the messenger will never reach his destination alive. Your messenger, however, has reached the manor house unharmed and brought you the news you have so eagerly awaited. How would I benefit from killing him? I did not sell myself to you to save my life and that of my siblings just to risk it recklessly a month later. I would rather have died with honour in Ledlinghe." Exhausted and despairing, I hang my head with a sigh. "But what do you know about honour?"

It is quiet for a while. *What are they going to do to me now? Can they execute me just like that? Without a trial? Who would want to defend me? I have no one here to stand by my side. No father to protect me. No Ulfgar to fight with me against the enemy.*

The memories hurt. I clench my teeth and close my eyes. A brief murmur then someone puts a warm hand on my shoulder. *Thibault.*

The others fall silent as he begins to speak. They eye me with disdain, but at least Thibault's words stop them from cutting my throat here and now. Even Lord Geoffrey nods in agreement before rising and leaving the room with his advisors.

Walchelin lingers on, taking a breath. "You've done well, Oswulf."

"What do you mean? What will happen to me now?"

"Don't worry, Oswulf," says the wealhstod. "Our master of arms is not so quick to surrender his – pardon my expression! – booty. But if you continue to make such speeches, you will not remain his helper for long."

A tremor goes through my body. *Of course. I was too bold. How often did father stop me when my tongue got the better of me!* "Forgive me, I didn't mean to—"

"We have nothing to forgive, Oswulf. Your English tongue is almost as sharp as the blade of your scramasax. If you learn to wield it like this in our language, fortune may favour you for a long time to come."

꩜

CENHELM AND THIBAULT have assured me that they will keep an eye on me, but the previous day has left its shadow on my soul. What a night! It will be a while before I can sleep peacefully again. I sit up and rub my face. *Wa la wa! My nose still hurts from the blow.*

With the scramasax, I cut through the dried poultices that Hild tied around my wrists yesterday and peel them off. I put the short sword back in the weapon belt – which I had left on overnight as a precaution – and leave the great hall.

In the yard outside the manor house, a servant harnesses an ox to a small cart, which two women load with buckets.

They are about to set off for the river to fetch water for cooking and for the animals. Luckily enough, the Fors Bekkr meanders not far from the palisade fence along the north and west sides of the manor house. Cenhelm said the current is not too strong at this time of year unless there has been a lot of rain or a late thaw. In the winter, the river can be treacherous, and sometimes in the summer, only a small trickle remains. Then they have to fetch the water from further away. Either northeast, at the edge of the woods, where the river flows a little more quietly, or further downstream in the village, south of the Benedictine monastery, where they use ropes to lower the buckets from the big bridge and scoop water.

A bunch of children comes towards me. They carry baskets filled with eggs and cluck at least as excitedly as the chickens from whose nests they have taken them.

Muttering indignantly, someone is cleaning his shoes near the stables. As I approach, that someone straightens up, his lower jaw grimly thrust forward so that his teeth protrude.

Stígandr. My heart beats faster, as I speed up without thinking about it. How I would love to ram my scramasax into his belly right now! *Will he forever haunt me wherever I go?*

The oxcart pulls away, accompanied by a Norse curse. As Stígandr looks up, his angry face changes to the goat grin that makes my blood boil.

I hesitate, speechless, even stunned. Only with difficulty do I resist the temptation to touch him to see if he is actually made of flesh and not just a figment of my tired and frightened mind. "You!"

The goat grin is as if frozen. "Well, look at that! Young Osfriðson! We haven't seen each other for a long time."

"I wish it had stayed that way."

"Now, now, is that how you greet an old friend?"

"You're not a friend anymore. You were once, before you started betraying me and everyone else. You're a rascal and a traitor! You knew the French were on their way to Ledlinghe. You knew it all along."

"I know a lot of things you don't know. You learn a lot when you travel."

"All these years, you have worked as a spy for our foe. Before the battle at Fuleforde, at Stanfordbrycge and then Ledlinghe. You spied on my father and his men and reported all to our enemies. Because of you, many good men had to die. And their families with them."

"Not everyone wants to live on the dark side of life just because they were not born, like you, into a rich, noble family. There are people who are happy to use my services and pay well for them."

"You're a traitor. You have betrayed the English in whose land you live. You have delivered my people to the axes of the Norþmenn and the spears of the French."

"That's life. Some win, some lose. Some are up, some are down. As the son of a nobleman, you ought to know that. After all, enough underlings and slaves worked for you while you collected taxes or administered justice for the king at your manor house. Tell me honestly, where would you rather be, at the top or the bottom?"

He looks around casually. "By the way, I hear you're working for the French now, too. How does it feel for an Englishman to join the enemy ranks? The very men who killed your family and friends? What would your father say if he saw you teaching the sons of his enemies how an Englishman fights? What do you think?"

"I am not a traitor. I did not sell my country to the enemy for money, as you did. I saved the lives of my brothers and sister by putting mine into the hands of the French. It was out of desperation and compassion, not greed, which is what made and still makes you do it."

"I commend you for your high principles, Osfriðson, and surely, you reproach yourself for having decided to join the French. Your English pride groans and moans like a wounded animal lying on the ground, writhing in agony. Your honour lies battered beside it." He grabs my shoulder and leans towards me. "But look at you! You're still alive. Well, you may have a few scratches right now, but you're alive! You've made it! You have defeated the enemy. You are here at this manor house, amidst all these Frenchmen, and you can go on fighting so that your father and your people will look upon you with pride. You can uphold the honour of the ðegnes, the huscarles, by becoming one yourself. You may not be called a huscarl, but you will show the French how an Englishman deals with defeat, he gets back up, holds his head high and fights on. That's how we must do it, Oswulf! So that Englaland's honour and glory may live on."

Stígandr stands in front of me with his eyes wide open, his lower jaw thrust forward and his fist clenched.

He has clearly gone insane. He is completely mad. First, he accuses me of stabbing my people in the back, and then he wants me to go on fighting to become a huscarl under the French? I knock his hand off my shoulder. "Don't touch me, you two-faced Loki! Just because you do business with the enemy and let them pay you doesn't mean others want to do the same. I am still alive because I wanted to save my siblings. I am here for an honourable reason, unlike you. After your uncle's betrayal, my father always said, 'Never trust a Viking!' When I finally realised, in Richale, what you had been up to since Fuleforde, I knew why he kept repeating those words. So, I will keep an eye on you until I know what you're plotting. And then I will not spare you, Stígandr. You will finally pay for all you have done to me and the English."

Stígandr gives a brief laugh. "Do you still believe that with your stubborn behaviour, King Harold will rise from the dead to save your glorious Englaland? Your king is dead, as are most of your countrymen who thought they could stand in the way of Englaland's future. Your new ruler is French, and you will have to bow to him whether you like it or not. The sooner you realise that, the better for you. Otherwise, you'll be wishing that the French had burnt you and the remnants of Ledlinghe to the ground like the rest of your wretched homeland."

The death scream of my beloved wife echoes in my ears as the Frenchman rams his sword into her belly. Images of the twisted, mutilated bodies of my parents and sisters, stained all over with blood, whirl before my eyes. A shiver freezes my skin.

"You'd better get on their good side. It may be your last chance to escape your fate." In a futile attempt to adjust his tunic and assume a dignified posture, Stígandr shakes his hunched shoulders as his gaze wanders off. "Now if you will excuse me. My services are needed elsewhere." He turns and leaves.

"Hi sculon gan libbende on helle!" I call after him half-heartedly. "They are cruel and bloodthirsty beasts," I say more to myself as I try to suppress the last memories.

"Ne ealle," a quiet voice says behind me.

I laugh briefly. "Ic ne cnawe—" The sentence gets stuck in my throat. Turning round, I look into Thibault's light brown eyes. "Ana hwa...?" I breathe and stare at him. "You speak English?"

The master of arms innocently raises his shoulders and eyebrows. "It never hurts to learn the language of the people you deal with every day."

Thibault understands my language. All the weeks I've been at the manor in Wilburgfos, he has understood every word I've let out in my mother tongue within earshot. I don't know whether to laugh or cry. The ground under my feet seems to be shaking, but I am still standing. *Surely, he would have told his liege lord long ago if my words had given him cause for concern. Or has he perhaps already done so? Does my life more than ever hang by a thread that Thibault can cut at any moment with a single word? Would he do so? He, of all people, who wanted Lord Geoffrey's men to spare me so that I would work for him? Would he use his power over me and my life to his advantage?*

The master of arms grins mischievously. "Have you lost your tongue, Oswulf? Or did you really think that all people outside Englaland are ignorant fools?"

Yes, I probably thought that. And the way the French behaved in Englaland, I certainly had a reason for it. "Why have you never spoken English to me, if you know the language?"

"As you can imagine, Sire Geoffrey is reluctant to have his men speak English unless it is to give short orders to the English servants. Many French do not speak your language anyway, not even a few words, and they do not want to learn the language. So, if I spoke English, no one would understand me except you and your countrymen. That would be highly suspicious, of course, so I have Walchelin translate if any Frenchmen are listening."

"You understood everything I've ever said."

"Mm-hm."

"Does Sire Geoffrey know about this?"

"You mean did I tell him what you said?"

"Have you?"

"What do you think?"

"You're not answering my question. It's not about what I think, it's whether you did it."

"Would I have had reason to?"

"So, you didn't understand everything after all?"

He's playing with me. Like a cat with a mouse. He knows he has me in his grip and is having a little fun with me.

"Do you think Sire Geoffrey must know everything you say?"

So he did understand everything! Wa me! If only I'd been more careful with what I've said! At this manor house, there are not only English ears to beware of but also French ears listening to my conversations.

"Do you believe that, Oswulf?"

I shrug my shoulders.

Thibault laughs. "You overestimate his curiosity about what his servants say about him. Unless you insult the king or conspire against him, he does not care, as long as you do what you are here for. Also, remember that I am responsible for you. Everything you say reflects on me. If you cause trouble, I will be the first whom Sire Geoffrey will hold to account. I insisted on bringing you here. We are in the same boat, so to speak, so be careful what you say, for a boat that capsizes is hard to keep afloat. And we both don't want to drown, do we?"

We're in the same boat. A Frenchman and me. As if it were the most normal thing in the world for us to work together, after all that we have both been through. I nod. "I will choose my words carefully, Thibault. I am already in your debt several times over. I will not disappoint you."

"I am sure of it, Oswulf. Otherwise, you would not have left Ledlinghe alive."

Not left alive? So he could have killed me then and chose not to? I feel sick.

Thibault waves me towards the armoury. "Come and tell me more about what happened yesterday."

Chapter 8

IN THE SUMMER Of THE YEAR Of OUR LORD
1070

Raindrops tap on the roof of the great hall. Thunder rumbles in the distance. Occasionally, a bright light flickers through the openings under the ceiling.

The thunderstorm fades at last, but the air continues to weigh heavily in the great hall. Most of the Frenchmen sit at the tables and pass the time playing board games they brought from their homeland.

The wealhstod sits opposite me and rubs his forehead while he strains to look at the Merelle board.

I stretch my legs, which are stiff from sitting, and wrinkle my nose. The stench of pig dung still clings to my shoes. *If I catch whoever shovelled that stuff into them while I was asleep! The smell will remind me for days to come that I am not wanted on this manor. The things they have tried! Dragged me into the woods, pushed me into the river, stole my scramasax and damaged the weapon stands with it. If it hadn't been for Thibault, I'm sure Lord Geoffrey would have thought of a different punishment for me rather than simply have me mend everything.*

Compared with that, pig dung in my shoes is almost a reward. If only I knew who slipped it in there!

"Are you dreaming of a beautiful woman, Oswulf?" asks Walchelin with raised eyebrows.

"What? No. I was just thinking about something."

"I noticed that. Your turn!" He points to the pieces between us.

There is a rumbling at the front door. "Fiz a putein!"

Thibault and the squires, with whom he had ridden out to go hunting, stagger in. Their clothes cling to their bodies like a wet sack. The youths approach and peel themselves out of their dripping tunics. They look like five puppies thrown into a trough of water. I almost feel sorry even for Roul when I see him like this.

The lisping Frenchman summons two servants, who light a fire and hang up the soaked clothes to dry. A young maidservant brings linen cloths and hands one to Jehan. Her cheeks glow red as her gaze follows his every move while he rubs his wet body dry.

Roul snatches a cloth from her hand. "What are you standing there staring at? Don't you have any work to do in the kitchen?"

Jehan laughs. "I assume naked men are a more pleasing sight than dead animals in the kitchen." Grinning, he beckons the maidservant to rub his back dry.

Roul rolls his eyes. "Those bloody Engleis take every opportunity to avoid working. Pereçous."

Eustace and Eudo giggle and whisper, like on the battleground. Jeannot is stuck in his linen shirt, which clings to him like a second skin. He looks to the older squires for help, but they don't pay any attention.

I walk over to him, grateful that I have a reason to get up from my seat. I hate idling around, even though Roul has just loudly denied that to my people. "I'll help you, Jeannot," I say in French, feeling rather proud that I master the language enough to hold easy conversations with my pupils and Frenchmen like Frederic. Most importantly, however, I understand quite a lot, and it seems to me that some have become considerably more careful about what they say in my presence. They must be afraid that I will overhear their conversation and catch them talking about me or discussing things that are none of my business. *Cenric is a good teacher, that's for sure.*

Jeannot's little face lights up as I grab the sleeves of his linen shirt. "Merci, munsire."

Roul throws the rest of his clothes at the servants and wraps the linen cloth around his hips. "Look, our Engleis should be working as a page rather than on the battleground."

I hand one of the servants Jeannot's tunic and linen shirt. "As long as I don't have to serve you, it would certainly be an honourable job."

Roul looks daggers at me. "You have no business among the Normans. You behave as if you were of the same rank as us."

"I *am* of the same rank as you, Roul. My father was an English nobleman."

He comes two steps closer, his thumbs tucked into the edge of the cloth around his hips and spits out to the side. "Don't you ever dare sully my father's name again by equating him with your father."

"I would never compare my father to yours."

Jeannot has meanwhile thrown the cloth over his back and is walking towards the fire. I sit down again at the table where

Walchelin is waiting for me with pricked ears and raised eyebrows.

"Because you know he can't stand up to the comparison." Roul saunters up to our table. The thunderstorm seems to have made him even grumpier than usual. "But I see you are quite in demand at the manor house. Do we have so few Normans here that we must invite the Engleis to sit at the table with us and pass the time playing games?"

"This Engleis is a worthy opponent, Roul," Walchelin replies. "He plays strategically well, and more often than not, he wins. What do you think? Is he in league with the goddess of fortune?"

Roul snorts. "You must mean with the Devil."

"It is not for you to correct my words, Roul," Walchelin says loudly enough for others to hear. "I mean what I said."

Roul's mouth turns into a thin line. I know from the practice lessons that he doesn't like to be reprimanded, especially not in front of others. He props his hands on the table and looks me in the eye. "One day, your luck will run out, Engleis."

With bulging veins on his neck and temples, he is standing in front of me like a hunting dog that wants to attack the game but is held back by the hunter. I wonder if he is behind the assaults.

"Then I hope that by then, I will have succeeded in making a good fighter out of you."

Roul jumps up. "How dare you? Did you hear this Engleis insult our master of arms? Claims that he could make a fighter out of me! Ha! What am I now, after more than two years' practice as a squire?" He leans towards me again. "Well, tell me! Tell everyone in this hall what you think of our master of arms! What has he made of me in these two years, if not a fighter?"

I wipe the droplets of spit from my face and clear my throat. "You haven't been a squire long, Roul. You still have much to learn. Thibault is a very good weapons master, but even he can't make a warhorse out of a donkey in two years."

Walchelin stifles a grin.

Roul's muscles tense. "You... you..."

I'm getting ready to jump.

A fist thunders on a table.

"Enough!" barks Lord Geoffrey, jumping up. "A Norman has better things to do than prate like a washerwoman. If you have complaints against the Engleis, take them to the master of arms. If not, spare me your whining and howling. Now, get out of my sight!"

Roul bends down to just in front of my face. "Don't mess with a Norman," he whispers. "That's what your king tried to do, and you know who won, don't you, Engleis?"

"Roul?" Walchelin's question makes the young Frenchman look up. "If you do not leave this table immediately, I will have you thrown out. Your behaviour is unworthy of a Norman."

The young man gives me one last venomous look before whirling around, snatching his damp clothes off the wooden trestles on which they lie to dry, and stomping away with long strides. Eustace and Eudo watch him leave and with a side glance towards me, put their heads together and start whispering. Jehan shakes his head, puts his arm around Jeannot and pulls him to the table. He grins as he sits down next to Walchelin.

"It's almost half a year that you've been at the manor house," growls the language master. "Even Roul should have got used to seeing you around here by now."

I move one of the flat pieces along the outer line on the board. "Do you think Roul has anything to do with what happened?"

The wealhstod and Jehan exchange a glance. Sighing, he puts one of his pieces where two lines cross. "No one seems to have observed anything that could help us in this matter."

"I doubt Roul has anything to do with it," says Jehan. "He hates the Engleis and he gets angry easily, but he wouldn't go that far. He doesn't like secrecy. He likes to be the centre of attention. He would rather challenge you to a duel in front of spectators than stab you in the back."

I run my thumb and forefinger over the ends of my moustache and stare at the Merelle board. "So it seems, and the Engleis at the manor house prefer to keep their mouths shut. They'd rather bite their tongues than get in trouble over a stranger by testifying against a Norman. Even if they did see something, they pretend they don't know what you're talking about. Same for the Normans. No one would accuse a fellow countryman of mistreating an Engleis. Life goes on as before, as if nothing had ever happened. May good fortune stand by me!"

Two hands gently squeeze my shoulders. "This is not the Engleis I fought in the last battle."

I listen up. It's as if I hear a second voice – my father's, echoing the words of the master of arms. Turning round, I see my father's kind but challenging gaze reflected in Thibault's face.

"Where is the fighter I got to know and appreciate back then?" asks the master of arms. "Where is the proud son of a ðegn who defends the honour of Englaland and his home village against the overpowering enemy with a burning bucket, if necessary?"

The corner of my mouth twitches upwards. *Strange what survivors of a battle remember for months.*

Thibault sits down and looks at me. "I know it's not easy for you to live at this manor house, Oswulf, and I beg your forgiveness for having put you in this position. But as master of arms and the one in charge of our squires, I would never have forgiven myself if I had not got you out of there alive. Many good men died in those battles, Engleis and Normans, so it is only fair that now and then one should escape with his life, even if it is with the help of the enemy. The times of war are over now. We must work together to bring this country back to where it was before all the battles. Getting along with people like Roul is not easy for us either. You have already earned some respect in the short time you've been here. Many looked down on you because you are Engleis and not much older than our squires. But you have a way with weapons that many here envy, though they would never admit it. You know how to share your gift with our squires. Look at the progress they've made: Eustace, who used to miss opponents with his spear unless they stood directly in front of him, can now hit targets further away with accuracy. Jeannot no longer backs away from the older squires' blows but takes advantage of being smaller and more agile than them to deceive and take them by surprise with nimble movements. Eudo has learned that if you are more disciplined in combat, you can not only defend yourself better, but also with less effort. Roul finally has another serious opponent besides Jehan and has become much more persevering and tough."

The master of arms falls silent. Frowning, Jehan holds out his hands as if begging. "What about me? Haven't I learned anything?"

Sighing, Thibault shrugs his shoulders. "Jehan is Jehan. With Oswulf's help, you could possibly be dubbed well before you are twenty-one years of age."

"You underestimate, Oswulf, what you have achieved so far," says Walchelin. "Have you not noticed that no Norman supported Roul in his accusations? Can you remember the noise they made the day you came to Wilburgfos and we introduced you to them? Look at them now! Not one of them complained about your sitting at the table. For months, no one has pressed the master of arms or Sire Geoffrey to chase you off the manor. Not everyone was on your side at first, and even now, many men still feel a decent reluctance towards you, but they have come to accept that you are here, and above all, they have learned to respect you for what you do. You are reliable, hardworking and carry out all your assignments impeccably. There is nothing we can find fault with."

"Except, perhaps, that you should stop feeling sorry for yourself all the time," Thibault adds. "Remember where you came from and what you do best, and act accordingly!"

∽

"We English must stick together." Stígandr's head seems to disappear between his shoulders as he whispers these words to me behind his hand. His gaze wanders over the Frenchmen who have gathered their horses in the yard to go hunting.

I run my hand down the saddle girth to make sure it fits properly. "That sounds strange coming from a Norþmann who has spent years being paid to betray his English neighbours to their enemies."

"Have you forgotten what the French did to your family and your home village? Now you would have the chance to take revenge on them. I could help you. They trust me. We could destroy them from within."

Revenge.

For a moment, my heart catches fire for this thought. *Revenge for Godgifu, my parents, my siblings. And for Ulfgar.*

Stígandr leans further towards me. "Should their deaths really go unpunished? Can you live with the burden that they died and you didn't even try to retaliate against the French for their deaths? Can you, huh?" He tugs at his chin beard.

Hatred, pain and the desire for vengeance fight in my chest as I watch him, wondering if the Fiend who seduces people does not have the horns and claws of a goat. "I tried, Stígandr. Ulfgar and I fought to the last to avenge them. Should I have thrown away the lives of my younger siblings like an old bone just to satisfy my thirst for revenge? If God had willed it, he would not have protected their lives until the French encircled me and demanded my life in exchange for theirs. I did my duty." I swing the reins over the horse's head and place them over the pommel of the saddle.

Stígandr looks around again and comes so close that we almost touch.

"Aren't you surprised that more and more often, they take you along on their hunting trips? After all that has already happened to you at the manor house, you should be more careful! An accident while hunting can happen quickly – if you know what I mean."

I attach the quiver with the arrows to my weapon belt and slide my bow onto my back. "Why don't you ride along if you care so much about my life?"

Stígandr thrusts his lower jaw forward, looking like a disgruntled goat. "That stubborn Frenchman doesn't want me to go hunting. He says I am a messenger and should see to delivering his messages."

"So you'd like to come along, but Lord Geoffrey has forbidden it?" Inside, I am falling about laughing. If Stígandr's looks could kill, we would now have one rider less amongst the hunters.

But the liege lord climbs into the saddle unconcerned. He couldn't care less what we think of him anyway. He has no interest in his underlings as long as everything at his manor house runs smoothly. Only if things don't go as usual is his interest aroused. Then God have mercy on the one who incurs the liege lord's displeasure! Only recently, he had a maidservant whipped because she tripped and accidentally spilled wine on him.

I lower my head to hide my gloating from Stígandr. "I am sorry for you, Stígandr. Surely you spend enough time in the saddle on your errand rides. You should be grateful for a break."

He snorts discontentedly. "Am I supposed to sit around in the manor house all day long?"

"I don't know. Maybe Lord Geoffrey will send you away again soon with a message." I grab the stirrup and mount. "Do you know where you're riding next yet?"

The expression on Stígandr's face freezes. "Maybe your French friends will tell you on your ride. Unless something unexpected happens to you."

He casts an evil glance at the liege lord and his men, turns round and slinks away like a lurking wolf.

"The French are not my friends," I call after him half aloud.

Unless something unexpected happens to me. The certainty in his voice makes me frown. Does he know something I don't? Am I coming along so they can get me out of the way? How will they do it? All the French nobles will ride with us, even Thibault and also the two oldest squires, Jehan and Roul. Who would harm me when there are so many witnesses? Wouldn't it be easier to overpower me in a smaller group? I should not ride too far away from Thibault or the language master, because if there is anyone at all amongst the French who will protect my life, it will be one of these two. Outwardly, I try to dissemble, but my stomach is tingling. I let my eyes wander over my companions. *Which one of them would want to kill me? Perhaps Stigandr only wanted to unsettle me, for being forbidden from coming along himself. Out of wounded pride. I shouldn't worry about his words. So far, all assaults on me have taken place near the manor house. Nothing has ever happened while we were out on horseback. Until now.* I grit my teeth. *Everything has gone well so far, nothing will happen today either. Why should I worry about something that is beyond my control? Only children and women are afraid of unseen dangers and ghost tales. And if an incident does occur, I still have the bow, my scramasax and a fast, agile horse.*

The hunt goes as expected. As the sun rises above the tree-tops, we pursue an enormous wild boar that searches in vain for a place to hide. My horse gallops through the bushes to-wards the low branches of a tree. I duck, my horse jumps to the side to dodge them. The next moment, something jerks me to the side with such force that my head barely misses one of the branches. The horse whinnies and rears. I squeeze my legs together to stay on, but I fall backwards, saddle and all. A hellish pain shoots through my head and shoulder as I crash to the ground. Everything goes black.

A flapping sound reaches my ears from far away. Some-thing is slapping my cheek. My head is buzzing as if someone had hit it with the blunt end of an axe. Breathing is difficult. I gasp, although I don't remember running.

"Oswulf?" I know this young voice, even though I cannot remember where from. A hand is touching my neck. "He's alive!"

I hear footsteps and excited chatter. *Who are these people? Where am I? What has happened?* I struggle to open at least one eye. Someone is squatting in front of me, but the outline is blurred.

"What happened?" a second young voice asks.

"I don't know," the first voice answers. "The horse reared and he slid off."

"I hope nothing is broken." The second voice approaches my face. "Oswulf? Oswulf! Do you hear me?"

I blink. Something red shimmers in front of me. "Jehan?" I groan.

"Yes, that's right. It's me. You fell off your horse. Are you all right?"

I try to move, but my whole body is heavy as lead. A sharp pain stretches from my shoulder to my neck. My head seems to burst. I feel sick. My stomach clenches. I swallow several times.

"Let me through!" The order comes unmistakably from the master of arms. With well-aimed grips, he checks my head, neck and shoulder. "He's lucky. Nothing seems to be broken. Can you move, Oswulf?"

I struggle to open my second eye and slowly recognise the face of Thibault, who is squatting in front of me. I gather all my strength and try to sit up. Thibault and Jehan put their arms under my head and back to lift my upper body. I groan like an old man as they pull me up gently to a sitting position.

I swallow again, but something wants to get out. Just in time, Thibault pulls his arm away as I turn to the side and throw up.

"Bring a water pouch!" shouts Thibault.

Clumsily, I wipe my mouth with my sleeve. I feel as if a herd of cows has run me over. My skull is pounding. My vision is blurred. I try to sit up straight on my own. My left shoulder throbs. My arm feels like a sack of potatoes. I slowly open and close my fingers. *All good.*

The master of arms hands me the water pouch. "Here, drink! Then we'll see if you can get up and ride."

It takes a while before I can grasp the pouch, which keeps blurring before my eyes. In wise foresight, Thibault has already opened it so that I only have to put my lips to it and drink.

"He will have to ride bareback." Roul approaches with the saddle on his arm. In one hand, he holds the girth. "It looks like someone cut the girth so it would break while he was riding."

"What?" Jehan jumps up and looks at the girth. "Someone wanted Oswulf to have an accident?"

The two of them look at me. While I can see horror in Jehan's face, Roul looks thoughtful.

Thibault stands up and examines the end of the strap. His gaze goes into the distance, where the other riders are continuing the hunt. "We didn't assign the horses until just before the ride. Whoever cut the girth must have been there when we assigned them."

"So, it was someone from the hunting group," Roul says.

Even though I cannot see clearly yet, I notice his wide-open eyes. *Is he really amazed? Could it not have been him who cut the girth? How else would he know to look at the saddle to find the reason for my fall?* I gasp. My head feels like a squishy pumpkin. My legs tremble as I try to straighten them. I struggle to get up onto my knees. My head is spinning. I squeeze my eyes shut and hope to see everything clearly again when I open them. *Where is my horse?* I put one foot on the ground and try to stand, but I can't. I hold out a hand. "I need help. Everything is spinning."

"Wait!" says Jehan. "I'm coming."

While he supports me, I rise bit by bit. My knees are as soft as barley mash, but with one arm on Jehan and the other on the tree, I stand up slowly. How I'm going to get through the ride back to Wilburgfos, I don't know. My horse will have to walk all the way, for anything faster without a saddle will shake all my bones even more. But I'd rather sit and endure the pain with a piece of wood between my teeth than be laid over the horse's back like half a pig being brought to the manor house for cooking.

"You checked the saddles just a short time ago, Oswulf," says Thibault, and I wonder if I hear a slight reproach in his words. "Didn't anything strike you about their condition then?"

I stop short of shaking my head, as it feels like it's tearing my brain apart. "Nothing at all. The girths were all flawless, too."

Thibault grumbles. "One of our own men! Can't we even trust our countrymen anymore? If I find out who did this...!" His thick fingers open and close hastily.

I don't want to think about what punishments he is coming up with for the offender. This time, my unknown foe has obviously gone too far. So far, his attacks have been limited to putting an Englishman in mortal danger or embarrassing him to other people. But deliberately damaging their property, a valuable saddle that is in constant use, is another matter and something the French cannot tolerate. This time, there will be consequences for the wrongdoer, and even if they only punish him for damaging the saddle, at least I will finally know who my secret adversary is. Then the game of hide and seek will be over.

Thibault casts a glance around. "I will find out who cut the girth. If anyone wants to tell me anything about it, they can do so when we have handed Oswulf over to the healer at the manor house. As for the saddle, whoever is found guilty will pay me the price of a new girth and the work on the saddle. Everything else will be decided by Sire Geoffrey."

Everything else? What else is there to discuss that would require a decision from the liege lord?

In the meantime, the language master has also arrived and is leading my horse back on the reins. Fortunately, the animal is unharmed.

While Walchelin listens to Thibault's explanations, Roul leads the horse to a tree stump, which I climb to get onto the horse's back as easily as possible. I slide into place, groaning and moaning, and take the reins from Roul.

His gaze is thoughtful, his nose wrinkled. "I have nothing to do with it."

Should I believe him? For the time being, there is nothing to prove that he has been involved in the incidents against me. Dogs that bark don't bite. Roul is one who likes to bark, but whether he also has the courage to bite, I don't know. "We'll see," I say.

"It wasn't me, do you hear?" A furrow of anger appears on Roul's forehead. His gaze wanders to the other three, who look at him silently. "Why are you looking at me like that? I didn't do it!"

Maybe he really is innocent.

But who else could have done it? Apart from the grooms, only Frenchmen stood around the horses before we rode off. And Stígandr. *Did he not say that something might happen to me? But how could he have cut the girth when I was standing beside him all the time? He must have done it earlier, before the grooms led the saddled horses out of the stables into the yard. Or was it one of the grooms? Did Stígandr promise him a reward for cutting the girth?*

Thibault and Jehan get up on their horses. Roul looks lost amidst the silence of the others. *How helpless he can be!*

"Mount!" orders the master of arms and lifts himself into the saddle. "We must bring Oswulf back to the manor house. We will deal with the culprit later. This time, I will personally see to it that we find him."

❧

IT WAS A long two weeks that I won't miss. I couldn't even hold the wooden practice weapons safely and was still staggering around like a drunk for days after my fall, so Thibault had ordered me to do work that was less dangerous for the bystanders and also for myself. Instead of teaching squires on the battleground, I therefore spent most of my time sitting in the armoury, thoroughly cleaning and mending all its contents. Even the saddles and bridles now shine as if Thibault had just bought them from the saddler. Today, I'm supposed to go back to the work I was brought here for. The bruise on my shoulder has healed enough for me to be able to hold the shield even against a blow from the stronger youths, and my legs obey me again as before.

With impatient steps, I go to the stables to check on the horses we need for today's exercises with the spear. The young bay at the very front greets me with a neigh as I enter. Otherwise, it is quiet in here. Every now and again, there is a snort as one of the horses blows the dust out of its nostrils, or the grinding of their teeth as they chew hay. I look at them one after another, then take two out into the stable aisle and tie them there. As I am about to get the saddles, a rider is just arriving in the yard.

Traitor! I press my lips together, clench my fists and stomp out between the horses towards the rider.

"Oswulf! Good to see you safe and sound!" His voice trembles.

"You won't escape me this time, Stígandr." I pull out my scramasax and speed up.

He lets go of the horse and stumbles in the other direction. "Why are you drawing your sword? What are you up to?"

"Don't try to fool me! You cut the girth that tore during the hunt a fortnight ago. Because of you, I fell off my horse and almost broke my neck."

"What are you talking about?" Stígandr backs off without taking his eyes off me. "I didn't even touch the saddle."

"You liar! I'm going to get you this time."

"You're making a mistake." He runs round a group of pigs and rushes towards the great hall. "Help! Help! Oswulf is trying to kill me!"

A few glances follow us as I continue to hurry after him. He disappears through the entrance to the great hall. I follow him. Stígandr bumps into a servant who falls over, cursing.

I try to avoid her and knock my thigh on the edge of a table. I flinch for a moment before I chase after the Norþmann again.

"Give up! Now, you will pay for your evil machinations!"

Like a rabbit fleeing from a fox, Stígandr tries to shake me off by turning corners through tables and benches. "This Englishman is mad! He wants to kill me! He'll kill you all!"

I reach out to Stígandr. His tunic is only a finger's length away from me. Leaping forward, I grab it and hold on to the fabric for dear life.

Stígandr tumbles backwards. "Help me! Help!"

We stumble and crash to the ground in a bundle. My scramasax slips out of my hand but remains within reach.

"I will kill you!"

I reach out for the short sword. As my fingers close around the hilt, I cry out. A foot presses my hand so hard to the ground that I can neither move it nor pick up the scramasax.

My gaze wanders upwards. Two ice-cold eyes stare at me. *Lord Geoffrey.*

Two Frenchmen grab me by the arms and pull me up.

"He has gone mad!" shouts Stígandr as he stands up and points his finger at me. "He tried to kill me! He is a danger to us all!"

"He cut the girth of the saddle!" I shout at least as loudly as Stígandr. "He wanted me to break my neck. He told me himself before the hunt that something was going to happen to me. He is behind all the attacks on me."

"I didn't cut the girth! That's a lie."

"Then you told one of the grooms to do it for you!"

"I did not!" Stígandr sweeps the dirt off his tunic with both hands before continuing, more confused than angry. "Why would I do that?"

"Why? Why?"

Exactly, why? What would he gain by my being dead? It wouldn't make any difference to him.

"Enough!" The liege lord glares at both of us. "You are here to work, not to fight. If I catch you doing it again, I'll throw you off my manor. Now, get out of here!"

I shake off the arms that still hold me in an iron grip and pick up the scramasax without taking my eyes off Lord Geoffrey. More than his commanding tone, I am annoyed by the way he speaks of *his* manor. He's the one who doesn't belong here. He should be the one thrown out of the manor house. He is the trespasser who caused this dispute in the first place.

Stígandr adjusts his clothes and looks at me suspiciously. I put my scramasax back into its scabbard and turn round.

Thibault is standing in front of me and looking at me with raised eyebrows. "Oswulf, Oswulf. You'll get yourself into a lot of trouble if you go on like this. And me too."

"Forgive me, Thibault, but when I saw Stígandr arrive, I thought—"

"You thought wrong, Oswulf."

"What do you mean by that?"

"I think as far as the girth is concerned, Stígandr is innocent."

"There you go!" exclaims Stígandr. "That's what I've been saying all along, but he won't listen to me."

"Who else would it have been?" I ask.

"I spoke to the grooms. One of them said that someone ordered him to cut the young bay's girth."

"Who?"

"He doesn't know. He wasn't allowed to turn around while the man was talking to him, so he didn't see his face."

"And the other grooms? Didn't they see him?"

"Unfortunately, no. They were busy with the other horses."

"But he might recognise him by his voice." I'm begging with the Lord that he can.

"That will be difficult. The man only whispered the order to him – but the groom still noticed that he sounded strange somehow."

"In what way?"

"The way he spoke sounded unusual. The servant wouldn't answer me any more questions because the man threatened to kill him if he betrayed him. So, we don't even know if he spoke Engleis or Norman. The grooms understand both languages well enough to take orders in them."

I glance at Stígandr, who is listening attentively. Stígandr is Norse, but he speaks English like an Englishman. The groom must mean someone with an unusual pronunciation.

Or with a speech impediment.

"Do you have any idea who it might have been?"

"Not really, and I still don't know why he wanted to kill me," replies Thibault.

I frown. "Kill you? But why? He cut *my* horse's girth, didn't he?"

"The bay is still young and has not often been on a hunt. In fact, *I* wanted to ride him that day, but when I noticed how restless he was, I decided to swap my horse with yours. That way, the bay would still take part in the hunt, but not right at the front, where he could have been easily spooked and passed on his fretfulness to the other horses."

My jaw drops. *Someone wanted to kill the master of arms, the only Frenchman who can protect me. Someone who wants to get rid of me and whose assaults on me personally have all been unsuccessful so far. Who now resorts to other means to achieve his goal at any cost. Who could be so obsessed with his hatred of me, of the English people, that he would even risk the life of a Frenchman for it?*

The master of arms growls. "As long as we only have the testimony of a groom who doesn't dare say anything more, we can't do much. From now on, we must be even more vigilant than before, Oswulf!"

Chapter 9

"Why have they still not found the churl who did this? Had plenty of time, didn't they?" Cenric shakes his head as he incessantly follows the circular line in the sand.

"I doubt they want to find the wrongdoer. Nothing happened to the master of arms, and what the groom told us applies to many men. They could all be guilty." I toss aside the dry twig I've been breaking in half over and over. "It's hopeless."

"What did Lord Geoffrey say?"

"He announced that someone tried to kill the master of arms, that he will not tolerate such conspiracies against his men in his manor house and that the culprit will face severe punishment should anything happen to the master of arms as a result of such actions."

"That's it?" Cenric ruffles his blonde hair and continues marching in a circle. "He's got a madman at the manor who thinks up a new ruse every month to put you in the ground, who has attacked the master of arms, and all he does about it is utter a threat? He's not usually so squeamish. The other day, they caught a beggar stealing a loaf of bread from the kitchen. Had his right hand chopped off. For a single loaf of bread! As if his French friends didn't have enough to eat! They're enjoying themselves while we have to fight for every crumb. But we're still lucky in Wilburgfos. A travelling merchant mentioned a terrible famine further north. Fields and fruit trees have been destroyed, villages burnt. Countless people dead. What the wolves and crows don't eat is rotting in the open air. The sight and the stench are unbearable. The survivors can't dig the graves as fast as people die from disease and weakness." He stops, directs his gaze upwards and folds his hands. "May the Lord spare us this fate!"

Just as he did with my family and Ulfgar.

Cenric puts his hands behind his back and continues on his trail. "We must find a way to prove him guilty. Make him reveal himself."

I laugh briefly. "How are you going to do that? Do you want to force him to surrender and tell Lord Geoffrey the truth?"

Cenric pauses again. "Do you have any idea who it could be?"

"I'm not entirely sure, but I noticed something."

"And that would be?"

"The groom said the voice sounded unfamiliar."

"Means little or nothing."

"Think about what is unusual for a groom, the voice of someone who doesn't often give him orders, who usually has nothing to do with him." I look around to make sure no one is eavesdropping on us. "I questioned the groom again, and do you know what he said?"

"No, what?"

"The voice was not only unfamiliar, it sounded somehow eerie. He didn't understand anything at first because the man was whispering, and his words sounded like the hissing of a snake. The groom already feared that Satan himself wanted to seduce him."

Cenric looks at me with a wrinkled nose.

"Have you ever heard someone whisper with a lisp, Cenric?"

He shrugs his shoulders. "Mostly, folk shout at me instead of whispering."

"There is only one Frenchman who has a lisp, and that is Quentin de Lisieues, Roul's uncle."

❧

THE FIRST AUTUMN winds sweep across the fields. Barns and sheds are filled with the yields of the late harvest. The fruit trees are heavy with pears and apples, which the peasants gather in baskets to store for the winter. Every day, children roam the surrounding woods to fill their baskets with mushrooms and firewood. Or to squeal along with the pigs that they drive through the woods in search of acorns, beechnuts and chestnuts to fatten the animals.

Letting our legs dangle, Jehan, Jeannot and I sit on the bridge that crosses the Fors Bekkr not far from the convent of the Benedictine nuns. At our feet, the hemp-nettle lines with their hooks dance gently in the river, which today looks more like a pond than the raging torrent that so often thunders under the bridge in the rainy autumn weather. We have already caught two tench and an eel.

The thought of a piece of smoked eel in winter makes my mouth water. *One thing is for sure, the French certainly know a thing or two about eating and preparing food, although I still prefer a good ale to their sour grape juice. At the same time, they praise me for the perseverance with which I endure all opposition and difficulties and have made myself useful – some even say indispensable – on the manor. I will never be a huscarl, but I share my knowledge with others as I used to do when I made bows and arrows with the children and taught the older ones how to use weapons. If only Godgifu were still alive... The days of war seem to be over at last. It would be a good time to raise children.*

I wipe the thought away and let my eyes wander into the distance, wondering how my brothers and sister are doing.

Wigstan is about the same age as Jeannot, old enough to be a squire and to bear arms as Father would have wanted him to. But he can probably call himself lucky if he has found a good home and does not have to endure the insults and humiliations that lie behind me. Did they bring my brothers to the same manor house? What about Little Eda, only nine winters old? They probably put her in a convent. There are plenty of English servant girls, after all, but what they really need is young men to make up for the losses on the battlefields. Maybe I'll at least see my brothers again one day.

On the path leading into Wilburgfos from the south, a group of horsemen emerges from the woods. Three armed men in battle dress and two women, sitting on their palfreys with billowing, ankle-length clothes and the hoods of their long cloaks pulled low over their faces. The dark fabric flutters in the wind, whose gusts pull individual dark strands out from under the hood. A single horse trots behind the group with an empty saddle.

"Look there, at the edge of the woods!" I say to the squires.

"Three warriors and two women," says Jehan. "I wonder what brings them to Wilburgfos."

I shrug my shoulders. "Maybe they're just passing through. Or they're taking the girl to the convent."

A cart appears, piled with sacks, boxes, baskets and chests.

I stand up and stroke my moustache thoughtfully. "That's quite a load, they must be on a long journey."

When the group reaches us, the first rider tells the others to stop.

"Messires, dites mei," he says addressing us, "what place is this?"

"You are in Wilburgfos, east of Eoforwic," I reply.

The Frenchman pauses. "Everwic?"

"That's what I meant. Everwic."

I look more closely at the travellers. The men are all wearing armour and carrying swords and shields. Even the carter is armed. The women's cloaks are made of dark blue woollen cloth, which is much finer than what most of the people at the manor house wear.

"We have been riding for more than three days and have come a long and dangerous way. We have been ambushed en route and have lost a man. Can you tell us where we can find a place to rest?"

"Our liege lord's manor is not far upstream from here, munsire." I indicate the direction with my head. Even from here, you can't miss the palisade fence.

I turn back to the rider and glance at the other members of the group. Under one of the hoods, two large eyes regard me. My skin tingles as if a thousand ants were crawling on it. The girl hastily lowers her eyes, but I can still make out that she is smiling. Confused, I try to remember what I actually wanted to say. I look at the group's leader, but my memory is blank.

"Do you think we could stay there for a few nights?"

"Where?"

"In your master's manor."

"I was just about to suggest that."

I cast a sideways glance at the girl, who is secretly watching me from under the hood.

The woman next to her, perhaps the girl's mother, looks at me with a mixture of haughtiness and suspicion. "We would be very much beholden to your liege, munsire, and would offer to repay his kindness, if at all possible."

Her words have an unfamiliar sound. She speaks French, but there is something foreign in the way she speaks that I have not heard before in either Frenchmen or Englishmen. I resist an unexpected urge to lead the troop of riders to the manor. Instead, I stretch out my arm towards it. "Beyond the palisade, you will find the manor house. Cenhelm or Frederic the seneschal will receive you there and take you to Sire Geoffrey."

The Frenchman nods deeply. "Jo vus en mercie, munsire. Aluns!"

The group starts to move. The woman nods at me with an imperious look. I catch a glimpse of the girl, who turns her head away when our eyes meet again. She rides past me, her gaze fixed firmly ahead, without turning round again. I continue to watch her for a long time. Jeannot's voice is lost in the rattle of the cartwheels.

"Huh?" I turn to him.

"Do we keep fishing or should we go and follow them?" asks Jeannot, sitting on the bridge and letting the fishing line hang in the river.

A glance at our buckets tells me that I should not be standing around, staring after travellers, if we want to fill them all today. I sit down on the bridge again and throw out the line. "You're right, Jeannot. The fish won't jump into our buckets on their own." Once more, I look back towards the manor, where the leader of the group is just passing through the gate of the palisade fence. "If Sire Geoffrey takes in the travellers, we will meet them again anyway."

We return to the manor with buckets brim-full. Lady Edeva will be pleased with what we have fished out of the river for the kitchen and the larder – and even more so Father Leofric when he comes from Cattune to Wilburgfos later for the evening mass. He certainly enjoys a good piece of fish, not only on Fridays.

In my mind, I picture the small and gaunt priest with his black robe and dark crown of hair in which the first silvery strands are showing; an Englishman who, even under the French, continues to work on the salvation of the people of Cattune and the surrounding area on holy days, at baptisms and death ceremonies. *Whenever there is a feast.* I sigh. *At times, I have the impression that his desire is more to fill his belly than to take care of his community, making him blind to the suffering and needs of his fellow human beings.*

While Jehan and Jeannot carry the fish to the kitchen, I stow the lines in one of the sheds where tools for harvesting and fieldwork – as well as those for chopping, sawing, hammering and drilling – are also stored.

As I lock the door, Cenric is pulling a handcart full of logs across the yard. He stops and beckons me to him. Patches on his clothes and the tips of his hair are darkened from sweat.

"Wel gesund, leof Cenric," I greet him.

He points to the huge cart near the stables. "Dear visitors from the southeast. Two noble women and three warriors. They must not go to bed hungry tonight, so my father has sent me to chop more wood."

"Are they staying here?"

Cenric shrugs and starts moving again. "Looks like it."

I walk next to him, although I was supposed to stop by the armoury. "How long are they staying?"

"Dunno. Judging by what they had on the cart, they packed enough for a longer stay."

"Mm-hm."

"Did you see them?"

"They passed us by when I was fishing with Jeannot and Jehan on the bridge near the monastery. I wasn't sure whether Lord Geoffrey would agree to feed as many as six strangers."

"You saw them and spoke to them?"

"Yes. Why?"

"Are the women pretty?"

"They were wearing long mantles with big hoods. How am I supposed to tell what they look like?"

"Just wondering."

"I expect they will stay a few days then travel on to wherever their destination is." Something inside me tightens at this thought. I slow my steps until I realise that we are already standing in front of the entrance to the great hall. *What am I doing here anyway?* "I should be in the armoury." I turn round and make my way there.

"Wait, Oswulf!" Cenric looks around, then whispers, "Have you heard from Roul's uncle?"

"As far as I know, he's still with his elder brother at the family manor in Eastengla." *Besides, I couldn't care less where he is, as long as he's not here.* "At the moment, they need him there more than we do in Wilburgfos. He may be an evil person who hates the English, but he's not a bad fighter."

Cenric looks at me for a long time. "Do you think they can win?" he asks quietly, and a glimmer of hope seems to flicker in his eyes.

He doesn't dare say it out loud, but even so, I know who he means when he says 'they'. *Does he really still believe that the English can win against the French? That Hereward, with his English and Danish allies, can once again turn back time to when there were no Frenchmen in this land? For months, the last rebel fighter of our people has been hiding in the marshy area around Elig in Eastengla, making fools of the French. But they are relentlessly pursuing him. Eventually, they will find him and his men in the inhospitable terrain and wipe out the last resistance to the French ruler. It is idle to conjecture about the outcome of the battles. Come what may. Up here, in Wilburgfos, there is nothing we can do about it anyway, and the French are just as powerless in this respect as we English. At least this once.* "We will know soon enough. Surely, Roul's uncle will return to Wilburgfos for Christmas. He's been away for weeks, and I doubt if Hereward and his men can withstand the French army for long. Danes and English fight for their own advantages. Their opponent is an army of highly skilled French riddan led by their king and a single, common goal."

I can see from the look on Cenric's face that he would have liked to hear a different answer, but it is only a matter of time before this attempt at resistance is also stifled by the French. The first months of the year made it clear what King Willelm is capable of in order to break our will for good. Even months later, people are still fleeing from the land up north, having barely escaped with their lives. Injured folks who narrowly escaped the wrath of the French. Starving families who can no longer cultivate their land, pillaged and laid to waste. Sick people, hoping to find a cure for their ailments somewhere. It is impossible to estimate how many fugitives reach the villages and towns south of the burnt areas in spite of hardship and misery, looking for food and work, or hoping for a release from their torments by healers, priests or the Lord himself.

Cenric kicks the sand, puffing a small cloud into the air. "At least there'll be no further assaults on you until then. But what if Roul's uncle comes back? Don't you think he'll keep trying to kill you?"

I shrug my shoulders. "Possibly. I have to be prepared for that." *He will hardly change his attitude towards the English as long as they keep rebelling against his king.*

"Are you sure Stígandr really had nothing to do with it?"

"You can never be sure with Stígandr. He just goes with the tide and bows to whichever lord looks most promising. He serves everyone and no one."

❧

How gracefully she moves. As if she were floating above the ground. Reluctantly, I turn my gaze away from her and thoughtfully scrape along the ash sapling that lies in my hand and will one day become an arrow.

Meanwhile, Cenhelm and his men are noisily hammering the wooden boards over the charred hole in the roof of the armoury. I had noticed the rotten spots in the back part of the roof beams, where the arrows are stored, some time ago.

However, we only found out what state the roof was really in two days ago, when a thunderstorm came. The beams might have withstood the storm longer, but the lightning that struck the rotten wood finished the old building off. It flared up like a torch of dry, thin twigs. We were lucky to put out the fire in time to save at least most of the armoury. The burning beams, however, fell on the arrows below and loosened weapons from their stands, which themselves destroyed even more arrows by tumbling on them.

Now, I am sitting with my pupils in a circle in front of the armoury. Each of us has a sharp knife in his hand. In front of us are string, arrowheads, feathers, glue and a pile of sticks, from which everyone takes what they need to make an arrow. Jeannot is there for the first time and keeps looking over at Jehan and Roul, who, with deft fingers, prepare one arrow after another in rapid succession. Eustace and Eudo are also slowly getting to grips with the individual steps, even though they confer in between about what comes next and how it could be done best and fastest.

For more than eight months now, I have been involved in teaching the squires. Although there were difficulties at first, even the most stubborn among them have realised now that I am neither a danger to them nor should they underestimate me in battle just because I am English. They would never admit it, but I am sure that Eustace, Eudo and especially Roul also appreciate my teaching. For a long time, they haven't complained when the master of arms orders me to continue the exercises in his place.

I take a deep breath. Having been initially defeated and cast out, I finally seem to be finding my place in Wilburgfos, where what I know and can do has been earning me the reputation and honour I have always dreamed of. In battle, I serve my country, even if it is now ruled by someone other than the one I once fought for.

And who do I have to thank for that? I utter a brief hollow laugh. *A Frenchman, of all people. What would Father say to that?*

My gaze wanders across the yard. She's standing next to the herb hut, searching through the contents of her basket, as if to make sure that she really hasn't forgotten any of the herbs she needs. Again and again, she throws me a glance.

She's looking at me. At me?

The corner of my mouth twitches. I watch as she turns again to the plants she has collected.

Solen. A beautiful name. Why does no one know where she and her mother come from and who the relative they are on their way to is? Everything about them is a big secret, or for some reason, they don't want it to reach strangers' ears. Perhaps, they are afraid of another assault in case it becomes known who they really are or where they are going. Would they not have been better off riding along with their armed guards a few weeks ago, who continued the journey northwards with a fully loaded cart? Lord Geoffrey would certainly have been pleased. His mood has worsened with every day that his guests linger. He probably slipped Father Leofric some delicacies from the kitchen to ask the Lord to rid him of the unwelcome company. But Solen and her mother have stayed. For the time being.

Her dark hair falls loosely over her shoulders, almost to her elbow. A shiny brooch flashes out from between the strands, holding her dark green cloak together on her left shoulder. From a distance, I cannot make out exactly what kind of brooch it is, but it has a peculiar shape that I've not seen before.

I glance at the feathers and the wooden stick, still unchanged in my hands, while the squires obediently go about their work and the pile of arrows grows steadily. Once more I look up. A smile is playing around the corners of her mouth. Hastily, she turns to the door and enters the hut to hand the herbs she collected to the two healers. She's bound to become a good healer herself one day, if she—

Why am I staring at her all the time? Father Leofric is right. Women confuse men's minds just by being there. They distract them from the truly important things in life. We need to replace the damaged arrows. What do I care who she is and what becomes of her? Her past and her future are none of my business. I should stop worrying about her. Once Roul's uncle returns from his trip, I will have other things to worry about anyway. Besides, it is not so long ago since Godgifu...

I close my eyes and see her face in front of me. She's smiling and looking at me with her clear eyes. *I cannot simply forget her, pretend she never existed!* With one last look at the closed door of the herb hut, I begin cutting the feathers in the middle.

"What do you think, Oswulf?" asks Roul. "Will my uncle be home soon?"

I frown. His uncle? *As far as I'm concerned, he can be hacked to pieces by the front-line warriors of the rebellious English and end his miserable days as crow food.* "I cannot tell you that, Roul. Until the messenger returns, we will have to wait for news. Why do you ask?" Still frowning, I regard the young man, who has so much changed for the better in the last few months. He is less choleric and condescending towards others and shows more prudence and foresight in battle. He also behaves more moderately towards me. For a long time, he fought against me with words because he failed to defeat me on the battleground. But he made no secret of his dislike for me and my fellow countrymen and always openly said what he thought. *In contrast to many others who secretly wished me into hell behind my back. Most have come to terms with the fact that I came here to help the master of arms and am now highly favoured by many Frenchmen. But some have never forgiven me that my fate was different from theirs.*

"If the rebels in Elig hold out against the Norman army, do you think they will eventually send us there, too?" Roul looks pensive rather than eager to make the journey to Eastengla to fight entrenched and ambushing hordes in the swamp.

"I'm sure the king will find enough skilled men there, Roul. He never goes into battle rashly and without a prospect of certain victory. I know that from experience."

"How long do you think the fight will last down there?" asks Jehan.

My gaze wanders over the questioning faces of the five youths. "If you want a prophecy, you have to ask someone else. I may be Engleis, but I neither throw rune sticks in the air nor do I read the flight of birds to predict the future. Find a witch for that!"

The five laugh. Outwardly I smile, but secretly I wish that I could actually see into the future; that I knew what was in store for me once Quentin has come back. Roul knows nothing of his uncle's conspiracies, at least not from Thibault, me and Cenric. The master of arms and I have agreed to keep him out of it, lest he do some foolish thing that could be dangerous. It's enough that my own life is in danger. We don't want to additionally put a squire's one at risk through careless talk.

❧

WHILE THE PEASANTS are sowing the winter wheat on the bare fields, all the animals for which there is not enough fodder to bring them through the winter are slaughtered in Wilburgfos. Only the geese are spared and fattened with what little the peasants can spare. On Saint Martin's Day, there will be a big feast, where the geese will be roasted on a spit and served with a sauce of garlic, onions and various herbs. Everyone can eat their fill one last time before the austere winter half of the year brings great privations to many of them.

To be honest, we have no reason to complain, with our barns, buttery, larders and pantries brim-full of stocks, but if fugitives continue to show up at the manor during winter, we will soon have little to share with them if we want to survive ourselves. Thibault now finds it more important that the squires prove themselves as skilled hunters and trappers in order to stock up on meat for the winter. I enjoy our common forays into the woods that surround the fields and meadows of Wilburgfos. Although some spots are not without danger, the woods are a place of tranquillity where one can discuss many things that would elsewhere attract the attention of too many ears.

"Still nothing?" Cenric looks at me in amazement as we examine, in groups of two, the traps we set two days ago. Although he is not allowed to take part in the weapons practice because he is not of noble birth, he accompanies us when we go into the woods to set traps or hunt small animals, such as rabbits, partridges or ducks. He knows the area around Wilburgfos better than any of us, as he grew up here and used to hunt extensively with his father Cenhelm, Kjetil and the other servants of the manor, or to look for firewood, building material, mushrooms, berries and nuts.

"The Lord seems to have mercy on me," I say, stalking over a cluster of thorny branches that spread out ankle-high across the ground. "Perhaps I should give Father Leofric some of our quarry if we have caught anything, so he puts in a good word for me to keep my luck going."

Cenric laughs. "Certainly wouldn't reject a fat hare. He's not picky about food, even though you can't really tell how much he can gobble up by simply looking at him."

"An English priest is far better than a French one. I'm sure Father Leofric cares more about the worries and needs of the people than someone from a foreign country would. Besides, he will do all he can to keep his office, and for that, he needs the people to trust him."

"Or a feudal lord to protect him, for whom he is nothing more than a means to strengthen their rule." Cenric's voice has a threatening undertone.

When did he learn to think and talk like that? Astonished, I look at my former challenger, who has become my best friend over the last few months. He is no longer the awkward braggart of four years ago who could not back up his big words with actions. He is only a few months younger than me. Almost a man, and if his parents hadn't been commoners but nobles, he would surely be dubbed next year. *But he will never have that honour. He will never fight in an army such as he could have done in the fyrd under an English king.*

Just as I start wondering whether I will ever become a knight, I hear someone rejoicing to my left.

"It looks like we're having roast hare tonight!" Jehan's red head glows above the undergrowth. He has his hands at his sides and is looking down with a broad grin at a wriggling something.

Jeannot swings the woollen bag off his back and opens it expectantly.

We join the two and look at the little animal desperately trying to free itself from the noose.

"It's puny," Cenric says disappointedly. "We don't need a woollen sack for that. A belt pouch will do. Couldn't his parents have walked into the trap?"

"Even small animals are good enough to eat, Cenric," says Jehan and pulls out his knife.

The crack of a branch makes him pause.

Between the trees, a woman's voice calls out, "Wait!"

About fifty paces from us, two slim figures in long cloaks are approaching light-footedly. Their cloaks are swinging back and forth with each step. The two figures almost seem to float through the undergrowth and between the trees, like beings from the Otherworld. A few strands of dark hair stick out from under their hoods. On the left arm of the figure in front, a basket made of fine wicker is gently swinging.

"Isn't that the Breton noblewoman with her daughter?" says Jeannot with a frown.

"You shouldn't go through the woods alone!" I shout at them.

"I am not alone," Morwenna replies, pointing to the younger figure. "My daughter, Solen, accompanies me, as you see."

"The woods are too dangerous for two women on their own," says Cenric. "Neither a robber nor a wild animal will be scared off by a herb knife."

"I don't need any explanations from you about dangers," Morwenna says with a stern look.

Cenric and I exchange a look while she bends down and frees the hare from the trap. She takes the little animal in her arms and strokes its fur.

"Have you at least told someone at the manor house where you were going?" I ask. "As your host, Sire Geoffrey is responsible for your welfare, especially since you sent your guards away."

"Where they have gone, they are needed more than here." Morwenna's tone is sharp and final.

As always. Nothing has changed since our first encounter at the bridge near the monastery.

She examines me closely before continuing in a softer voice. "But if you are so concerned about our lives, perhaps you would like to offer to protect them with yours?"

I am to serve as a personal guard for two guests? Confused, I look at the squires, who look back just as astonished.

Morwenna's eyebrows furrow. "You hesitate."

There is more contempt in those two words than Lord Geoffrey could express in a whole sentence or Cenric in one of his rambling speeches.

She says it as if she expected nothing else from me. But I am not her underling and owe her no service. Who does she think she is, daring to ask, even demand, such a thing from me? I straighten up. "I don't see why I should do that. You are not part of my family nor that of my liege lord. I am under no obligation to you."

Just as I have spoken the words, Solen's and my eyes meet. Her dark blue eyes sparkle like two gems under the large hood. Something in me is writhing at what I have just said. *I am under no obligation to you,* my voice echoes through my mind, mingling with a lighter voice, *"Your blood ties and* oaths of allegiance bind you, and what of your honour?" I frown. *Was that in my head or did she actually ask me that?*

Without taking her eyes off me, Morwenna is holding the little hare in her arms.

I clear my throat. "We should get going. We don't have time to stand around here."

"What about the hare?" asks Cenric, pointing to the bundle of fur in Morwenna's arms.

"It is only small," says Morwenna, "and I advise you to release it. If you have no sense of honour, at least show reverence for the old goddesses. If you spare the hare, you could obtain the favour of Abnoba, the great goddess of hunting, and ask her for good luck in the hunt. Besides," her gaze becomes even more insistent, "you will appease the goddess Ostara, to whom the hare serves as a symbol of fertility and rebirth. That's what you want, isn't it?"

I swallow. My heart is pounding in my chest as if my life were at stake. *What is this woman talking about? Is she trying to bewitch me with words? Why is she looking at me all the time? What about the squires? Wouldn't they also have reason to hope for luck while hunting?*

Cenric takes a step forward and stands between Morwenna and me, ready to snatch the hare from her hands, if need be. He had to bear witness to the misery of his countrymen for too long to let a defeated quarry slip away before winter.

"Are we taking the hare or not? We have other traps to look at."

Jehan pulls back Jeannot, who is still expectantly holding out the sack, and waves it off. "Oh, leave little long-ears alone. I'm sure we have some bigger fur wearers in the other traps."

Cenric sighs as Jehan and Jeannot continue on their way.

I nod hastily, embarrassed that Jehan has caught me off guard with his decision. "He's right. We should move on. Keep the hare."

Morwenna's voice floods my head with words dancing around. *"Abnoba", "hunting luck", "Ostara", "fertility".* I take one last look at Solen, who smiles silently at me. Feeling a sudden flush of heat, I tug at the collar of my tunic for more air. "You should go back to the manor house. You never know who or what might be prowling the woods at this time of day. God bless you." I pull Cenric with me and follow the other two.

There's something creepy about Morwenna, even if I would never say so in front of the others. She's hiding a secret. Something that happened in the past that has brought her up north, just herself and her daughter. She speaks, but her words are as dense as the morning mists above the river.

∂∾

After Mass on Saint Martin's Day, Solen and her mother join the stream of people beside me, pushing their way through the portal out of the festively decorated church. Amid the throng, Solen is pressed so close to me that I feel her body at my side. She smiles at me. Her eyes resemble the waters of the Fors Bekkr on a day in early summer, a deep dark blue surrounded by the light, almost creamy tone of her face, which in turn is framed by her dark hair. Only now do I realise how beautiful she is, even though I have seen her many times before. This time, she is so close that her beauty literally leaps into my face. Only a blind man could still miss it.

"I have watched you at your work," Morwenna says.

"Was there any particular reason why you did?"

Morwenna purses her lips. "I happened to be in the yard when your weapons practice took place. I must say that you are a skilled fighter."

As if a woman can judge that! Besides, most of the men I have ever fought or who have seen me fight would say that I am the best of them all. "Do you think so?"

"One thing astonished me, though."

"And that would be?"

"How is it that an Engleis is teaching squires at a Norman manor house?"

I take a deep breath to suppress the memories of Ledlinghe. Morwenna doesn't need to know what really happened, and that the events of that time still wake me up at night after all these months. "It turned out that way."

"A divine providence?"

"If you want to call it that."

"Do you think you are chosen?"

"Only God knows. I would never dare to call myself the Chosen One." Angered by Morwenna's enigmatic questions, I look down to Solen, who bashfully avoids my gaze and lowers her head. A dark curl slides forward from her shoulder. I feel a deep urge to brush it back over her shoulder so that she straightens her face and looks at me.

"It must be hard to live as an Engleis in a Norman manor house. After all that your countrymen have experienced."

"It is not harder than before. I am alive, and I earn a living."

"You work with Normans."

"And with the English at the manor house."

Annoyed, Morwenna shakes her head. "Servants and slaves. You tend to spend most of your time with the Norman nobles and their sons."

"Dame Edeva is a noble Englesse. Do you also count her as an underling?"

"She is the wife of a Norman baron. He rules over her as he rules over his followers. I understand, however, that you are under the personal protection of the Norman master of arms and must account for your deeds only to him. That is remarkable indeed."

Is she making fun of me, or does she really admire me? Her expression is just as haughty as on the day I first saw her on horseback. Not a trace of humility. Whatever she has experienced in her homeland, it has not taken away anything of her disparaging attitude towards others.

"I am the son of Ðegn Osfrið of Ledlinghe, who served Eorl Morkere and thus King Harold. My father himself taught me everything he knew about fighting and warfare. I need not hide from any Norman."

Morwenna's lips form a thin line. She nods graciously. "The son of a ðegn, you say. A noble Engleis among Norman barons. Does it not bother you that you can never become one of them? That you, as an Engleis among Normans, will always be seeking the likes of you as a leper does among the healthy?"

Father Leofric is right when he says that women, like the serpent in the Bible, want to sow discord between God and man. "As a Breton, you yourself know how it feels to be alone among Normans. But you seem to master your life, too."

A faint smile crosses Morwenna's mouth. "I see you are not only good with weapons."

From somewhere I hear a voice speaking in a foreign language. Only when I see Solen's gaze move from her mother to me do I realise that it must have been her who spoke. She looks at me expectantly, almost impatiently.

"What?" I ask, completely taken aback.

Morwenna shakes her head. "My daughter suggested that you might accompany us if you feel as outcast in this manor house as we do."

I look into Solen's eyes, in which there is so much hope. My throat tightens. Solen is young. Even younger than Godgifu, maybe fourteen or fifteen winters. *Young, but old enough to get married.* The thought hits me like a thunderbolt. *Perhaps they are on their way to meet her betrothed, who lives somewhere further north. Some rich Frenchman who is looking for a young woman of noble descent.* "Where should I accompany you?" My heart hammers in my chest as if preparing to burst at an unwanted answer.

"We need to go further north, but at the moment, our healing skills are more urgently needed here. When winter is over and Dame Edeva is better, we will move on, God willing."

"What about the warriors who accompanied you?"

"They have long since gone where we need to go. I sent them on while I stayed here to help the healer. A few weeks ago, I asked your liege lord for riders, so that we could continue our journey. Sire Geoffrey refused to provide even a single one of his men. He said he needed them for more important matters."

Solen grabs my arm. "My mother and I will never reach the end of our journey alive without armed guards."

My heart pounds all the way into my ears. In my head, I see Godgifu, my sisters and my mother lying on the ground, violated, bloody, dirty and mutilated. Without thinking about it, I put my hand on Solen's finger. "I can't leave this manor.

I owe my life to the master of arms, and in return, I owe him service on the battleground. He might give me leave for some time, but Sire Geoffrey will not allow it." I swallow hard. "I'm sorry."

We look at each other for what feels like an eternity, my hand on hers, as if we were an old, close couple. If it weren't daylight and her mother weren't standing next to us, I would kiss Solen right now. I clear my throat and hastily pull my hand away.

Morwenna has been watching us with raised eyebrows. "Winter has just begun. Many things will change in the coming months."

She says this with a certainty as if she can actually see into the future. Maybe she really is a witch.

❧

It is a cold winter day when Roul's uncle returns to the manor. Stígandr already told Lord Geoffrey a few days ago that the arrival of the men he sent off was imminent.

My two mortal enemies are back home. I vigorously scrub the sword blade with the linen cloth, without paying much attention to where I am wiping and whether the blade is not already clean enough. *"Many things will change in the coming months."* Morwenna's words buzz through my head like flies attracted by a badly wounded animal. An uneasy feeling creeps over me that my life will soon no longer be the same. I think of my father and our last conversations before the French invaded southern Englaland – the unknown danger that had been lurking out there, waiting to crash into our lives, over-turning and completely destroying them. An invisible fist presses on my stomach and makes it difficult to breathe.

Slowly, I lean the sword against the bench, fold up the cloth and put it on my leg. *It's not a whole army waiting for me out there somewhere. It's just two men. One who hates the English to the bone, and one who has neither honour nor sense of duty and will sell his services to anyone who pays him highly enough. If only Ulfgar were alive!* A tremor runs through my body when I see the image of my big, bearded friend in front of me. *Why did he have to die?* I clench my teeth and bury my face in my hands.

"Are you not well, Oswulf?"

I slide my hands down my face and try to make an indifferent face that doesn't show the pain of the memory.

Stooping down, Roul looks at me as if he were checking for signs of illness. He himself is pale as a sheet and has been complaining since yesterday that he keeps throwing up. I hope he's doing all right and that his food is not coming up at this very moment.

I find it difficult to swallow. It's as if all the horrors of the past were trying to make their way out through my throat, blocking the way for my voice. "It's..." I croak, clearing my throat and trying to sound determined and confident. "It's all right, Roul. Don't worry."

"Hastez vus!" Jeannot waves from the door of the armoury. "I want to hear what he says." He's already off and running after the others to hear the latest French exploits against the rebellious English, told in glowing colours.

By one who lisps and is not man enough to confront a single Englishman, but instead orders his henchmen to kill him stealthily. What a brave warrior! I shake my head, take the linen cloth from my thigh and throw it over the sword pommel. "He's right. We should go and listen too. Perhaps, at last, there will be peace in Englaland." *Dead silence. Who am I trying to fool? Certainly not Roul. He knows how I feel about his uncle and what his uncle thinks of me. Do I need to encourage myself by telling myself that my beloved homeland is no longer a cauldron of war and ruin for my countrymen? That the unbridled and ruthless murder and plunder of the French will finally come to an end? That I too will finally find peace? Peace! How can I live in peace when someone is trying to kill me and I must expect them to strike again every day?*

Roul regards me with tired eyes. He is too sick to question my words. I push him forwards in front of me. Surely, he wants to greet his glorious and praiseworthy uncle, no matter how ill he himself is.

Outside in the yard, a motley crowd of children and youths has gathered around Quentin, greedily demanding and soaking up all the gory details of the battles against the rebels. From what I can gather from their faces and cheers at the door of the armoury, the French achieved a decisive victory against Hereward and his men.

While Roul is staggering towards the cluster of people and making his way to his uncle, I turn away and hasten to the nearby shed. There are some tools that have been affected by the damp late autumn. Cenric has also asked me to help him mend a fence later. His father, Cenhelm, has been in bed with a fever for a week, like many others who have been taken ill. A light can be seen from the herb hut almost all the time these days. The weather also leaves its mark on the people. Hild and Morwenna have their hands full, and Solen helps them where she can.

I imagine what it would be like to be injured in one of Quentin's assaults and brought into the herb hut, with Solen examining the wound and her delicate hands roaming over my skin.

"...thtill here?" I hear a voice ask.

I startle and look around as if I've been caught in the act. In the yard, Quentin is walking with Hugues de Borre and the group of attentive listeners to the great hall, where Lord Geoffrey will receive him with pomp and glory. *Celebrating a defender of the French order against the stubborn and unruly defeated.* I spit out and continue on my way.

"If it had been up to me, I would have chased the Engleith from the manor a long time ago."

I slow my step and prick up my ears. *Đu wyrma gifl! Speaking up on purpose so that I cannot but hear it. Yet what would you say if you were not surrounded by your ardent followers?*

"How long will Sire Geoffrey let the master of arms have his way? An Engleith teaching Norman squires! Why not sell the souls of our children to the Devil?"

I stop and turn to Roul's uncle. "Haven't you sent him enough English souls in the last few weeks?"

Quentin pauses. His pursuers jostle each other before the whole bunch of chickens comes to rest. Roul's uncle peels out of the crowd and, with his cloak billowing, takes a few steps towards me, though not fully leaving the protection of the group. With each step, the rings of his hauberk clink under his wide cloak.

"Did you say something, Engleith?"

I regard the burly man in front of me, who yearns to crush me with his foot like an annoying insect and yet has failed at every attempt. *So far.*

"Forgive me. I didn't know you were hard of hearing or else I would have spoken louder."

Quentin's chest heaves as if he wants to blow me away when he breathes out. The fingers of his sword hand twitch. I only have my scramasax with me, but if it came down to it, that would be all I'd need.

"You think you are very clever because you have learned our language, don't you? But you have no business in this manor house, Engleith. I know it, you know it, and everybody else knows it."

"Everybody also knows very well what you think of me."

His brow furrows as if he is weighing what I know and how far I would get with that knowledge in case of a dispute. "Then thank the Lord that the master of arms is so high in the favour of your liege," he hisses, half-closing his left eye as if aiming an arrow at me, "for there's plenty of us who think as I do."

I cast a glance over the people gathered in the yard to see if I could hope for help, should he decide to attack me. Next to Quentin is Hugues, whose dark hair seems to stand up more with each sentence. Three more of Lord Geoffrey's men are with him. Some servants, who have taken the horses and weapons from Roul's uncle and his companions. A handful of children and English youths who have interrupted their monotonous work routine as underlings of the French to hear tidings from the far end of Englaland. As if it were necessary, the news will only rob them of any remaining hope that they will ever be able to shake off the French yoke. At the back of the group, the squires are raising their heads in the air. Neither Thibault nor Walchelin are near. The squires are unarmed. Roul is ill – but I could hardly expect him to help against his uncle anyway. "But not everyone would try to kill me because of that." I hold my breath and watch every little movement of my opponent to be ready for an attack. From what I've seen of him so far, he's not going to engage in single combat against me. He is a good fighter, but he needs the backing of an army to prove it. I would defeat him in no time.

"Are you really sure about that, Engleith?" Quentin grabs the side of his cloak and throws the corner over his shoulder. He turns, waving his hand at Hugues. "Let's go! We have more important things to do than talk to peasants."

"I'm very sure of it indeed!" I shout after him. "I have proof."

Roul's uncle slows his pace briefly but then continues on his way without turning round again.

I have no proof, but maybe this will cause him to make a mistake. Maybe, then I can finally catch him and make his stalking stop. The thought makes me smile to myself. I should be teaching squires, but now, I'm chasing a Frenchman who wants me dead.

"Hear, hear, he has proof," grumbles a voice beside me. Stígandr appears out of nowhere, running bony fingers over his chin beard. "What crime has our noble Frenchman committed that you are gathering evidence against him?"

"I don't see how that's any of your business, Stígandr."

"Maybe I could help you against him, you know, we English must—"

"You're not English, and you never will be."

Stígandr continues to stroke his beard as he looks at me. "Do you think you are in a position where you can be picky about who helps you and who doesn't?"

Most of the crowd has now dispersed. Only Jehan and Roul linger, regarding us indecisively. *Would Jehan fight on my side if need be? Even if he did, he is only a squire, albeit a very good one. Cenric would defend me with claws and teeth, but he is merely the son of the English cupbearer – who is in bed with a fever at the moment and exempt from any work. Whom else could I trust? Would Thibault save me again from the wrath of a countryman? What about Walchelin or Frederic the seneschal? Perhaps Stígandr could be useful to me after all. He travels a lot, gets around the country, perhaps knows the right people.* A bitter taste spreads through my mouth. I feel a tugging in my chest. *"Never trust a Viking,"* my father's voice echoes through my head. I see him in front of me, pronouncing these words with a raised forefinger. *"Never trust a Viking!"*

"My situation is not so bad that I need your help." I turn around and walk to the tool shed.

"You're afraid of this Frenchman, aren't you?"

"I'm not."

"Then what do you need proof for?"

"It's none of your business."

"He tried to kill you."

Ic hine wergðo on mine sette. He got it all. Stígandr, of all people!

"Your silence tells me that I am right."

"So what!" I open the door to the tool shed. "It's got nothing to do with you."

Stígandr puts his hand on his heart. "You may not believe it, but since your father's death – may God have mercy on his soul! – I feel responsible for you."

"You feel responsible for me? Don't make me laugh! You are responsible for the death of Godgifu, Ulfgar and my whole family."

"Now, now! Aren't you doing me wrong? You know yourself that the French would have reached Ledlinghe sooner or

273

later. How could one man have prevented that?" He puts his arm around my shoulders. "Now, let us forget the past, and together, think how you can get rid of this Frenchman."

I shake off his arm and step into the shed. "I don't want to get rid of him. I just want to make sure he gets his just deserts for what he did to me. I just need to get him to actually admit his deeds."

"You should talk to him alone. Or at least, it must seem to him that you are alone. Thinking that he's not admitting guilt in front of witnesses will loosen his tongue."

"Talk to him alone? How am I meant to do that? Do you want me to invite him to a meeting in the hayloft?"

Stígandr creeps far too close to me and leans towards my ear. "He prays alone in the chapel every night after dinner," he whispers. "You could meet him there and try to extract a confession from him. There's no one else there at that time. He'll feel safe and might tell you more than he wants you to know."

"What good would that do me if no one else heard it? I could never prove that he admitted his shameful deeds to me."

Stígandr straightens up, adjusts his mantle and purses his lips. "Well, your old friend Stígandr might happen to pass by the chapel and overhear the conversation. I am Lord Geoffrey's messenger. My word carries weight at the manor."

I look at the goat face between the hunched shoulders. The eyebrows are arching expectantly over the flashing eyes. *"Never trust a Viking!"* Never... "Why would you do that? What would you get out of it?"

He spreads his arms. "But Oswulf, aren't you listening to me? I've told you that I feel responsible f—"

"Yes, yes, I know. Stop blathering and tell me what you really want! You don't do anything without asking for something in return. So?"

Stígandr looks at me silently.

Did he think that I would just accept his proposal? After all that has happened in the past?

"Your question does you honour. You want to know exactly what might be driving me to help you. You think I am working against you because it must have seemed that way to you in the past. There have been many unfortunate coincidences that have led you to this belief. I can't change that. But look at our situation: we are two defeated people in a French manor house. We are being oppressed and used by the French for their purposes. Is this our true destiny? As the son of a great English ðegn, should you not aspire to something higher than running away day after day from a hateful Frenchman and his devious assaults? What would your father do if he were in your place? Would he not face the danger and take up the fight? Would he not challenge the Frenchman face to face and show him that the better man wins? That law and justice are on his side and will lead him to victory against baseness and jealousy? Would he not do that, do you think, Osfriðson?"

Images race through my head. I see Father taking up the fight in full battle wear. Over and over again. How he strikes down his opponents one by one. How he finally raises his spear in the air and roars out the victory to put the last surviving opponents to flight. My father would not be frightened by a single Frenchman. He would not run away. He would not wait for chance to bring his tormentor to justice. He would confront him here and now. And if necessary, he would also take up arms against him and go into battle for his right and his life. I have hesitated far too long. *"He who does not fight is worth nothing." I must put an end to this game. For good. And if Stígandr could bear witness to everything, I would soon have peace at last.*

"Well?"

"Are you sure we will be able to prove his guilt?"

"Of course." Stígandr looks at his fingernails. "But perhaps, you would prefer one of your French friends to help you?"

"What French friends?"

"Well, the squires and the master of arms seem to think very highly of you."

"The squires are too young. They cannot help me. Besides, they are my pupils and trust me. I couldn't possibly let them in on this and put them in danger while still keeping a clear conscience. And Roul? He would warn his uncle that I am trying to trap him."

"And the master of arms?"

I shake my head. "I'm already too deeply in his debt. I can't ask him for any more help."

Stígandr folds his arms. "You don't owe me anything. You could ask me for help."

Help from Stígandr?

"Never trust a Viking!"

Do I have a choice? What about Cenric? Cenric is brave and doesn't shun work, but he also acts rashly and imprudently. He would put himself in danger, and I cannot fight a skilled French warrior for Cenric's life and my own at the same time. With Ulfgar, that was possible. But Cenric is not Ulfgar.

"Come on! What have you got to lose? If Roul's uncle talks a little too openly, you have a witness. If not, at least you tried." He tugs at his beard. The teeth of his lower jaw push out from behind his lip. The goat smile spreads across his face. "And if you need my help, I will be there."

The wind drives through the door into the shed. I feel a cold breeze on my cheeks, but inside, I am on fire. My heart is pounding as if before a decisive battle. My fingers tingle. They long to do something. To get something done and over with. *Life is constantly changing. People live and die, that's just the way it is. Must I therefore submit to being stalked by a Frenchman who, even after many months, still hates me, just because I'm English?* The image of a young woman with dark curls and deep blue eyes appears in my mind. My heartbeat speeds up. *Solen. Didn't Morwenna want me to protect her daughter? How am I supposed to do that if I'm dead? Must I trust a Viking to free me from Quentin? Do I have a choice? Father, forgive me!*

"Agreed, Stígandr."

"A good decision!"

"But if you betray me, I will kill you. This time, it won't be just a threat. I will not rest until you're lying on the ground covered in blood."

"Have faith in your old friend Stígandr. He will take care of everything to your satisfaction. Go to the chapel tonight after dinner. I will wait for you there and give you a sign. When you enter the chapel, see that you leave the door open behind you, so that I can easily hear all that you discuss." He throws one side of his cloak over his shoulder and straightens up as far as his hunched shoulders will allow. "You have made an important decision, young Osfriðson. Tonight, your life will change forever." Like a shadow, he disappears from the shed.

I stare after him for a long time before I search for the tools that need mending. I try to swallow the metallic taste in my mouth. As I reach for a bucket of small tools, I pause. My hands are shaking, even though I am not cold. After a moment's hesitation, I grip the bucket all the more firmly. *Even if Roul's uncle confesses, how can we go on? I can't work as a helper to the master of arms forever! This manor is too small for two teachers. Thibault is French. Lord Geoffrey would never replace him with an Englishman as long as he can help it.* I turn my gaze to the sky, ignoring the dark wooden beams of the ceiling. *What is to become of me, Father? I should be sitting on a proud steed and fighting in full battle dress for Eorl Morkere and King Harold to defend Englaland against its enemies. Instead, I am working for those who killed our king and shared out our land between themselves. Whose henchmen laid waste our villages and destroyed our homes. Who took my family from me and brought me to this manor house as a stranger. What am I doing here?*

I drop onto a barrel and bury my face in my hands.

"You were born to fight, Oswulf. Never forget that," I hear a voice say.

I look up, but there is no one in the shed but me.

"You have always been a keen and ambitious pupil."

"Father?" I sit up straight and look around. *How can this be? He is not here, and yet I hear him loud and clear.*

"I never promised you that your path would be easy. You are on your own now, and you have to show what you are made of. Fight, my son, and find your way!"

I nod in disbelief. "I will, Father."

"But beware of false friends, Oswulf!" My father's voice is slowly fading. His last words are but a whisper.

"Never trust a Viking!"

An icy gust sweeps in through the door and tugs at my mantle. I rise heavily from the barrel and clench my fists. "I have no choice, Father," I breathe. "I have to do it. Just this once."

❧

DARK CLOUDS DRIFT across the night sky, dimming the moonlight to a glimmer just enough to illuminate the ground on which I tread with unsteady steps. From the great hall, the hustle and bustle after the end of dinner breaks the silence of the evening. In the kitchen, the maids are chattering and clattering as they wash and stow away the pots and cutlery. Many are already busy looking for a place to sleep, while the servants once again stoke the fire in the middle of the hall so that it will continue to burn during the night.

With everyone moving about in the dim light, no one pays attention to me as I sneak out. Only two servants are in the yard at this hour to check on the animals one last time and make sure the doors and gates are locked. I wait in the shade of a hut until they have disappeared and then skulk on.

A faint light shines through the small windows of the chapel. Roul's uncle must already be there. I hesitate. *How do I know it's him and if there is no one else around?*

A slender shadow appears behind the chapel. I duck and squint my eyes. The shadow hovers next to one of the windows. For a moment, his face is illuminated. A tingling sensation runs through my stomach. *Stígandr.* I look around in all directions before venturing out of my hiding place. Stígandr gives me a sign. I tiptoe towards him, past the houses and to the side of the chapel. Cautiously, I peek through the window.

"He's alone," I whisper. My breath and heartbeat race. I wipe my hands on my tunic and run them over my scramasax. The grip feels cool, but I am unbearably hot.

"Your short sword," whispers Stígandr.

"What about it?"

"You don't want to go to church armed – or do you think that will help you loosen his tongue?"

"You're right." I loosen the weapon belt and hand it to Stígandr. "Quentin must feel completely safe, otherwise he will never betray himself."

Stígandr's face glows ghostly white in the dim moonlight as he accepts my scramasax. "Don't forget to leave the door open so I can hear and see you well."

I nod, take another deep breath and open the chapel door. It creaks softly. I go in and pretend to think hard about something while I push the door as far as it will go. It swings gently towards me again. I push it open again. Another soft creak. An annoyed hiss comes from the front. I watch the swing of the door, which becomes slower and slower until it stops altogether. Now, the door is open wide enough for a man to easily walk through. I carefully approach the altar in front of which someone kneels under a wide-spread mantle with their head bowed, seemingly absorbed in prayer. I kneel beside them, direct my gaze to the cross above the altar and fold my hands. *Leof dryhten, give me strength and courage tonight to expose this man and bring him to his just punishment.* I lower my head and close my eyes. *Father, forgive me!*

For a while, we kneel in silence next to each other, each preoccupied with his own thoughts.

"Do you think that our God hears your prayerth?"

"Maybe. And you?"

Quentin fixes his gaze on the cross and pinches his lips together.

"It seems you are also praying in vain."

His eyebrow twitches ever so slightly. "How do you know?"

"I'm still alive."

Quentin gives me a disparaging sideways glance. "Death comes when you least expect it."

"From the looks of it, I'm at the top of his list, but I've already escaped him several times this year." I look for telltale signs in Quentin's motionless face. "Did you know that someone at this manor house wants to kill me?"

"Why should I care?"

"Five times this man's henchmen have attacked me, abused me and tried to bring shame on me, but in vain. It must be terrible to watch your underlings fail to accomplish such small assignments. Realising how little success you have against a single Engleis, even though you are among the best warriors in great battles. Don't you agree?"

Quentin scowls at me. "I don't know why you're telling me all this."

"Yes, you do."

He turns away.

"I've had a few months' rest because there were Englishmen to be defeated in the east of Englaland who continue to resist Norman rule. Sire Geoffrey sent men there. They all survived and are now back at the manor, most certainly including the man who wants to end not only my life, but also that of the master of arms. Because he hates the Engleis and cannot bear to see his nephew taught by an Engleis."

"We have a Norman master of arms. Why do we need an Engleith?" He rises and turns towards the door.

I jump up and claw at his mantle. "You actually tried to kill Thibault."

Quentin snatches the cloak from my hands. "That was a mistake." He turns his face away. His shoulders are heaving.

"What have I done to you that you keep on trying to kill me?" I do not expect to get an answer to my question.

He looks at me with angry eyes, holding his hand with the tip of his mantle in front of his body as if for protection. While I search for a sword scabbard that might be peeking out from under his cloak, he takes a step back without taking his eyes off me.

He probably came to prayer unarmed, but under his cloak, he might be carrying a dagger. I must be vigilant.

Quentin's gaze wanders restlessly over my body, as if he too is looking for a weapon on me.

I open my arms. "I have no weapon. I have come to talk, not to fight."

Quentin nods. Even though the frown on his forehead remains, his voice suddenly sounds calm, almost gentle. "My nephew told me about you."

Of course he did, and I can guess how the conversations between the two went. A heated exchange of hateful words and curses. It's surprising that there hasn't been an assault lately. Quentin must have been too busy to prepare more attacks on me. *Or does he no longer find niþingas to carry out his orders?*

"He says you're a good man."

"Roul?"

"He hated you at first – many of us did."

"Then it is him who is responsible for the attacks on me?"

"No. He has nothing to do with it. I'm the only one to blame for that."

We look at each other. *A confession! He actually admitted that he ordered the attacks. That he wanted to kill not only me, but in his desperation and hatred also the master of arms, my protector. I hope Stígandr heard everything well.* I should be happy now, but I don't feel anything, except a strange tugging in my stomach, a tension, a bad premonition. "I thank you for your honesty, Quentin."

"I have treated you unfairly. You are doing very good work with our squires. Sire Geoffrey and Thibault are very pleased with you, and so is Roul."

My ears are ringing as if someone next to me is hammering incessantly with a blacksmith's hammer on a hot iron on the anvil. *Roul's uncle admits his guilt and injustice and even praises me?* I am about to say something when Stígandr enters the church.

Quentin turns round. His questioning gaze wanders from Stígandr to me.

"Did you hear everything, Stígandr?" My heart is pounding.

Stígandr approaches calmly. In his hand dangles my weapon belt with the scramasax. "Indeed."

A smile wants to get out, but my lips are frozen. I reach out my hand, trembling. Something is pushing me away from here. "Good. You can give me my belt back now. We can go."

Quentin looks from one to the other. "What's going on?"

Stígandr hands me the weapon belt but holds on to the handle of the scramasax.

As I take the belt, the sword is pulled out of the scabbard. "My scrama—"

"You won't need it where you're going." With a broad grin, Stígandr rams my sword into Quentin's body.

"Wha—" groans Quentin, slouching forward.

"What have you done?" I catch Quentin and try to hold his weight in my arms. "Stígandr!" I can just see the Norþmann's cloak fluttering in the doorway. The sand is crunching under his hasty steps.

"Help!" I hear him shout outside in the yard.

I heave Quentin onto a chair and try to keep him upright. My scramasax protrudes from his blood-covered belly.

"Quentin? Quentin, I didn't plan this. Stígandr was only supposed to overhear our conversation. There was never any question of killing you. Do you hear me?"

Quentin looks at me with half-closed eyes and a distorted face. "You're a good man, Oswulf," he gasps before his strength fails him. "I know that now. But it is too late. Forgive me." His head falls to the side. His body goes limp.

"Quentin! You can't die now!" Desperately, I shake his shoulders, but to no avail. You can't stir a dead man back to life.

I hesitantly release my grip. The body leans to the side and slowly slides onto the adjacent chairs. Helplessly, I sink to my knees and rub my face. I hear voices from the yard. *He never wanted to help me. It was supposed to look like I killed Quentin from the start. He set a trap for me, and fool that I am, I blindly walked into it. They'll arrest me and convict me.* I press my lips together. *"Never trust a Viking!"* my father's voice echoes through my head.

A whisper interrupts the voice. "Oswulf."

At the chapel door, Roul's blonde hair shimmers in the candlelight. He leans against the door as he staggers into the chapel. His face is white as chalk, his gait unsteady. His gaze wanders to the body on the chairs. "Uncle Quentin," he breathes and continues to crawl towards us.

My thoughts fly from Roul to Thibault, the rest of the squires, Cenric, Lady Edeva, Lord Geoffrey. *What will Solen think of me?*

Leaning on the back of a chair, Roul reaches out a trembling hand to his uncle. His voice is no more than a hoarse squeak. "Uncle Quentin." A tear is rolling down his cheek. He looks at me.

I swallow and slowly shake my head. "I didn't kill him, Roul. You have to believe me."

"Hastez vus, Roul, e alez hors de la chapele!" a voice bellows. Two armed Frenchmen rush through the chapel door and point their swords at me. "Lieve toi, engleis!"

"I didn't kill him," I say again to Roul as I stand up. "You're capturing the wrong man. Stígandr stabbed him."

One of the Frenchmen points to Quentin's body. "And whose sword is that?"

"You still have your weapon belt in your hand, too," says the second.

"I gave Stígandr my sword when I went into the chapel. He was supposed to give it back to me, but instead, he killed Quentin with it. It was supposed to look like—"

"Stígandr was watching everything from outside." The two of them shove me forward with their swords. "It's just as well he let us know before you skewered more men."

I stumble outside, where half the people of the manor are waiting for me, wrapped in blankets.

"Stígandr killed him when he was supposed to give me back my scramasax."

The Frenchman laughs briefly. "What reason would he have? We know you hated Quentin."

"What? That's a lie! Who told you that?"

"You told Stígandr yourself."

"I never said I hated Quentin. I just wanted his confession that he ordered the attacks on me. I never wanted to kill him."

The Frenchman pushes me further. "You can tell that to Sire Geoffrey when you stand trial. Va dunc!"

They drive me on like a piece of cattle being led to slaughter. Everyone's staring at me. I catch sight of Jehan and Cenric. At the end of the crowd, I see the master of arms. "Ne ic hine cwealde, Thibault."

"Ic cnawe."

Chapter 10

The cockcrow rouses me from my sleep. I arch my back and stretch my legs before tightly huddling into the two woollen blankets again. For three weeks, I've been idling about in this draughty and damp shed while everyone else is celebrating Christmas by the fire in the great hall with copious amounts of ale and food. Their chants are ringing in my ears. The smell of roast meat and spices is stuck in my nose like an arrow whose barbs are hooked into my skin.

How many have staggered drunkenly in front of the shed, laughing and grunting while they relieved themselves right in front of the door, or vomiting up the fatty food so that it splashed through under the door! They mocked me, laughed at me and in their drunkenness threw bones at me as if I were a dog. Yet as soon as they were gone, I greedily picked up the bones, gnawed them down to the last bit and thanked God for letting me celebrate the birth of the Lord with this feast in my prison.

May He also have mercy on me today and make me strong for what lies ahead. I pull up my knees to warm my feet, which are stiff from the night frost, under the blankets. During the weeks of my captivity, I have seen who really stands by me and whom I can trust. *And who can't wait for the French to finally condemn me.* If it weren't for the master of arms, they would have done this many months ago. Once again, I owe my life to him and it is through him that it has lasted until now, even if it should end today. Every day for the past few weeks, he has come to see me. Asked if I needed anything. Brought me woollen blankets to protect me from the cold and personally trimmed my moustache every week.

"Many consider what happened in the chapel as proof that you are still the savage Engleis they always thought you were," Thibault said as he carefully cut the ends of my whiskers with the knife. "You should not let your appearance confirm that view."

"Why are you doing all this for me?"

Thibault shrugged his shoulders. "I respect you as a warrior. You are skilled, clever, brave and tough. These are all qualities our squires need if they are to become good fighters."

"Surely, there are many warriors to whom that applies."

"Perhaps, but when I saw you fight, you were just nineteen years old – an age when most of our squires still have at least two years of practice ahead of them. Look at you, you haven't even been dubbed and yet you are teaching our squires, who are barely younger than you, how to wield weapons. Your father would be proud of you, Oswulf."

Tears well in my eyes as I remember Thibault's words. Pain and pride form a lump in my throat. I wriggle against the hard wooden slats of the wall. My backside aches from sitting for so long, but in this cold weather, I didn't dare lie down to sleep. I would not have survived the night.

288

But I woke up every morning. And every morning, except on the Lord's days, Thibault took me out of the shed under strict guard so that I could instruct the squires. He said that I was still needed at the manor and that this was a predicament for everyone, forcing him to make changes to his journey. When I asked what those changes were, he evaded my question. Nothing had been decided yet. All possibilities were still open, he said, with an undertone that made it clear that he wished no further enquiries.

I have not been able to find out more from the squires either. We only speak what little is necessary during the weapons practice. Roul was absent for a long time and only returned to the group a few days ago. He still looked pale. Whether it was due to his illness or the death of his uncle, I cannot say. He needs all his strength to hold even the smallest weapon and not trip over his own two feet. Talking to him is almost impossible in this state, but with the low mood amongst the others and the grim looks of my guards, words were sparse on the battleground anyway. At first, our fights looked as if we were all carrying a heavy stone on our shoulders. Our movements were slower than usual, our attacks more hesitant, our defences half-hearted – until one day, Thibault interrupted our fighting.

"What has happened to you? You fight like washerwomen lashing out at each other with wet laundry! Where has your fighting spirit gone? Your ambition? Your will to win? You think you're worthy of being called warriors? Then prove it to me! Show me! Fight for your right, your reputation and your honour! I once met a young Engleis who, in the face of death, stood shoulder to shoulder with his friend and challenged an entire force of heavily armed Normans. At the time, his home village was in flames, much of his family dead, the ground covered with his countrymen. Death seemed inevitable for him too, and yet, the young Engleis would not surrender to his fate without a fight. He fought back till the very end. He could not save his friend, but he himself survived because he believed in himself, because he never forgot that he was the son of a ðegn and born to fight. No warrior worth anything gives himself up until he has drawn his last breath."

He who does not fight is worth nothing.

In the darkness, I see Thibault's penetrating gaze, as if the master of arms were standing before me. As his face fades away, my life passes me by. My years as the son and heir of an English ðegn. The battles I fought with Ulfgar at my side. The great battles we survived together. Our last stand at Ledlinghe. I relive the attacks, but also the few moments of happiness I have had here in Wilburgfos. Thibault's face has become distorted behind all these images. It has become more elongated and ugly, with a pointed beard and a protruding lower jaw.

"Stígandr!" I startle.

The first glimpse of light falls through the small window in the door. I look around to make sure that it was all just a bad dream, a delusion of my mind, and that Stígandr is not actually skulking around the shed. As I stand up awkwardly, my left ankle cracks as I stretch out on my tiptoes to warm up my cold and stiff muscles. I glance out of the window. No one there. *Not yet.*

From the great hall come the first sounds of the morning. Two servants shuffle across the yard with a large basket to fetch firewood. Soon, more servants will swarm out to feed the animals, milk the cows and collect the hens' eggs. Slowly, life awakens in Wilburgfos. *Life!*

My hands are clammy. I let go of the corners of the blanket and rub my hands together. My stomach growls. A warm meal would do me good. Most of the time, I get leftover stale bread and a bowl of cold oat mash left by the barons. There is only water to drink, and even that tastes stale and bland. How fortunate I am that Cenric is the cupbearer's son and can wander along the storage rooms without anyone suspecting, making it easier for him to slip a piece of bacon or a sausage or two to me during one of his visits.

With a grin, I picture my English friend outsmarting his French rulers once again. The Lord may have taken away my family and my home in Ledlinghe, but He has also blessed me with a few people in Wilburgfos who make me feel not entirely lonely. People who trust me and who give me the comfort and closeness I had in Ledlinghe. People like Thibault and Cenric... and Solen. I remember her standing outside the door of my prison one day with a worried face and a few soothing words. All too soon, she had to sneak away again because one of Lord Geoffrey's men turned up, and it was imperative for her not to be seen with me. No one but the master of arms and my prison guards were allowed to visit me. Cenric did it anyway, as did Solen.

She is young, beautiful and virtuous. Like Godgifu. I lower my head as the memory returns. *I am to blame for her death. How could I ever think about another woman again when the remorse of having put my beloved wife into an early grave is still so fresh?* The more I try to chase Solen from my mind, the harder it is to think of something else. Morwenna keeps us in the dark about her family, but it is obvious that Solen is the daughter of a nobleman and of high lineage. Surely, more than one of the French barons at the manor has asked for Solen's hand in marriage. The thought that someone else might have her tears my heart apart. *What can I offer her? I have lost everything that a husband should give her, my rank, my manor, my reputation. Even my scramasax they have taken from me.*

A sigh wells up inside me, but a whispering voice in my head makes me stop in mid-breath, so that I stand there as if swollen with pride –

"...survived because he believed in himself, because he never forgot that he was the son of a ðegn and born to fight."

I let the air escape noisily from my mouth. *What is the worst that can happen to me in court? That they sentence me to death on the testimony of a Norþmann? He has no witnesses. Only a few other than the three of us were out on the yard at that late hour, and those who still had work to do were trying to finish it quickly. No one would have been bothered about a light in the chapel. However, I can just as little prove that I am innocent. The French will have to decide who they believe more, an Englishman or a Norþmann.*

"Are you awake, Oswulf?" a voice asks.

The metallic click of a key in the lock sounds. The door opens a crack.

"Thibault! What are you doing here at this hour?"

The master of arms hands me a bundle and a cup. "Here! Take this! You will need it today."

I look into the cup, take a sip and feel a tingling in my throat. "Ale!" Several large gulps of the delicious barley juice follow the tentative sip.

"I will come and get you later," Thibault says with a serious look. "Sire Geoffrey has scheduled your trial will be up first this morning."

I wipe my moustache. "First, right, thank you."

The master of arms points to the sack in my hand. "Eat and drink! You'll need all your strength today. The charges against you are heavy, and you're not facing an easy opponent."

I nod obediently. Thibault glances at the two guards standing next to him. *Does Lord Geoffrey think that the master of arms will help me escape if they send him with the key to my prison by himself? Or that I will try to overpower him in order to flee?*

"I have a few things to do, Oswulf," Thibault says. "Be prepared."

One of the guards closes the door and locks it. As the footsteps move away, I open the bag in which I find fresh bread, a sausage and a piece of smoked eel.

"Si bletsung Drihtnes ofer þe, Thibault," I mutter, sit down and greedily bite into the fish. *If I have to fight for my right and my life today, let it not be to your shame.* I raise the cup in the air. "Wæs hal! For Englaland, my father and the French master of arms."

❧

"HERE THEY COME!"

The murmuring in the great hall swells as two Frenchmen lead me inside. They have tied my hands together with a thick rope, not knowing that I can wield a weapon even with my hands in shackles. But resistance would not get me far in this crowd of armed men. Besides, even with my hands tied, the guards won't let me out of their sight until the trial is over.

Many put their heads together and whisper. In their faces I read concern rather than anger or vindictiveness. Quentin was not a popular man, but that is true of most French barons here and at other manor houses. Lord Geoffrey may be married to an Englishwoman, as are many of his countrymen, who use marriage to justify their claims to English lands. But our peoples are separated by a deep gulf of suspicion and contempt. I pray to God that this gulf will not be my downfall today.

The squires are sitting in the second row – all except Roul. Can he not bear to see his uncle's alleged murderer? Or is he saving his strength for more important things than the conviction of another Englishman? The boys' faces are petrified. I don't know if they think I'm guilty or innocent, but what difference would it make? They are only squires. What weight would their word have in court?

In front of the squires, in the very first row, Walchelin and Thibault sit with serious faces. The master of arms nods encouragingly at me.

An unpleasant feeling spreads over my back. I look to the end of the row, where a figure with a diabolical grin above the chin beard and eyes narrowed to slits lolls about like Satan himself. The man who is responsible for all my misfortune and who has put me in this position. *Stígandr. If I ever get my hands free again, I will reach for the first weapon I can find and use it to send him back to hell where he came from. If only I had killed that snake in the grass at Stanfordbrycge, or in Ledlinghe in the three years since! All these years, he has been working to bring envy and misery to the son of the ðegn who had everything he did not possess. Would that I had split his skull when I had the chance! Leof dryhten, if I cannot save my own life, let me at least take Stígandr with me into the afterlife and avenge all the misdeeds that have come upon my people and my family through him!*

My guards stop me in front of the raised table. Up there sit the accusers who will decide about my guilt and my life:

Frederic the seneschal, Lord Geoffrey and Hugues de Borre, the bailiff. Frederic's face is relaxed, while the other two Frenchmen look at me grimly. *Can I put my hope on the twelve jurors who, together with my judges, will pass sentence? Half of them are French, and I can expect little clemency from them. But the other half are English – will they vote for the innocence of their fellow countryman?*

My gaze meets Cenhelm's, a brief smile of despair flitting across his face. He takes a deep breath as if his own life is at stake.

While the seneschal asks for silence, I turn around. I wonder where Cenric is. For a moment, concern for my friend blots out my own misfortune, but the sound of the barrel-shaped reeve clearing his throat brings me back to cruel reality.

He struts along in front of me and thunders the following speech at his listeners: "Sire Geoffrey de Bernaium, Messires, men of Wilburgfos. It is our duty today to decide on the dastardly and despicable murder of the esteemed Baron Quentin de Lisieues at the hands of an Engleis who has grossly abused our trust and respect for his base purposes."

I can just about refrain from laughing out loud. *Trust and respect from the French? From individuals, perhaps, but for Lord Geoffrey and his advisors, I have always been the hateful enemy they had to live with as long as I have the master of arms' favour.*

In a large gesture, the reeve extends his arm in my direction. "You see here the accused, Oswulf, son of Osfrið of Ledlinghe, whom the master of arms, Thibault Braz de fer, rescued from a battle that would have meant his certain death. Thibault also brought him to this manor house, where the accused received bread and lodging in return for his work with the squires. The defendant owes his life and welfare to a Norman. He repays him by luring an excellent warrior and compatriot of our generous and just liege lord into the chapel and there – in a place of worship! – treacherously stabbing him to death with a short sword. He could have killed even more men, had not our messenger, who happened to observe the evil deed, stepped in."

Happened to? He had it all figured out to the last detail!

"Who knows who his next victim would have been?" The reeve pauses before addressing the jury. "It is your duty, honourable jurors, to restore justice to this manor house and to bring the culprit to the punishment he deserves."

He waddles over to me and plants himself on the space just in front of me. "I ask you, Oswulf, do you plead guilty to having fraudulently deceived, entrapped and murdered Quentin de Lisieues?"

Wordwringa! Your words are as swollen as your belly. "I am innocent, munsire. I myself was lured into a trap. Your messenger did not observe the deed but carried it out himself."

There's a murmur in the hall. The reeve looks at me as if I had spoken to him in English and he didn't understand a word of it.

Before he can say anything, Frederic jumps at the chance. "Could you be more specific about who you mean by 'your messenger', Oswulf?"

"The Noreis Stígandr, who has served you as a messenger for a long time."

Stígandr gives a brief laugh. "What a laughable idea! Everybody knows what Quentin and the accused thought about each other. My only regret is that I didn't pass by sooner. Perhaps I could have saved Quentin, and he would still be alive now."

"You were standing outside the door all the while, just waiting for an opportunity to kill Quentin with my scramasax. You wanted it to look like I killed him."

The murmur grows louder.

Frederic raises his hand and turns to me again. "Are you saying that Stígandr killed Quentin and not you?"

"That's right, munsire."

Stígandr waves his hand. "There you go, he's clearly mad. He killed an innocent man and wants another one condemned for his outrage. You must not allow this! The accused must realise that in this manor house, law and order also apply to Englishmen."

Frederic, Lord Geoffrey and Hugues de Borre exchange a quick glance.

"So you plead not guilty?" the seneschal asks.

"That's right, munsire. I did not kill Quentin."

Frederic gives the two guards a wave to lead me to the side. "Then I suggest we begin the questioning to find out which of you is telling the truth. Hugues?"

The bailiff nods. "We call Thibault, the master of arms, as our first witness."

He would probably have preferred to call another witness. The master of arms will do everything to defend me. But they have to hear him out because he is responsible for me.

Thibault gives me a look and steps forward.

"You saved the accused from death in February this year and brought him to this manor house. Why did you do that?"

"I had never seen a young warrior fight like him before. I brought him here to pass on his fighting skills to our squires."

"Did you never worry that he might seek revenge?"

"No."

"What makes you so sure?"

"Who would he have wanted to take revenge on? He was a stranger when he came and completely on his own in a manor house full of Norman warriors. Revenge would have been hopeless from the start. Tell me a single incident that has given you the slightest cause for concern since his arrival!"

The judges look at each other puzzled. Frederic turns his palms upwards and shrugs his shoulders. Lord Geoffrey shakes his head imperceptibly. Hugues raises an eyebrow and turns back to Thibault.

"It seems we have no complaints about the Engleis. Yet he is accused of killing a respected Norman. How do you explain that?"

"It is not for me to explain, but I very much doubt that he would commit such a crime."

"His short sword was stuck in Quentin's body when our messenger found them."

"That is correct, but not sufficient to convict him."

A murmur sweeps through the rows again. My skin tingles.

"The testimony of our messenger is clear. He was a witness to the event."

"So was Oswulf, and he says the messenger killed Quentin."

The murmuring in the hall grows louder. Hugues leans back with the corners of his mouth pulled down.

God bless the master of arms! He's fighting for my life even in the face of defeat.

"I think we have heard everything we wanted to know, Thibault," Frederic says. "Please sit down again. Would you like to proceed, Hugues?"

"I call the squires Eudo FitzRou and Eustace Landry as my next witnesses!"

298

Eudo and Eustace? Of all people, the two who can hardly say a word to your face and instead prefer to whisper behind their hands?

Eudo and Eustace stagger to the judges' table and stop awkwardly.

"Eudo FitzRou, Eustace Landry, you are squires under the command of the master of arms. Since February, the accused has also been responsible for teaching you in warfare and the use of weapons. How do you feel about an Engleis as your instructor?"

The two of them cast a shy glance at me. Eudo nibbles at his fingernails. Eustace whispers something in his ear.

"Parlés haltement!" thunders Hugues. "You are in court, not with the babbling women in the kitchen."

Scared, the two stand straight. Eustace is the first to calm down enough to speak. "We thought it was a strange idea."

"What do you mean by that, strange? Par Deu, why don't you say clearly what you mean?"

"He's an Engleis. We are Normans."

"Exactly." Eudo nods eagerly. "We don't need an Engleis to teach us how to fight. The Engleis have lost to us."

"How did the accused behave towards you and the other squires?"

Eudo shrugs his shoulders. "He didn't say much at the beginning. He didn't know our language, after all. He ordered us around with the weapons."

"What do you mean? What did he do exactly?"

"If he thought we were standing the wrong way, he would hit us on the leg with the wooden sword," says Eudo. "Or if we attacked, he knocked us over or just stepped aside so that we ran into the void."

Eustace takes a step forward. "Wherever he could, he made fools of us when we fought. He always wanted to show that he was better than us. Any ruse was good enough for him."

Niþingas.

"I did not make a fool of you. I showed you what you still have to learn. That was my duty."

"Thibault has never embarrassed us like this in front of the others," Eudo barks.

"You amuse yourself by making us look like dolts," adds Eustace.

"Pes, messires!" says Frederic. "You are not here to quarrel, but to answer truthfully the questions of the court."

Eudo and Eustace fall silent, grumbling, and give me an evil look.

"If I understand correctly, you claim that Oswulf not only used ruses on the battleground but also took pleasure in exposing you in front of the others, is that correct?"

The two youths nod. "Yes, exactly."

"Then why didn't the master of arms intervene? As far as I know, he was always present at the weapons practice. Didn't you complain to him about the new teacher?"

The two examine their feet in dismayed silence.

"Responez!" barks Hugues de Borre with such force that his unruly hair is shaking wildly.

"We talked to him, but he said that was exactly what he expected," Eudo replies.

"And that it was exactly what he wanted, because that way, we would learn much faster," says Eustace.

Frederic exchanges a glance with Thibault and the other two judges. Lord Geoffrey is still sitting in the chair with his arms folded as if the trial is none of his business.

"Roul cannot attend the trial today because he is still seriously ill," Frederic tells the squires. "You know him well. How does he feel about Oswulf?"

Eudo waves it off. "The two of them couldn't stand each other from the beginning. Everyone could see it. More than once, they butted heads on the battleground, calling each other names and hitting each other like savages. We thought they were going to kill each other."

"Those were practice fights," I say. "He is more advanced than you, so I had to fight him differently."

"Outside the battleground, they also argued," says Eustace. "Everyone in here can testify to that."

"They hated each other, and that's why Oswulf also hated Roul's uncle," says Eudo. "He is an Engleis and will always be one."

"I didn't hate Roul, and I didn't hate his uncle, even though he tried to kill me several times."

The men in the hall audibly suck in their breath. The murmuring swells; even the three judges exchange a few words before Frederic raises his hands to silence the men.

When the noise dies down to a tolerable level, Frederic looks at me. "Who tried to kill you, Oswulf?"

I look around uneasily. Maybe it wasn't a good idea to mention the assaults. "Quentin tried, munsire. He hired people to get me out of the way."

The seneschal struggles to stop the interjections, which range from simple insults to demands for punishment.

"How do you know it was Quentin who instigated the attacks?" shouts Hugues over the hecklers.

I hesitate. If I mention the name of the groom who put us on his tracks, they might take revenge on him. "One of his henchmen had noticed that the man from whom they received secret orders sounded strange. He said the words sounded like a hiss. At the manor house, there is only one whose speech sounds like that."

A whisper spreads. Eudo cautiously raises his hand. "Are we still needed, munsire?"

"No, my boy," the seneschal replies. "You can sit down."

"As you can see, he had reason enough to kill the baron," Stígandr says loud enough that no one can miss it.

"What were those attacks, Oswulf?" asks Frederic.

I shrug my shoulders. Outwardly, I try to look calm and in control so that they can't accuse me of bad behaviour in court, but inwardly, a storm is raging through my body, making it tremble. "Once, they dragged me into the woods at night, beat me up there and tied me to a tree. Another time, someone pushed me into the river. In the last attack, the girth of my saddle was cut so I fell off my horse. I can only thank God and your healer that I am still alive."

Frederic looks at Lord Geoffrey as if expecting a comment from him. He turns back to me, frowning. "Can you prove these accusations?"

"I have witnesses who were there and rescued me, munsire."

The noise in the hall is now deafening. The audience is waving their hands around wildly and discussing loudly. Frederic wrings his hands as he watches Hugues talking to Lord Geoffrey. My heart pounds loudly as if entering the great battle of Stanfordbrycge a second time. A bead of sweat runs down my temple, tickling me. I hastily wipe my face with my tied-up hands.

"Silence!" Lord Geoffrey slams his fist on the table. "We are not here to judge a dead man, but to punish his murderer."

"Who, according to the evidence, is standing before us," says Hugues de Borre. His hair is blazing like flames on his head.

"I didn't kill Quentin!"

Is there no one here who speaks for me? Doesn't anyone trust what I say? Do not even those whom I worked with daily believe me?

"It is my word against the Norþmann's. Do you believe him more than me?" I look at Thibault seeking help, but his gaze is thoughtful.

If he has the slightest doubt about what I say, I am lost. Then my fate is sealed. I will die today. I lower my head. Tears well up in my eyes. *Father, what have I done? How could I even dare to ignore your warning? What a fool I was to ever believe that a Viking would help me! Now, I will have to pay for it. I deserve it. If only I could see Solen one more time! What will she think of me when she learns that they executed me like a common, vile robber?*

I sniff and hold my head up high. If I die today, let it be with dignity and not as a beggar whose life is worth nothing and who yet whimpers for mercy.

"Let's hear what the messenger has to say about this!" says Hugues, gesturing with his head for Stígandr to step forward.

Without haste, Stígandr leaves his throne and ambles along the judges' table as if I were already dangling from the nearest tree. His goat face reflects all the arrogance and deceitfulness he has never shed since our quarrel while out hunting almost five years ago.

"Stígandr Olafsson, shoemaker from Ledlinghe, you have served Sire Geoffrey as a messenger for some years and know the accused from your home village," said Hugues.

God sceal forlætan þe to ðam ecan forwyrde.

"Indeed, we grew up together," says Stígandr. "But in the last few years, Oswulf has changed a lot, and somehow, I sensed that one day, he would come to a sad end." He casts his eyes down, shaking his head. "That he would furtively stab someone to death in a place of worship, however, no one could have guessed."

"Lygewyrhta!" I call out. "We used to be friends, until you became jealous because I am the son of a nobleman and because your uncle acquired land and wealth through fraud. When it was certain that I would become a huscarl, while you would remain the son of a shoemaker forever, you could not bear the thought of it, and now, you want to pay me back and have me condemned for a murder I didn't commit."

Stígandr puts his hand on his chest and stares at the judges. "Do I need to suffer the insults of the defendant? I am only telling the truth, which I am obliged to do in court."

"You don't even know what that is, truth!"

"Please hold your tongue, Oswulf!" says Frederic. "You will be permitted to give us your opinion in a moment." He nods to Stígandr. "Please tell us what you observed that night."

"Well, I had suspected for some time that the accused was up to something bad. I often found him talking to the son of the English cupbearer, away from everyone else. This struck me as odd, so I decided to find out what the two of them were talking about that clearly no one else was supposed to overhear."

"You eavesdropped on us and sounded us out, just as you did with everyone you subsequently betrayed!"

"Oswulf?" Frederic gives me a reproving look. "I told you not to interrupt. Please let Stígandr finish, or I will have you escorted from the hall."

Wordwringa! He twists everything so that it looks like I have been planning Quentin's death for a long time.

"The accused told me about the alleged assaults on him and that he assumed Quentin wanted to kill him. If you ask me, these conflicts were unfortunate coincidences that unsettled him so much that he saw an enemy in everyone here at the manor house. Gradually, he aimed his hatred at Roul and his uncle, and he made up stories which he himself eventually believed to be true."

My soul screams, my muscles quiver, my teeth grind against each other. I want to pounce on Stígandr and shove his false words back down his throat with my fist, but I hold back. I want to hear what he says so that I know what he will pay for once I get my hands on him.

"I casually asked the accused what he wanted to do now, and he answered that he wanted to confront Quentin at his prayer time. But in his eyes, I saw his lust to kill glimmering, and I suspected that he was up to evil. That is why I crept after the accused when I saw him leaving the hall that evening shortly after Quentin. I saw him follow his victim to the chapel and that he had his scramasax with him. That's when it all became clear to me. He wasn't going to talk to Quentin. He wanted to kill him."

Breathless silence. Countless pairs of eyes are staring at me.

Leof Dryhten, help me! A bead of sweat burns its way down my chest, as if someone were cutting my skin open with a sword, as a taste to the torment awaiting me, until finally the merciful death stroke puts an end to my misery. *I don't want to die for a wrong I did not commit.*

"And when you came to the chapel, Stígandr, what did you observe there?" asks Frederic after a long pause.

"The accused harassed the poor baron with words. When Quentin wanted to leave the chapel – probably because he suspected what Oswulf was up to – the latter held him back. Without taking heed of my own safety, I rushed into the chapel. The accused told me to leave, but when I stood firm, he drew his sword and stabbed Quentin to death before my very eyes."

"Death seemed inevitable for him too, and yet, the young Engleis would not surrender to his fate without a fight. He fought back till the very end... No warrior worth anything gives himself up until he has drawn his last breath."

"I didn't stab him!" I shout with all my might. Looking at the seneschal, I take a breath before continuing in a calmer voice. "Please let me speak, munsire, and tell you what really happened."

The three judges exchange glances.

Are they wondering whether it's even worth it to let me have my say? Isn't the evidence clear? Clearly against me? Everyone watching has already decided who they believe more. After all, most of them are French and therefore on the side of Quentin and the story as Stígandr has told it. What prospects do I have?

Thibault rises, and immediately, all eyes turn to the master of arms. "If you will allow me, Frederic, Sire Geoffrey, I would like to give you my thoughts on this."

I rub my knuckles. My heart is hammering. The linen vest sticks to my chest. My gaze wanders restlessly between the faces of the judges and that of the master of arms.

Lord Geoffrey nods. Frederic beckons. "Please, Thibault. You know Oswulf best of all of us. Let us hear what you think of the incident."

The master of arms turns to the assembled men. "One of our compatriots has been killed, messires, and we must find the one who did it. You have heard from the reeve what happened. The only witness has told us what he saw. But we cannot stop here. The law and justice require that we also hear the accused, whether you believe him guilty or not. I know Oswulf better than anyone in this hall. I have seen him fight, and I brought him to this manor to assist me in teaching the squires. I know that many resisted my decision at first and that Oswulf was met with hatred and rejection, and not only by Normans. But that has never kept him from dutifully and impeccably performing the task for which he is here in Wilburgfos. Others have treated him disrespectfully and with contempt, but he has shown a poise and integrity rarely seen in a man of his young age. Instead of returning like with like, he took care of what he does best: to fight. Many complained to me that he is an Engleis, but apart from that, I have heard no other accusations since his arrival. Nothing to suggest in the slightest that he harboured such hatred for Quentin that he plotted his death and brought it about in the chapel. Only two men were there at the time, and we must question them both." He turns to Frederic. "Let him speak, messires. You have heard a Noreis. The same right is due to an Engleis."

The judges confer and nod unanimously.

"Step forward, Oswulf, and tell us what you have to say," Frederic says with a conciliatory look from his kind eyes.

The stares from the audience feel like hundreds of little stings on my skin. I see haughty disapproval in the faces of the jurors, as if they doubt that I can still save myself by talking, and as if I am only wasting their time and dragging out the trial unnecessarily. I swallow, rub my wrists together, which are slowly going numb from the tightly wrapped shackles, and stand before the judges with the courage of despair.

"No warrior worth anything gives himself up until he has drawn his last breath."

"Messires, I have known Stígandr since I was a little boy. He wants to accuse me of murder because he hates me."

Stígandr raises his hands defensively. "I'm just saying what I saw."

"Of a murder not committed by me, but by himself."

"Ha! The culprit accuses me! He is mad, messires, and a danger to us all."

"Please refrain from interrupting, Stígandr!" says Frederic. "You were allowed to speak undisturbed. Grant Oswulf the same right."

Stígandr smiles disparagingly. "Of course, munsire."

He feels so safe there, out of my reach and knowing that my hands are tied and I have no sword within reach. If I don't control myself now, they will throw me out, and the jury will pass their verdict without having heard me first.

I take a deep breath and turn to the three Frenchmen at the judges' table.

"I hated neither Roul nor Quentin, messires. One day, I was thinking with Cenric, the cupbearer's son, how we could convict Quentin of the assaults against me. Stígandr overheard us. It was he who suggested that I seek Quentin out in the chapel at evening prayer, and who offered to listen in on our talk, hiding by the door. If Quentin confessed, Stígandr could testify as an earwitness. But he never intended to do that. He deliberately lured me into a trap."

"How could I know he would kill him?"

"I urge you again to be silent, Stígandr," Frederic says. "You have had a chance to speak. If we have any questions at the end, we will call upon you. Please, Oswulf, go on!"

"I had my scramasax with me that night because since the assaults started, I haven't taken it off, even when I sleep. I handed it to Stígandr before entering the church. He told me to do so himself." A hiss spreads amongst the audience. "Then I went to Quentin and spoke to him. At first, he resisted, but when I showed him I was unarmed, he began to talk. He told me his nephew thought I was a good man, and he too had seen that I was doing good work with the squires. He admitted he had treated me unfairly and even Sire Geoffrey and Thibault were very pleased with me, like his nephew, Roul. At that moment, Stígandr appeared in the chapel, saying he had heard everything. This was all I needed, so I asked for my weapons belt and wanted to leave. Stígandr made to hand it over, but would not release his hand from the scramasax, saying I didn't need one where I was going then stabbed Quentin in his belly with the sword. He died in my arms. 'Forgive me!' were his last words. The man who at first hated me so much that he wanted me dead, begged my forgiveness with his last breath. While the one who hates me ran off to conclude his betrayal."

The hall is filled with the murmurs and incredulous interjections of the audience. Frederic, Hugues and Lord Geoffrey look at each other helplessly. *It's my word against the Norþmann's. Whom will they believe? Stígandr has done them no wrong. His reputation is impeccable, as far as I can tell. But didn't Thibault just make the same point for me? That my only fault is being English? What is left for them to make a judgement? Two assertions and their own opinion.*

"Thank you, Oswulf," says Frederic. "We have no further questions for you. You may return to your seat. Do you have any more witnesses to question, Hugues?"

The bailiff shakes his head.

Frederic's gaze sweeps over the liege lord before turning to the jury. "Good, then I will hereby close the questioning. The jury will retire to deliberate and then return a verdict."

I wipe the sweat from my forehead. My guards lead me to the edge of the hall, far away from the judges' table. The jurors leave their seats and walk past me to confer undisturbed outside. They try not to look at me, and when my gaze meets theirs, they hastily turn their heads away. It is impossible to tell from their faces how they will decide. *Were they convinced by what I said? Or was I allowed to speak only to satisfy the court's protocol? Have they already made their decision?* My hands tremble. Since I cannot fold them because of my shackles, I clench them into fists and close my eyes for a moment. *Fæder ure þu þe eart on heofonum, gewurþe ðin willa, on eorðan swa swa on heofonum.*

Many people in the audience are talking in low voices, some are standing, others are leaving the hall. Thibault and Walchelin have joined the judges at their table. Hugues and Thibault are talking animatedly, accompanying each of their sentences with a nod or a shake of the head. The squires exchange words eagerly.

"Beo strang, Oswulf!" A figure flits past me and hurries to the squires.

Cenric! Where has he been all this time?

Images flash through my mind. My father taking me on one of his errands for the first time when I was a boy. Ulfgar frolicking with Bargest, his long shaggy hair twirling in the air. Godgifu laughing in the sunshine, running towards me to embrace me. My mother fetching fresh bread from the oven. My sisters Æðelflæd, Wassa and little Eda, laughing and dancing. My brothers Wigstan and Oswine, fighting with wooden swords on the manor in Ledlinghe. The shields, spears, axes and banners with which our men and the Norþmenn fight fierce battles. The dying. The corpses on the battlefield. The mutilation of my father. The French invasion of Ledlinghe. The burning houses. Screaming women and children. My home village in flames as it gets smaller and smaller behind me. My battles and the assaults here in Wilburgfos. And finally, Solen. I want to swallow, but my throat feels tight.

Solen.

I remember the day I sat with the squires making arrows and watching her float light-footedly across the yard. Her dark brown curls swing freely with every step. She gives me a look from her dark blue eyes which make me forget everything around me. *If I could at least see her one more time before they condemn me to death! Just once, before I have to leave her forever. I would have been her protector if Morwenna had had her way. Now I leave her defenceless, like Godgifu.*

The commotion in the hall makes me prick up my ears. I feel a hand on my arm.

"Aluns!" One of my guards makes a head movement forward and pulls me with him.

The jurors take their seats. The empty space in the hall fills up. Stígandr swings his cloak around him with a sweeping gesture of his hand and settles down in his chair with relish. The teeth of his lower jaw protrude from the sneering smile. He rests his elbow on the back of the neighbouring chair and twirls his beard, which I would like to wrap around his throat and pull so hard that the smile freezes on his goaty face. *What a satisfaction for him to see his arch-enemy like this, accused of murder with his hands bound and soon to be sentenced to death by the false testimony of a Norþmann. If only I were allowed to fight for my life!*

Frederic stands and raises his hands. "Silence, messires! We will proceed with the pronouncement of the verdict. Silence!" He turns to the jury. "Messires, have you reached a decision?"

A Frenchman rises and nods. "We have, munsire."

Frederic looks at me. "Would you like to say something before the verdict is declared and the sentence is pronounced?"

"And yet, the young Engleis would not surrender to his fate without a fight." I lick my dry lips and straighten up. *I am the son of a ðegn and born to fight.* "I am innocent, messires, and I will fight to prove it."

A faint smile flits across Frederic's face. Lord Geoffrey watches everything silently and without moving. Hugues de Borre scowls at me. Thibault and Walchelin sit on the edge of their chairs, ready to jump. The squires keep looking towards the entrance of the great hall.

"We'll see what the jury has to say about that." Frederic makes a gesture towards the jury and takes his seat. "Please, tell us what you have decided."

The Frenchman, still standing, squares his shoulders. "Sire Geoffrey de Bernaium, messires, men of Wilburgfos. After deliberation, the jury have reached the following verdict. We find the accused Engleis—"

"Wait!" shouts someone from nowhere. "We've someone here who's seen everything."

Cenric appears in the doorway, supporting a young man with his arm. Roul. Amid the murmur of the people, the two make their way forward, followed by Hild the healer.

Cenric? Roul? What's going on? A flutter spreads through my chest.

Thibault waves the two of them over. Cenric lets Roul slide onto the chair. The boy is pale as a linen sheet.

Hild bows to the judges. "Forgive us for disturbing the proceedings, messires, but it was not possible to bring Roul to the trial earlier. The illness is sapping his strength, but he has something important to tell you."

"Are you trying to make fools of us?" Hugues points at Roul. "The boy is sick. He doesn't know what he's saying."

Hild looks straight at him. "His mind is less clouded than that of many a healthy person."

Cenric points to Roul. "Besides, he's an eyewitness."

"An eyewitness?" Frederic exchanges a puzzled look with his table neighbours. "Neither Oswulf nor Stígandr mentioned that anyone else was in the chapel that night."

"They couldn't, because they didn't know he was there." Cenric looks at Roul and makes a motion with his hand. "But you should tell 'em yourself."

Roul sits up. His movements are slow. He looks haggard, but he smiles weakly at me.

"Women are not allowed at court hearings," grunts Hugues.

"The boy is sick," says Hild, planting herself in front of the judge's table. "If I can't stay, I'll take him back to the herb hut. Then you can question him there."

"She can stay." Lord Geoffrey waves his hand. "Let the boy talk."

All eyes turn to Roul, who begins to speak haltingly. "When my uncle heard that an Engleis was to teach us squires, he was beside himself. I too was horrified that one of those we had defeated should teach us how to fight successfully. Hadn't the Engleis just proved that they were inferior to us Normans on the battlefield? This Engleis, however, fought better than

I did. He also fought better than all the other squires. Even Jehan could do nothing against him. I tried again and again to win against the Engleis, but it was impossible, which only made me more angry with him. I often talked to my uncle about how the Engleis embarrasses us. How he enjoys making fools of us and humiliating us on the battleground. My uncle found this humiliation unworthy of a Norman and tried everything to make the Engleis disappear. Anything, really. He even paid people to kill him. He wanted to silence the Engleis, for he had realised that protesting would get him nowhere. It had to look like an accident or be done secretly so that no one would see it. The master of arms has always stood by Oswulf, and even Sire Geoffrey was not inclined to let the Engleis go because of resistance amongst his vassals." He groans and catches his breath. "I know that the master of arms even threatened to leave the manor if the Engleis was sent away. I also know that my uncle was responsible for the assaults on the Engleis. But I only found that out when I got used to Oswulf's ways and realised that in many ways, I was fighting better than before. He was an enemy, but he knew exactly what mattered in battle. He knew every attack and every defensive move and showed us steps and ruses that we could use to make our opponent miss or surprise him. I had to admit to myself that my anger and pride stood in the way of my progress and that this Engleis was the best thing that had happened to us squires. A few days before my uncle..." he swallows, "died, I had a long talk with him. I told him all that the Engleis had done for us and that his masters were also pleased with him. And that I didn't want him to kill the Engleis."

"Asez!" Hugues sweeps his hand through the air. "Will you tell us now what you saw that night?"

"I had not been well for a few days. I even had to miss the weapons practice again because I was suffering from vomiting and fever. That evening, I was so sick that I had to get out into the yard as quickly as possible. I just about made it outside the door before I threw up. Then I saw the light in the chapel. I knew it was my uncle at his evening prayers. But then I noticed that the chapel door was open and that a figure was lurking nearby, repeatedly peering into the chapel. They had something in their hand, but I couldn't see what it was. So, I crept closer to the chapel in the shadow of the houses until I found a spot behind the bushes from where I could watch the figure. From within the chapel came two voices – my uncle's and a voice that spoke Norman with an accent that sounded familiar. It was Oswulf's."

The glares from the audience hit me like arrows. I start to sweat. *What he says now will decide my fate.*

"So, you knew that Oswulf was in the chapel with your uncle," says Frederic. "Were you able to hear what they were talking about?"

"No, I was too far away. They didn't speak very loudly."

"Did you see who was standing outside the chapel?"

"Not at first. Then I crept closer. I saw that the Noreis, Sire Geoffrey's messenger, was standing there. I also recognised what he had in his hand."

"What was that?"

"It was Oswulf's weapons belt, and he was holding on to the short sword."

"How did you know it was Oswulf's weapon?"

"He is the only one with a scramasax at the manor house. Besides, the decorated leather scabbard is unmistakable."

"What happened next?"

"The Noreis entered the chapel. I left my hiding place and crept to the gate, even though I was sick again and could hardly walk upright. But it was not only my illness that caused my stomach pain. I had a bad premonition that something terrible was about to happen." Roul lowers his head. His shoulders rise with a long, heavy breath.

Cenric pats him on the back. "Almost there, Roul," he says quietly. "Just these last words."

Roul rubs his face with his sleeve and looks up with tired eyes. "I made it to the church door where I sat down for a moment to rest. Oswulf asked Stígandr if he had heard everything. I looked cautiously around the corner. My uncle was standing between the two of them. Oswulf asked the Noreis to give him the weapon belt he was still holding. He said that they could go now, like they had achieved all they wanted. But the Noreis held on to the sword." Roul's chin trembles. "He said Oswulf wouldn't need it anymore. Then he killed Uncle Quentin with it. Oswulf caught my uncle and called after the Noreis, but he had long since run past me. He was going to blame Oswulf for my uncle's death. But I saw who the real culprit was." He jumps up and lunges at Stígandr. "You killed him, you cursed fiz a putein! Go to hell, felun!"

Cenric grabs Roul by the sleeve and holds him while Roul lashes out.

"Let go of me! I'll send him back to hell myself. Let him pay for killing my uncle! Let go of me!"

Hild and Thibault come to Cenric's aid to restrain the raging youth.

Stígandr no longer looks as confident as he did when the trial began.

"Silence!" barks Hugues.

The men fall silent. Thibault pushes the exhausted Roul towards Hild, who takes hold of him with open arms.

"Thank you, Roul," says the seneschal. "I think you have cleared up the last uncertainties with your words."

"The boy is clearly not in his right mind." Stígandr waves his hand in the air. "You saw how he tried to come at me. He is sick. You can't believe his words."

Hild resolutely straightens up beside Roul and looks at the judges with a stern gaze. "Roul's body is sick, messires, but his mind is perfectly clear."

"She probably clouded his mind with some herbs," says Stígandr, "so that he would tell us a story that saves an English murderer. Do not forget that she's English too. You will not take the word of a sick boy and a herb witch, will you?"

"How dare you?" Hild gasps. "People come from far and wide to be healed by me."

"With all due respect, messires," says Thibault, stepping forward, "Roul has been my pupil for many years, and I do not have the impression that he is under the influence of mysterious herbs. Moreover, what he says corroborates what Oswulf has told us."

My clothes are as sweaty as on a hot summer day. My ears are smouldering, my wrists burning from the restless rubbing of my hands in the tight rope. "Munsire! Munsire!" I shout to get the attention of the seneschal.

Frederic turns his head towards me. "Yes, Oswulf?"

I take a step forward. "Munsire, if you want God to judge whether Roul is telling the truth, then I will fight in his place."

Frederic nods thoughtfully. "Perhaps the jury should deliberate again first, to take Roul's words into account when making their decision."

The French spokesman for the jury rises again. "Munsire, we have already reached a decision after the young man's testimony."

"Well then, let us hear what judgement you have come to."

The spokesman lets his eyes wander over the judges, the listeners and finally me. "Sire Geoffrey de Bernaium, messires, men of Wilburgfos. After the words of Squire Roul le Blanc, we have come to the following verdict. The accused Engleis Oswulf did not kill Quentin de Lisieues and is, therefore, not guilty."

My ears are buzzing. *They acquit me? I am innocent?*

Frederic smiles contentedly. Lord Geoffrey and Hugues de Borre put their heads together. They look in Stígandr's direction. My gaze wanders to Thibault. The master of arms nods briefly and clenches his fist. Someone slaps me on the back while one of the guards cuts my shackles. I rub my wrists and look to the side. In front of me is Cenric, grinning from ear to ear.

"Eala min freond! You didn't think good ol' Cenric would abandon you, did you?"

For the first time in a long while, I feel the corners of my mouth move upwards. "Cenric! To be honest, I had already finished with my life. You saved me!"

Cenric taps my arm with his elbow. "We English must stick together, don't we?" He points to Roul, who briefly raises his hand as Hild leads him out of the hall. "And have good friends."

I hug Cenric and pat him on the back. "Ic ðancige ðe, Cenric! I will never forget this. Tell Roul that I will visit him later to thank him, too. I never thought that he, of all people, would be the one to save me from death."

Frederic stands up and raises his hands. "Silence, messires, silence! Sire Geoffrey still has something to say."

I am breaking into a sweat. *The liege lord? Does he not want to accept the verdict? Yet they have already cut my shackles.*

Lord Geoffrey rises. "Messires, we have heard the jury's decision and recognise it in the light of the testimony of the Norman eyewitness."

I take a breath. Stígandr, on the other hand, is sitting on his chair, legs crossed, elbow propped up on his thigh, thumb and two fingers at the root of his nose, eyes closed. He is shaking his head. *He was so sure of his victory. He would never have thought it possible that a sick squire of all people would spoil his revenge. And yet it happened. Ðe ic herige, Drihten ælmihtne!*

"I hereby absolve the Engleis Oswulf of his guilt. Now, it remains for us to try the murderer of Quentin, who sits over there." Lord Geoffrey points his finger at Stígandr, who looks up and sees himself surrounded by the two Frenchmen who, until moments ago, had been guarding me.

"What?" The Norþmann puts his fingers to his chest and sits up. "I'm supposed to have killed Quentin?"

Lord Geoffrey wipes his hand through the air. "Save your words! What we have heard has clearly convicted you as the culprit."

Stígandr jumps up. "You believe the confused tales of a sick child?"

"You're talking about the son of a Norman baron, felun. I could have your cheeky tongue cut off for that."

Stígandr makes a bow. "Forgive me, my lord, but as you have seen, the boy is gravely ill. How do you know that he really saw—"

"Silence! The healer said that his mind is unclouded by the illness."

"She is just a woman. How can she tell—?"

"Teisez vus! You will fight for your life. If you win, I'll chase you from my manor house. If you lose, I have one thing less to worry about."

Stígandr looks around in disbelief. "Fight? Against whom?"

I step before Lord Geoffrey. "I will fight the Noreis, sire."
This time Stígandr will not escape me. Today, the Norþmann is going to die by my hand.

The liege lord examines me briefly, then nods. "So be it!"

I give Stígandr a look and make my way to the door. *How long I have waited for this day! Revenge for Englaland, for my family, for Ulfgar.*

~

In the yard, the men form a ring around the battleground, onto which fine snowflakes drizzle down from a light grey sky. I slide my foot forwards and backwards on the ground. The earth is hard, the layer of snow still too thin to slip on, unless the snowfall thickens. My breath forms a white cloud of mist in the frosty air. The cold encloses my face and hands like an iron glove, but I don't freeze. I take off my heavy woollen cloak and hand it to Thibault. For far too long, I have remained idle in this cloak in my prison. In one long breath, I suck in the freedom that lies just one last battle away from me.

Thibault puts his hand on my shoulder. "I know you have to do it. Be careful, though!"

I nod. *I will be careful. Until my blade pierces the Norþmann's body.*

Jeannot comes hurrying from the armoury. He walks awkwardly, loaded like a donkey with two swords and two round shields. I would have preferred a battle-axe, but the weapon will make no difference. Stígandr will not survive this day. The young squire holds out the weapons to Thibault.

"Each of you chooses a sword and a shield," the master of arms announces, waving Stígandr over to us.

The Norþmann strokes his chin beard as he saunters towards us, watching me.

"You pick one first, Stígandr," I say. "It will be the last choice you'll ever make."

"Oh, our young Englishman is as generous as a king. But perhaps he's overestimating his capabilities a little, after more than three weeks of captivity, eh?"

"You'll be the first to answer that question, Viking."

Stígandr examines one of the swords and takes a shield to go with it. "The last few weeks have surely made you sluggish, Osfriðson. Think carefully about what you do." He walks back to the far end of the battleground.

"I did, Stígandr," I call after him as I pick up my shield and sword. "You know that as well as I do." My fingers close tightly around the cool leather that surrounds the wooden handle. An unexpected strength floods my whole body. I feel a warmth inside me that I haven't felt for a long time. That was missing in all the time I sat locked up in the shed.

We stand facing each other, swords halfway up, shields protecting our left sides. Only now do I notice Father Leofric. Glancing at each of us, he steps into the middle of the battleground.

The fact that he has to stand in the cold until the battle is over and he can give the last sacrament will certainly annoy him. But what do I care, as long as he gets out of my way quickly?

Father Leofric slowly raises his hands. "The Lord will protect the innocent and punish the guilty for their sins. Our Father who art in heaven, Thy will be done on earth as it is in heaven. Let the battle begin!" He strides back into the human ring and stands next to Lord Geoffrey.

I raise the shield and walk towards Stígandr, who is still wearing the thick cloak that conceals but at the same time restricts his movements. He moves aside without taking his eyes off me. I let him have his way until I am only two steps away from him. Then I leap forward, aiming for his left thigh. He lowers his shield just in time. My sword crashes onto the wood. I throw myself against him with the shield. Stígandr staggers backwards, catches himself and lunges with his sword. I pull up my shield, flinging his sword aside. I thread my sword between us and swing it to the right. Stígandr grunts. He pulls the shield in front of him.

I circle him slowly. "Do you remember what I said the last time we met, when you killed Quentin, Stígandr, do you remember? I promised you then that I would kill you if you betrayed me. I also promised you that this time it wouldn't be just a threat, like the times before when you escaped me. Do you remember? Do you also remember that I said I would not rest until you were lying on the ground covered in blood? That moment has come. This day will be your last. You will die and atone for all that you have done to me, to my family, to my village, to my homeland."

"Even if I should die today, you will never find peace."

Stígandr surveys his wound, then straightens up behind the shield and turns in my direction. "You are the one who betrayed his village. The one who abandoned his village because he wanted to play spies. If it hadn't been for me, you wouldn't have reached your village until everyone was already dead."

I clench my teeth. My fingers tighten around the hilt of the sword.

"You know my words are true, Osfriðson. But you think that by accusing me, you can wash your hands clean of the blood of your wife, your parents and your brothers and sisters. You know as well as I do that you will not succeed. You will be eternally guilty of the death of your family."

"Swiga, niþing!" I rush forward and stab at his neck with my sword.

Stígandr deflects with his shield, strikes at my head with his sword. I go down on my knees and catch the blow with the shield. From the outside, I swing the sword into his left leg, just below the edge of the shield. Stígandr cries out again. A large, dark red stain forms on the cloth strips around his leg.

I take a step back and look at my opponent. "Today, God is on my side, Stígandr. You have taken advantage of his mercy long enough to lure others into destruction." I let the sword circle in my hand.

Stígandr stands before me, bent over and breathing heavily. One could almost feel sorry for him, but before my eyes appear all the faces of those to whom his treacherous behaviour has brought death. *How many times has he himself escaped death, while so many good men have died? So many women and children.* I'm about to walk towards him again when he raises his sword hand.

"Wait! The jury has found you not guilty, and I am defeated." He looks at Lord Geoffrey, Frederic and Hugues de Borre.

"I will pay you the wergeld for Quentin and leave the manor house forever."

"So you admit that you killed him?" I ask, taken aback by the sudden confession.

"Yes, I killed him! I wanted to get rid of you for good because you were finding more favour with the French than I did. You were about to jeopardise my office at the manor house. You were going to destroy everything I had worked for, for so long."

"You've already destroyed everything I've worked for. You don't think you can buy your way out so easily, do you?"

"Call this fight off, messires. I will pay you for the damage."

"This fight will continue, Stígandr."

Stígandr spreads his arms. His tunic has a dark stain on the belly. "Look at me, Oswulf! I am wounded. You have won. We need fight no more."

"Yes, we must, Stígandr. The two of us will fight until one of us is dead on the ground. And that will be you."

"I'm sure we can come to an agreement." Stígandr's gaze wanders desperately over the faces of those who surround us, watching in stony silence. No one intervenes. No one wants to end the fight prematurely. "How much is the wergeld for Quentin? Five hundred shillings? A thousand? I'll give it to you. I can pay it, whatever it is."

How lost he stands there in the midst of the dancing snow-flakes. A man lost in the woods, unable to find his way out and desperately calling for help. But no one is there to give him an answer. He will have to find the way himself or die.

"You would sneak away before you paid the money." I pick up my sword and shield and walk towards Stígandr. "Save your words! You have only ever thought of yourself. The fate of those you betrayed for gold and empty promises meant nothing to you. Expect no mercy for yourself when you have denied it to others all your life."

I swing the sword at Stígandr's shoulder. He just about raises his shield to intercept the blade and stumbles to the side. I follow up with a blow from the front. He deflects and swings the sword into my side. My shield trembles under the impact. Stígandr pushes me backwards. I catch myself, leap to the side to avoid a thrust and aim for Stígandr's snow-covered head. He raises his shield. My sword crunches on the metal shield boss. I kick Stígandr in the unprotected belly. He grunts and staggers backwards.

"You have betrayed me for the last time," I say. "Now, I'm keeping the promise I made to you the last time we met."

"I'll give you money, Oswulf," groans Stígandr. We stand so close to each other that I can see the beads of sweat on his face. His lower jaw is trembling.

"You cannot buy your way out, Stígandr. No gold in the world is enough to make up for what you have done to me and my country. You will pay for your treachery with your life."

I jump sideways. Stígandr stumbles forward. I want to strike his back with my sword, but trampling upon the snowy ground has made it slippery. *Wa la wa!* My foot slides forward. I lean towards the side. Stígandr jumps up and kicks my shield. I fall onto my back, my arms wide open to catch myself. Little more than an arm's length above me appears the grinning face of the Norþmann. He lunges with his sword. Despite the thick snowfall, I see the evil glint in his eyes. The sword is coming down on me. I pull the shield in front of me and stab upwards with the sword.

"Argh!"

An ice-cold hand descends on my chest and squeezes the air out of me. Something heavy hits my head, followed by a thud. My sword is pressed to the ground. The shield slams into my face. I writhe in fear of death, trying to lift the sword again. My breathing is shallow and hurried. I feel like I'm choking and breathe even faster. With all my strength, I push the shield away from me and try to free my legs. Over the edge of the shield, a distorted caprine face is glaring at me, flashing the teeth in its lower jaw. *His sword? Where's his sword?* I look around frantically, try to feel where I am injured. I cannot move my sword, no matter how hard I try.

Stígandr's eyelids twitch. I can feel his breath coming in bursts. "You have won, Oswulf," he whispers.

Is he trying his wiles on me again? My head wants to burst as I heave the shield up and pull my legs out from under the weight. Stígandr groans again. Only now do I see that my sword has pierced through his belly. *He is dying.* "I've kept my promise," I say, more to my father than Stígandr.

The Norþmann rolls his eyes. His body trembles, then his head hits the shield.

It takes a while for my breathing to calm down. I struggle free and slowly stand up, eyeing Stígandr suspiciously. I expect him to sit up again at any moment and tell me with a grin that I've only dreamed it all.

"Eslevez le!"

I turn round. Hugues de Borre beckons two men. Next to Lord Geoffrey stands Father Leofric with folded hands. His lips move silently.

"Where should we take him?" one of the men asks as they lift Stígandr.

Lord Geoffrey waves his hand. "Throw him in the river!"

The men nod wordlessly and leave with the dead man.

"Will he not be buried in the cemetery?" asks the seneschal.

The liege lord shakes his head. "There is no place for traitors in my manor. He has profited long enough without being much use to me."

Father Leofric raises his hands. "We thank the Almighty for showing us the right way and for punishing injustice. We pray for the soul of the deceased, that one day it may find its way to the kingdom of heaven."

Frederic looks around in confusion. "Well, then, that's settled, so, I hereby declare the hearing closed." He turns to me. "You are free, Oswulf."

Free.

The circle around the battleground dissolves.

I feel as if someone is pulling an icicle across my skin. My teeth begin to chatter. My limbs tremble. I look up into the white flakes falling ceaselessly from the sky. My father's face appears in the snow flurry. He's smiling.

Someone throws a cloak over my shoulders and pats me on the back. "I'm sure your father would be proud of you now, Oswulf." Thibault smiles at me encouragingly.

I nod. "Yes, I guess he would be."

Thibault pushes me forward, and I see two figures with hoods pulled low over their faces, covered in a layer of white. We walk slowly towards them. Under one hood is a smile between two cheeks reddened by the cold. A dimple flashes in the left cheek. *Solen.* I feel the cold on my skin, but I'm getting warm from the inside. My heartbeat is pounding in my ears. My mouth is dry.

"We feared for your life," Solen says softly, and her cheeks glow even more.

The blood in my temples rushes like a waterfall. "Did you?"

Solen's mother nods appreciatively. "You were imprisoned for a long time, but it doesn't show when you fight."

I look at Morwenna. She looks pale, haggard, as if weighed down by sorrows. "Fighting badly can be fatal, dame. It was very important to me to win this one."

"A personal feud?"

"A matter of honour."

"I am pleased to see that the Engleis also place great importance on protecting their honour from shame and disgrace."

I nod, frowning. A shiver runs through my whole body. I am grateful to Thibault for pulling me along.

"Come, Oswulf! I have a few things to discuss with you."

Chapter 11

IN THE LATE WINTER OF THE YEAR OF OUR
LORD 1071

It is a clear winter's day as I set off on the final journey in search of my destiny. The fresh snow is crunching under my leather shoes.

Cenric is pacing forwards and backwards beside me. "Ðæt is forwundorlic wundor! Never has anything like that happened here in Wilburgfos. An Englishman, of all people, at a French manor house! The most noble lord of Cattune himself has come to Wilburgfos to pay his respects to you. Can't believe it!"

"You're exaggerating, Cenric." I try to sound calm, but my heart is fluttering.

"Exaggerating?" Cenric props his hands on his hips as we continue towards the chapel. "The great William Als Gernuns de Perci rides all the way to his vassal's manor house to dub an Englishman captured in the wilderness and now tamed? This is Wilburgfos, Oswulf, not Wincestre, where they're always crowning some king."

We enter the chapel, festively decorated for Candlemas. Father Leofric gives final instructions to the altar boys. Lord

Geoffrey and Thibault have put their heads together with a man in chain mail and heraldic tunic, on which five yellow lozenges shine on a blue background.

That must be William de Perci. The man before whom I will bend the knee. The man who will deal me the only blow I will ever receive without fighting back after being dubbed.

More and more people crowd into the chapel – Frenchmen like Walchelin, but also Englishmen like Cenhelm. I even catch sight of a few women at the back: Lady Edeva, in spite of her poor condition, has taken the trouble to attend the dubbing of a fellow countryman. Next to her, Hild is keeping a watchful eye on her mistress. Behind the herb woman and right next to Morwenna stands Solen, looking around the chapel with wide eyes. She spies me, and a smile crosses her face until her dimple appears. Her skin is not quite as rosy as usual, but the radiance of her eyes brightens the chapel more than all the candles placed along the walls and on the altar.

Godgifu I have lost forever, but Solen is here. Within reach. Close enough to hold on to. Never would I leave her alone, as I did Godgifu. I made that mistake once and regretted it bitterly. I'll never make it again. If only she will have me.

"Stop making eyes at the women!" Cenric nudges me to the side. "C'mon, get over there! Father Leofric wants to start."

Giving Solen one last look, I put myself next to Walchelin. I hear Leofric's muffled words. My thoughts wander. Only when I hear my name do I listen. William de Perci beckons me. The master of arms is standing next to him. I step forward. My hands are trembling. Images of Ledlinghe well up in my mind. Ulfgar and I, surrounded by Frenchmen, all eyes on us and our movements. This time, I stand here alone and have nothing to fear from the French. From this day, I am a recognised warrior, not a ðegn nor a huscarl, but a servant of the King of Englaland. *I have made it.*

Father Leofric holds out the Bible to me, on which I place my hand.

"By the holy writ and by the Lord, I, Oswulf of Ledlinghe, vow that I will be faithful and honourable to my liege lord, William de Perci, and love all that he loves and shun all that he shuns, according to God's law and according to worldly custom, and never, willingly or intentionally, either by word or work, do aught which is dishonourable to him, on condition that he respect me as I am willing to deserve."

William de Perci turns to the master of arms, who takes off his belt, sword and all, and hands it over to the liege lord after Father Leofric has blessed it.

"Oswulf of Ledlinghe, you have proven yourself to be a fearless and worthy fighter and are henceforth a warrior of the king. Take this sword as a gift and a reward for what you have done for your country and your king." He girds me with the sword while I look questioningly at Thibault.

When William de Perci has finished, he makes way for the master of arms. Thibault steps forward and turns me around to face those assembled. "Messires, you see before you the new master of arms of Wilburgfos."

Who? Me?

"That he is a brave and skilful warrior is known to all who have ever faced him in battle. Having been dubbed, he is now a vassal of the king. He will from now on take over teaching the squires by himself."

"Amen," Leofric says aloud and folds his hands.

While the first ones push their way out through the chapel door, I linger on, confused.

"But *you* are the master of arms of Wilburgfos." I look at Thibault, frowning.

"Only until I have fully handed over my office to you."

"But...?"

"I am going back to Normandig as soon as the weather permits, to receive the inheritance of my father, who has recently died."

"You are leaving Wilburgfos? I am to teach the squires alone?" Loss, fear, uncertainty buzz through my head like flies.

The master of arms puts his hand on my shoulder. "You know this is your destiny, Oswulf. You will be a worthy successor. I can think of no one to whom I would rather hand over my duty. The same goes for my sword, by the way, which has always served me well in battle." He points to the sword hanging at my side.

I look at him. His brown eyes have a warm, friendly glow that encourages me, and yet, I feel as if the ground has been pulled out from under my feet. "You're leaving."

Thibault smiles. "Wilburgfos is too small for two masters of arms. Besides, you have my sword. I will always be at your side as long as you carry it."

I nod, even though his words do not give me the comfort I need right now. An emptiness spreads through me, smaller than the one that befell me after the death of my family and the parting from Ledlinghe, but still similar.

"We should hurry." Thibault pushes me forward. "Father Leofric is already on his way to the great hall, and you know what a hungry lion that puny priest becomes when asked to a feast."

The churchman is just stepping out through the chapel door, turning his head sideways. His gaze wanders downwards and slowly upwards again. He's licking his lips. *Swa gifre swa swine. Slobbering already from his sleazy mouth, although he has not even set foot in the great hall.*

"Now, now! Who's gonna make a face like that on their day of honour?" Cenric makes a deep bow, abjectly waving his hand in the air. "I bow to you, hlaford min. May you teach the French to fight and put the fear of God into them for many years to come!"

I roll my eyes, but I can't help grinning. "Sometimes, you remind me of one of those jugglers who fool their audience with magic and words, Cenric."

Cenric frowns. "Do I hear envy in your words? Ah, c'mon, Oswulf!" He slaps me on the back. "You may be a servant to a Frenchman here in Wilburgfos, but you also work for the King of Englaland. It's what you always wanted, isn't it?"

The picture of my parents appears in front of me. They're both smiling at me. "I guess you're right, Cenric."

Before I can speak further, the squires surround us, cheering me as their new master, even if they regret Thibault's decision. Somehow, we are able to squeeze through the door of the great hall in a cluster, where the smell of roast duck wafts towards us.

As we enter, Roul stands wide-legged in front of me and props his hands on his hips. His blonde hair shines in the glow of the fire, and his face is back to its usual colour. He looks at me seriously. "If you are now the sole master of arms, does that mean that we must now exclusively follow the orders of an Engleis?"

I stroke my moustache. "Indeed. And now that Thibault is no longer protecting you, I will make you work even harder than before."

"Quei?" Roul's mouth remains open.

Jehan puts his arm around Roul's shoulders and laughs. "Calm down! The harder we work, the better we get, and the better we get, the sooner we'll be dubbed and need not listen to him anymore."

"This is your fault, Roul." I hold out my right hand to him. "If it hadn't been for you, there would be no English master of arms now. There wouldn't even be the Engleis anymore. I don't know how to thank you for that."

Roul pauses, but then a smile crosses his face. "Just let me win a fight every now and again." He takes my hand and squeezes it tightly.

I look around, see the faces of Cenric, Thibault, Jehan, Roul, Jeannot, Walchelin, Cenhelm and all the other inhabitants of the manor. How much things have changed in the last twelve months! Initially outcast and abandoned, I have finally found my place in life and know where I belong. The silly bowl cuts and French singsong are no longer foreign and mysterious. They have become part of my new home. I have a place to sleep, I have food and drink, I've been dubbed and have become an integral part of society here at the manor house.

What more could someone like me want?

౿

I wonder what Morwenna would like to discuss with me. She's making such a secret of it! And we're meeting in the middle of the woods, of all places, at this time of year! I shake my head as I steer my horse towards the small clearing in the woods east of Wilburgfos. *Apart from squirrels or a hungry fox, no one will overhear us there, that's for sure.*

Through the bare, snow-covered trees, I follow the small trail that leads to the clearing, where two shadows are pacing back and forth.

As they catch sight of me, they stop and watch. Morwenna looks at me with raised eyebrows. Against the white background of the winter woods, it strikes me only now how pale she looks, even though I have long had the impression that she has changed. Her cheeks are more hollow than usual, but her bearing is as erect as ever, commanding respect and reverence. Solen keeps lowering her head or looking uncertainly in another direction when I look at her. Even though her cloak covers her completely, I can see that she's fidgeting underneath.

A dull feeling of tightness rises in my stomach. "You wanted to see me, dame."

"Indeed." Morwenna looks around as if to make sure that we are alone. "Dismount, so we can talk."

Obediently, I get off my horse and step forward. "I'm listening."

"I appreciate your complying with my wish, Oswulf. I expected nothing else from you, and now, I see that I have come to the right decision."

"A decision?"

"I had to take it. It's a matter of life and death."

Dryhten min! Solen is fatally ill and will die soon. A tremor runs over my skin as if I were standing naked in a snowstorm. Solen lowers her eyes, but I think I saw a fleeting smile. "Then speak, dame!"

"You could do me a great service."

I hold my breath as if bracing myself to receive a blow to the bare skull with a two-handed battle axe in a fight.

"Times have changed, as I predicted. However, not in the way I wanted. There are some... changes at the manor house that force me to act."

The woman speaks in riddles. Just like back then. She drives me mad with her double talk.

"Do you remember our first encounter in the woods last year, Oswulf? At that time, you and your fellow Engleis told me that the woods were too dangerous for two women."

Abnoba, luck in the hunt, Ostara, fertility. I nod.

"Also, I asked you if you would be willing to protect our lives with yours, but you refused."

I shake my head in despair. *This woman is worse than any English riddle! Why can't women ever speak in a way that can be understood?* "What exactly do you want from me?" I ask irritably, but a glance at Solen makes me immediately regret my outburst. I bite my lips.

Morwenna stares at me silently, as if considering whether to answer my question at all.

I feel like a little boy who has to withstand his mother's stern look after he has done something stupid and she has found out. "Forgive me, I—"

"You are impatient. That is also a good sign. I do not want to take up your time unnecessarily. Therefore, grant me this single request." She puts her arm around Solen. "My daughter is the only thing I have left in this life. I've lost everything else. I guard her like a treasure, but where I go I cannot take her with me."

"You're leaving? Where to?"

"That doesn't matter. What matters is that someone takes care of my daughter in my absence and stands by her in dangerous times."

I wait, but she says nothing else, while Solen looks at me coyly from below. "You want me to look after your daughter? I am a master of arms, I teach squires, not girls."

"She does not need any teaching from you. She has mastered everything to run a household. She needs your protection."

"What are you talking about?"

"Solen is obedient, hard-working and gifted, and also of noble birth. You will not regret it. If you promise to see to it that no harm comes to her, I want to give her into your care and for her to become your wife."

I look at her as if she has lost her mind. "You want me to... marry Solen?"

"I see you have understood. Well?"

I'm freezing and sweating at the same time, I feel dizzy, my vision is blurred, the blood rushes through my ears, my heart threatens to burst. I look at Solen from top to bottom and back again. Her eyes shine like dark crystals. "I... I..." *Dryhten min!* I clear my throat and straighten up, but my voice trembles. "Certainly, I will take care of your daughter if that is your wish."

"Good, then we are in agreement." Morwenna takes Solen's right hand and motions for me to hold out my right hand. Solen's delicate white fingers brush my skin as Morwenna places her daughter's hand in mine and then clasps both our hands with hers. "By virtue of my authority as my husband's widow, I hereby give you my daughter's hand in marriage. Do you pledge to protect her from all harm and uphold her honour until death do you part?"

My heart tightens at the thought of this beautiful girl being touched by someone else. *Godgifu has been dead for almost a year. Don't I deserve a second chance to prove myself as a husband, now that I have earned the highest honour as a warrior?* "I vow by all that is sacred to me to protect Solen. My vengeance will befall anyone who tries to do her an injustice. This I swear on my honour."

NO ONE NOTICES how Solen and I leave the great hall. The people are too busy eating to pay attention to us. I pull Solen along behind the armoury, where we won't be disturbed at this time of day. The sun has disappeared below the horizon, but it is still bright enough to see how beautiful my betrothed is. I brush a strand of hair behind her ear and look deep into her eyes. "Why did I have to find out about this through a messenger from her half-brother? Your mother never said anything about her origins."

Solen shrugs. "She thought it would be too dangerous if others knew about it before we reached the end of our journey."

"Sire Geoffrey told the messenger that he would let you continue your journey as soon as you were no longer needed at the manor house. Does he know where your mother is?"

"No. Nobody knows."

"Not even you?"

Solen looks at me, pressing her lips together. I'm sure she knows, or does she?

"You can't tell me."

She remains silent.

"Eventually, we will know where she is. She wrote in her farewell letter that she hopes to be able to requite Sire Geoffrey at some point for what he has done to the two of you." As Solen lowers her head, I take her hands and stroke them with my fingers. "All that matters now is that you are here. When

William de Perci dubbed me and Thibault appointed me master of arms of Wilburgfos, I thought there was nothing more I could wish for. Now, I know there was something missing to bring my happiness to perfection." I place her hands on my chest and clasp her in my arms. "You must not leave me. We are going to get married soon. Father Leofric will—"

"No, not Father Leofric! He... My mother doesn't want him to marry us. She says we will get married where the end of our journey is. She's just not ready to continue the way there. Not yet. But soon. She promised me. Until then, it's your duty to protect me."

I stroke Solen's hair. "I swore that to your mother, yes. I will prove to you that she made a wise decision."

"I trust my mother's decision, and I will do everything I can to make you happy and pay my debt for your protection."

Slowly, I lift Solen's chin and bend down to her. "I would not mind if you started right now, deorling."

Afterword

8 September 1066 was the beginning of the end of Anglo-Saxon England. On that day, the Norwegian King Harald and his English ally Tostig, brother of the English King Harold, set off from Tynemouth with three hundred ships, sailing south along the northern English coast and plundering everything they found on their way. Scarborough, little more than a day's march from Leavening, tried to resist and was completely burned down. The Norwegian army continued their raids until the huge fleet advanced inland on the River Humber.

At this time, King Harold, who was waiting in the south for the Normans to invade England, had already disbanded his assembled army. The peasants who made up the fyrd had to go home for the harvest in August, so the king had to release them. However, this did not stop him from riding north with his huscarls – heavily armed elite warriors – when he heard of the invasion and raids of the Norwegian king.

After the victory at Fulford on 20 September 1066, the Norse army became reckless and only took the bare minimum of armour and weapons to Stamford Bridge, where they waited for hostages and supplies to be brought to them by the residents of York. Instead, however, they soon found themselves facing the overwhelming English army in full battle dress, led by King Harold and his huscarls.

While the English king defeated the Norse army and killed King Harald Hardrada, his warriors engaged in another battle with the Norwegian rearguard, led by King Harald's prospective son-in-law Øystein Orre. King Harold also won this battle, but the fighting had taken its toll on the English army, too.

Together with Olaf, the son of the Norwegian king, and Paul Thorfinnsson, the Earl of Orkney, King Harold agreed to a truce, which he accepted on the condition that the two and their followers swear never to attack England again. Only then would he allow them and their surviving army to depart. Otherwise, he would continue to fight them until the last one of them lay dead on the battlefield. Olaf and Thorfinnsson gave him their word that they would immediately leave England and never return.

With his father's lifeless body and just over a thousand men, Olaf subsequently set off for Riccall, where he dismantled the camp and sailed home with barely twenty-five of the original three hundred ships, never to be seen on the English coasts again.

Decades later, it was still reported that the battlefield at Stamford Bridge was white with all the bones of the fallen warriors.

But the winners did not have much time to catch their breath, for soon after, the threat they had been waiting for all summer in the south arrived: Duke William and his Normans landed in Pevensey and began plundering and burning the land. With his exhausted huscarls, the English king set off on his final journey.

Even after the Norman conquest of England, peace was fickle. Numerous uprisings in Wales, East Anglia – where the

English rebel fighter Hereward the Wake made life difficult for the Norman troops – and Northumbria kept King William on his toes for years after his coronation.

In December 1069, the new king ordered a campaign whose cruelty shocked even hardened warriors as well as loyal supporters and advocates, and which would go down in English history as the "Harrying of the North".

For two months, the Norman troops ravaged the land between Nottingham, Durham and York, causing a famine of unprecedented proportions. The death toll is estimated to be in the tens of thousands, with significant social, cultural and economic damage to the entire region. Out of desperation, survivors fled as far as Evesham Abbey, 250 km south of York, where records were kept of the starving.

At Easter 1070, William was crowned again to demonstrate his power. Sixteen years later, the Domesday Book, a survey of England listing (almost) all places along with inhabitants, animals and resources, still described the state of many places in the affected areas as "wasta" (vasta: laid to waste/destroyed).

William had defeated the English of the north, but neither he nor his kingdom would have peace for very long.

Places

Unless indicated otherwise, placenames are in Old English.

N = (Anglo-)Norman
ON = Old Norse

Aluertune – Northallerton, North Yorkshire
Cantwarebyri – Canterbury, Kent
Cattune – High and Low Catton, North Yorkshire
Chercam – Kirkham, Lancashire, one of the many fiefs of
　　Earl Walþeof
Chileburne – Kilburn, (south)west of the North Yorkshire
　　Moors
Deorwente – Derwent, Derbyshire and Yorkshire, river west
　　of Leavening and Wilberfoss
Dunholm – Durham, Durham County
Eastengla – East Anglia, East of England
Elig – Ely, Cambridgeshire
Englaland – England
Escumetorp (ON) – Scunthorpe, North Lincolnshire, south
　　of the Humber
Eoforwic (Everwic N), Eoforwicscire – York, North Yorkshire
Fors Bekkr (ON) – Foss Beck, North Yorkshire, river through
　　Wilberfoss
Fuleforde – Gate Fuleforde, North Yorkshire near York

Hæstinga – Hastings, East Sussex, where the decisive battle
for England between Norman and English forces was
fought on 14 October 1066

Humbre – Humber, river between Yorkshire and Lincolnshire

Huson – Howsham, North Yorkshire, west of Leavening

Ledlinghe – Leavening, North Yorkshire, south of Malton

Lunden – London

Maltun – (Old) Malton, North Yorkshire

Melduna – Maldon, Essex

Myrce – Mercia, Staffordshire, Derbyshire, Nottinghamshire, northern West Midlands, Warwickshire, old Anglo-
Saxon kingdom between Northumbria and Wessex

Normandig – Normandy, France

Norþhymbre – Northumbria, Northumberland, County
Durham, Tyne and Wear, old Anglo-Saxon kingdom between the river Humber and the river Forth, largely inde-
pendent from southern England

Norþ-Walas – Wales

Nortone – Norton, County Durham, south of Malton

Norweg – Norway

Pevenesel – Pevensey Bay, East Sussex

Redrestorp – Raisthorpe, North Yorkshire

Renliton – Rillington, North Yorkshire, east of Malton

Richale – Riccall, North Yorkshire, last navigable place on
the Humber, south of York

Sandwice – Sandwich, Kent

Scotland – Scotland

Snotingeham – Nottingham, Nottinghamshire

Stanfordbrycge – Stamford Bridge, East Riding of Yorkshire,
site of The Battle of 1066 between English forces and the
Norse army of King Harald Hardrada

Tatecastre – Tadcaster, North Yorkshire, southwest of York

Use – Ouse, North Yorkshire, one of the rivers running through York

Waruuic – Warwick, Warwickshire

Westseaxa – Wessex, Hampshire, Dorset, Wiltshire, Somerset, Berkshire, Avon, old Anglo-Saxon kingdom, from which the kings of all England emerged, descending from King Alfred the Great and, in particular, his grandson, King Athelstan, around the turn of the 9th/10th century

Wiht – Isle of Wight, Hampshire

Wilburgfos – Wilberfoss, East Riding of Yorkshire

Wincestre – Winchester, Hampshire

Glossary

Unless indicated otherwise, words and phrases are in Old English.

The form of address changes in the text from "Lord" to "Sire" and from "Lady" to "Dame", respectively, depending on whether a male or female noble person is meant in the context (speaker, listener). "Lord" and "Lady" are the Old English terms, "Sire" and "Dame" the (Anglo-)Norman terms.

Text in brackets is the literal translation of the word or phrase.

N = (Anglo-)Norman
ON = Old Norse

Aluns (N) – Let's go
Arestez! (N) – Stop! / Enough!
Beo ðu hal, leof cyning! – (Be healthy, dear king) Long live the king!
Beo strang! – (Be strong / determined!) Hold on!
Chevaler (N) – rider, in particular a knight.
Cnæpling – a youth
Ða Frenciscan sculon deaþe sweltan – (The French shall die from death) Death to the Normans!

The Normans are usually called French (Frenciscan) in Old English. The term "Norþmann", "man from the north" (see below) is used for Scandinavians in general and for Norwegians or Danes in particular.

Ðæt is forwundorlic wundor – (That is really a wonderous wonder) That's absolutely amazing

Ðe ic herige, Drihten ælmihtne, forðam þu bist swiðe rummod and swiðe mildheort! – I praise thee, almighty God, for thou art benevolent and merciful!

Ðegn, plural: ðegnes – thane, vassal of a king, between a freeman and lower nobility.

Deorling – Darling

Ðis is laðlic! – (This is disgusting!) Yuck!

Dites mei (N) – Tell me

Dryhten min – Dear Lord

Ðu scealt gan libbende on helle! – (Thou shalt go living [alive] into hell!) Go to hell!

Ðu wyrma gifl – You worm food

Eala – Oh! Oh dear!
    Exclamation of surprise or pity.

Eala ðu wundorwiga – O wonder warrior
    A warrior who does wonderous deeds or fights in a wonderous way.

Eala min freond! – Oh, my friend!

Engleis (m), Englesse (f) (N) – inhabitant of England / speaker of English; the English language

Eorl, plural: eorles – earl
    High-ranking nobleman and military leader right below the king. The title usually follows the name in Old English, but for modern readers, the title has been placed before the name.

Eslevez le! (N) – Take him away!

Fæder ure þu þe eart on heofonum, gewurþe ðin willa, on
  eorðan swa swa on heofonum – Our Father who art in
  heaven, Thy will be done on earth as it is in heaven

Felun (N) – evildoer, wicked person, traitor, felon

Fiz a putein! (N) – Son of a bitch!

Frenciscan – Frenchmen, including (Anglo-)Normans

Fyrd – Anglo-Saxon army of freemen
  The king would assemble fyrds in times of war, and they
  complemented the army of his bodyguards.

Git hildlatan – (You two war slouches) You two cowards

Gleoman – medieval entertainer
  A Gleoman could be anything from a travelling minstrel,
  musician, juggler and thespian to a jester and fool.

God sceal forlætan þe to ðam ecan forwyrde – (May God surrender you to eternal damnation) May thou burn in hell

God þin feorg freoðie, min sunu – (May God protect your
  life) Bless you, my son

Hastez vus (N) – Hurry up

Hastez vus e alez hors de la chapele! (N) – (Hurry up and
  leave the chapel!) Get out of here!

Hi sculon gan libbende on helle! – (They shall go living
  [alive] into hell!) Go to hell!

Hlaford min – my lord
  Form of address for a ruler or military leader / superior

Hlafordswica! – traitor (of a [liege] lord)

Hu eald eart ðu? – How old are you?

Huscarl, plural: huscarles – elite warrior and bodyguard of
  the Anglo-Saxon king
  Later, also of the powerful earls, until the 11th century.
  He was heavily armed – with the fierce, two-handed battle

axe as his weapon of choice – and rode to battle on his warhorse.

Hwær is Hen? – Where is Hen (the animal's name)?

Hwær sind þine ældran? – Where are your parents?

Hwæt dest ðu, Hroðgar? – What are you doing, Roger?

Hwæt is þin nama? – What is your name?

Ic cnawe – I know

Ic ðancige ðe, Dryhten min – I thank you, dear Lord

Ic ðancige eow – I thank you (plural)

Ic ðe wilcume – (I welcome you) Welcome

Ic eom Frederic. Wilcume! – I am Frederic. Welcome!

Ic eom nigontinewintre – I am nineteen winters (years) old

Ic hatte Oswulf – My name is Oswulf

Ic hine wergðo on mine sette – (I put my curse on him) Curse him

Ic ne cnawe ana hwa...? – I don't know a single one who...?

Jo vus en mercie (N) – I thank you (plural)

Leof Cenric – Dear Cenric

Leof Dryhten – Dear God

Lieve toi, engleis! (N) – Stand up, Englishman!

Lygewyrhta – Liar

Merelle (N) – Norman medieval version of Nine Men's Morris

Min fædre wæs Osfrið, Morkere eorles and Harold cyninges ðegn, þe ge acwealdon – My father was Osfrið, a thane of Earl Morkere and King Harold, whom you killed

Min nama is Oswulf – My name is Oswulf

Munsire, plural: messires (N) – sir
Form of address for a man of high status or nobility. See also "Sire".

Næfre ic sceal wigan for wuldre Angla banan – Never I shall fight for the honour of the slaughterers of the English

Ne ealle – Not all

Ne ic hine cwealde – I did not kill him

Niþing, plural: niþingas – outlaw, rogue, coward
> Originally used for discredited huscarls whose rank had been revoked.

Norþmann, plural: Norþmenn – inhabitant of a northern European (Scandinavian) country, in particular, a Norwegian or Dane

Noreis (N) – inhabitant of a northern European (Scandinavian) country, in particular a Norwegian

Osfriðson (ON) – son of Osfrið
> The suffix 'son' would be added to the Old Norse patronym (father's name).

Par Deu! (N) – By God!

Parlés haltement! (N) – Speak up!

Pereçous (N) – sluggish, lazy person or people; lazybones

Pes, messires! (N) – Peace, my lords!

Quei? (N) – What?

Responez! (N) – Answer!

Riddan – riders, knights

Scirgerefa – (shire-reeve) sheriff, royal administrator of a town or district (shire) in Anglo-Saxon England

Si bletsung Drihtnes ofer þe – (May God's blessing be over you) God bless you

Silence! – Silence!

Sire (N) – Sir
> Form of address for the liege lord as opposed to "munsire".

Swa gifre swa swine – Greedy as a pig

Swiga! – Shut up!

Teisez vus! (N) – Shut up! (plural)

Teng recene! – (Hurry at once) Run! Get lost!

Uncle (N) – uncle

Ungeleafful – infidel

Valhǫll (ON) – Valhalla
> Old Norse mythic home of the warriors who had died in battle.

Va dunc! (N) – Off you go!

Wa la wa! – Oh dear! Oh no!
> An exclamation of pain or distress.

Wa me! – Woe is me!

Wælwulfas – war wolf, death wolf
> This was an epithet of a warrior.

Wæs hal! – (Be healthy!) Cheers / To your health!
> An old English toast, usually answered with, "Drinc hal!" – Drink in good health!

Wealhstod – language mediator, interpreter

Wel gesund, hlaford min – (Be healthy) Greetings, my lord
> An old English greeting.

Witan – (the wise men) council of the Anglo-Saxon kings.
> The Witan advised on political, legal and social matters and comprised a varying number each of bishops and men from the upper nobility. The Witan also decided who would be the next king.

Wiþertrod! – Retreat!

Wodon þa wælwulfas, for wætere ne murnon (The Battle of Maldon, line 96) – The death wolves waded through (the river Panta), they did not care about the water

Wordwringa – (word wringer) sophist

Yfel gesiþ – evil companion

Acknowledgments

Thank you for reading Oswulf's story. If you enjoyed the book, please tell others about it by leaving a review on your favourite book portal. It can be as brief as you like, but your feedback is important and valuable for authors and, of course, other readers. Thanks a lot!

If you would like additional, exclusive reading material, go to **www.birgitconstant.com** and subscribe to my monthly newsletter *Medieval Motes*.

Many thanks go to my editor Miranda Summers-Pritchard for her subtle corrections and for polishing my prose, to my cover-designer Patrick Knowles, who did a great job at transforming my pedantic and picky demands into superb covers for the whole series, and, last but not least, to John Wyatt Greenlee for redesigning my maps.

FIND OUT HOW THE STORY CONTINUES

For Lord and Liege. Book 2 of the Northumbria Trilogy
– coming in 2025

Printed in Great Britain
by Amazon

59867992R00211